The
Universal Language of Mind

The Book of Matthew Interpreted

by

Daniel R. Condron
D.M., D.D., M.S.

SOM Publishing
Windyville, Missouri 65783

The Universal Language of Mind
Book of Matthew Interpreted

© July, 1994
by the School of Metaphysics No. 100150

Cover Design by Dave Lappin

ISBN: 0-944386-15-6

Library of Congress Catalogue Number pending

PRINTED IN THE UNITED STATES OF AMERICA

If you desire to learn more about the research and
teachings in this book, write to School of Metaphysics,
National Headquarters, Windyville, Missouri 65783.
Or call 417-345-8411.

Contents

The
Universal Language of Mind Principles

1
Thought is cause, everything else is sub-cause or effect.

2
The physical reflects the mental.

3
All creation begins with a thought-idea.

4
All ideas are images or mental pictures held in the mind's eye of the individual creator.

5
The Universal Language of Mind is the Language of Function.

6
The language of physical existence is the Language of Form.

7
In order to interpret from the language of the inner, subconscious mind to the outer, conscious mind, one must translate the communication from function (use and application) to form (which is slow change and inertia) and vice versa.

The Universal Language of Mind
The Book of Matthew Interpreted

The Universal Language of Mind
The *Book of Matthew* Inner Secrets Interpreted

The Universal Language of Mind has been discovered and is hereby revealed in this book. It is a symbolic language due to the nature of the difference in the duties of the conscious and subconscious minds. Physical language, the language of the conscious mind, proceeds from the need to utilize the five senses. These are the very factors that contributed to entrapment in the physical body and our thousands of years of evolution since that time.

A thought is produced in the conscious mind of the individual. Words are chosen and formulated in such a way as to describe the mental image. The mental image, the thought, that has been described in the conscious mind of the person with words is next expressed as verbal sounds through the mouth of the thinker. These verbal sounds then travel as vibration through the air as sound waves. These air or sound waves may be received in the ear of the listener, the receiving individual, striking the ear drum and causing a like vibration in the inner ear where it is then transformed into electrochemical units of coded energy that report to the brain. The electrochemical units of coded energy are "decoded" by the pituitary gland in the brain which then draws stored images of memory together in order to formulate a workable image similar to the image originally verbalized.

The degree of accuracy with which the recreated mental image or thought is formulated in the receiver's (listener's) conscious mind and brain is the degree to which effective communication transpires. At times the receiver's mental image may closely resemble the speaker's mental image. In other situations the two images may be worlds apart. The latter leads to confusion, reaction, frustration and, in general, inefficiency.

The language of the subconscious mind, which dreams and scriptures of Holy Books such as the Bible use for communication, is also initiated with a mental image. However, in the process of dream communication the mental image is relayed from subconscious mind directly to the conscious mind via the pituitary gland in the brain. The pituitary gland is the part of the brain that has as its function to interpret energies. It is the interpreter of energies. The pituitary, having received the mental image from the subconscious mind, then draws out of the brain a collection of stored mental images called memory of past events. This memory, these mental images stored in the brain, are then chosen, collected, orchestrated in such a fashion as to form a collective, moving image or message of the communication which the inner or subconscious mind is attempting to convey to the conscious waking mind.

Since mind to mind communication, such as one's subconscious mind to one's conscious mind, does not require the inefficient vehicle of words, the message is given in symbolical or picture image form and is received in like or similar manner. Therefore, it is of utmost importance that each individual, each person, come to understand this Universal Language of Mind which is the language of mental images, pictures or symbols.

The Bible, and in fact any truly Holy Book or Scripture, can be and is to be accurately interpreted in the universal, symbolic, language of mind for its deepest spiritual and evolutionary significance. This is the language of picture-images. This book uses exactly that interpretation in the language of mind. It recognizes the universal symbols and connects them to form a mental image of creation and evolution to our ultimate quest — Enlightenment.

Each chapter presents the symbols given for the first time in the *Book of Matthew* as well as their meaning. The symbols can be combined as the pieces of a puzzle until a coherent image appears as a result of the combination of all the pieces of the puzzle.

The people who originally wrote the Bible understood this universal language and therefore penned *Matthew* and other books of the Bible utilizing this universal symbolic language. The language of the conscious mind is the language of *form* and *structure*. The language of the subconscious mind is the language of *function*.

For example, a physical house is made of wood, stone, brick or some other type of physical material. We recognize a house by its structure and form. A house has doors, windows, a roof, walls, floors, and a foundation. In the conditional, conscious mind we recognize a house by these indicators of its structure. In the language of the subconscious mind a house is recognized by its *function*. A house's function is to serve as a protector of its inhabitants. A house is a place where people live. Mind serves a similar function in that the mind is where I AM, the identity of the thinker, resides. Thus, it is seen that the function of a house in the physical existence and the function of mind in the metaphysical existence serve the similar function as a place to exist, to live, and to use. The Universal Language of Mind has as its symbol for the mind, a house. When a house appears in a person's night dreams, it symbolizes that person's mind and the condition or state of that mind. In fact, dream symbols are messages conveyed in the language of mind. They are given in the same language of *function* used in the world's Holy Works including the Bible.

Another example of the use of function as the apparatus of the Universal Language of Mind is money. Money can take the form of metal coins, paper currency, gold or silver bullion, or anything else that is commonly recognized to have a certain value. Money serves as a vehicle or medium for the exchange of value. Money promotes a more efficient means of exchange than bartering because the second party may not desire the product of the first party. When money is exchanged, the person receiving money for goods or services (such as shoes) can use the money to purchase a different product, say oranges, which would have been very difficult to procure otherwise.

Thus, in the Bible, money, as well as gold, silver, and coins, represent value. The value symbolized in the Bible is the value of Self. The structure of money in the physical existence is available as printed paper or it may exist in a bank account, or value may be measured in gold, silver, or other possessions. The function of money is achieved as it is used as an exchange of value. The language of the inner or subconscious mind is the language of *function*.

The structure of a mountain may be described as a very large mass of rock and stone jutting up above the surrounding area. The function of a mountain in relation to people is to provide an obstacle or challenge in order to move or travel to the destination of desires. When the peak of a mountain has been achieved one stands above the surrounding territory and can see or perceive what was not previously visible.

The structure of clothing is as a covering of cloth over the body. The function of clothing, other than to protect the body, is to express one's Self outwardly to others in the environment. This is true for anyone who has a choice as to the kind, type, style or color of clothing they wear.

The structure people use while living and existing in a physical lifetime is a physical body. The function of people in regards to each other is to provide an avenue, a way we can mirror ourselves to see and understand various aspects of ourselves through our interactions with others. People, as a symbol using the Universal Language of Mind, represent aspects of Self.

Stones and rocks in the Bible represent will. Stones are used to build houses. Most importantly any house (mind) that is to last (be permanent), must be built on a solid rock foundation (or other substance just as supportive, like concrete). The supporting foundation for one who is to learn to use the whole mind is the development of a strong (but not stubborn) will and will power. Will power is the ability to cause continuous forward motion so learning and growth can occur. Stubbornness is the strenuous effort to remain in one place and condition with limiting attitudes. It is the refusal to move and change. Stubbornness creates stagnancy and non-motion.

Food provides nourishment for the physical body. Food is *constructed* and *structured* in such a manner as to be broken down by the digestive organs of the body into its constituent parts. Then the food can feed or nourish the body fulfilling the body's needs for vitamins, minerals, proteins, carbohydrates, fats, and so forth. Thus, the function of food is to provide nourishment for the body. The function of knowledge is to provide nourishment for the soul. Thus food, in the <u>Bible</u> or a dream symbolizes knowledge that nourishes the soul.

Grapes, grain, meat, honey, as well as other foods in the <u>Bible</u> represent knowledge. This is knowledge gleaned from experience that adds to the permanent soul memory. Knowledge is not information. Information is mental images stored in the brain that dissolve when the physical body dies. Knowledge is permanent memory gained from experience that heightens, increases, and enhances one's awareness. Knowledge is produced when learning of Self and creation is gained and gleaned from experience. This then leads to expansion of consciousness.

Information

Information called sensory experience is received from the environment through the five senses.

$\downarrow$

Knowledge

The information is applied in one's daily life. The information is utilized to produce successes and creations.

$\downarrow$

Wisdom

The valuable knowledge you have gained is taught to others thereby gaining understanding of the universal secrets of success and creation.

$\downarrow$

Complete Understanding

The people who you have taught then, in turn, teach others the Universal Truths and Universal Laws you have taught them generation after generation. Gradually, or rapidly this Truth that is universal becomes available and utilized by all of humanity.

At the time of death the physical body ceases to function or dies. No motion is then evident within the body. This is a change. The soul that existed within the body withdraws from that body and resides in subconscious mind where it had existed before incarning in a physical body. Death is a change, a transition from one form of existence, entrapment in a physical body, to another form of existence, soul awareness in subconscious mind. This is the structure of death. The function of death is change and motion. Death as a symbol in the Universal Language of Mind represents change. This holds true when interpreting dreams, as do all interpretations of symbols given in this book.

Learning <u>Bible</u> interpretation is like learning a new language. In fact, it is learning a new language! When learning a new language, first one learns basic words with common usage. Often nouns are learned first. Next, one learns to connect words into sentences so one can convey a whole picture or message. Also, when one is first learning to translate from one language to another, one translates word-for-word literally which can sometimes lead to misinterpretations. However, as one becomes fluent in the second language one translates not word-for-word but meaning to meaning. The interpreter chooses words in one language which most aptly describe the mental picture or image created by the words of the first language. For example, the phrase "a bird in the hand is worth two in the bush" can be translated literally but often when the phrase is used it has nothing to do with a physical bird or a bush.

<u>Bible</u> interpretation using the Universal Language of Mind, which is the language of symbols or pictures, follows a similar structure of levels of learning.

First the student memorizes the symbols presented and attempts to use the message in his or her life.

Second, the student, through gaining greater fluency in the use of the Universal Language of Mind, the sacred language of the ancients, begins to use the symbols to form a coherent picture or image of a universal message and Truth useful in one's life.

Third, through the regular, daily, applied, and practiced spiritual disciplines of concentration, meditation, imaging, and dream interpretation one gains intuitive awareness and insights into the inner meanings of the symbolical or Holy language.

The *fourth* stage is reached when one enters into the inner mind and understands the essence of the Truth portrayed in any Holy Book. Thus, one is actually changed and transformed through the use of this language.

The Symbolical Meaning
of the *Book of Matthew* Interpreted in the
Universal Language of Mind

A young boy attended Sunday School regularly at his local church. He enjoyed singing and hearing the spiritual hymns. He appreciated the good company of his friends and those who taught him what they knew of the Bible. Most of all he loved the Bible stories. In public school, history was always his favorite subject, particularly ancient history. In reading and studying Bible passages it seemed as if the history of the Bible and its people would come alive. He would commit the stories to memory, intuitively realizing they held tremendous significance for himself and others, now and especially in the future.

One of his greatest loves of Sunday School was the weekly newsletter, presented in comic book or picture form and format, which he received weekly. This "Sunday Pix" as it was called, described one of the stories of the Bible each week in picture form. "Pix" was a short form for the word pictures, although the young boy did not realize this at the time. He began to preserve and collect these "Sunday Pix". He thought, "Wouldn't it be great to have the whole Bible in pictures," not realizing how prophetic those words were.

That boy was myself. As I matured, and long after I had collected most of those "Sunday Pix" comics, I always kept that dream of the Bible in pictures alive, holding it close to my heart with the desire to understand fully the ideas or pictures created by the authors of the Bible. The authors of the Bible desired that those individuals who had developed their perception and intuitive faculties to a high level would be able to intuit the deeper meaning of the Bible passages through use of the Universal Language of Mind which is based on the form and structure of mental images and ideas or pictures. The language of mind is the picture language or the language of pictures and images. It is the language of *function* whereas physical language is the language of *structure* and physical *form*.

This is the secret key to the understanding of individual dreams as well as the Universal Language of Mind as presented symbolically in the Bible and other Holy Books of the world. The Language of Mind, the inner subconscious mind, is the language of *function*, whereas the language of the physical, conscious mind is the language of *form*. If you remember nothing else from this book, remember this key. This, reduced to its simplest equation, is my gift to the World. The Universal Language of Mind is the language of *function*. This Truth ties in directly with another Truth I have given the world which is expressed as *thought is cause, everything else is subcause*.

I attended Sunday School for over 12 years going through more than seven years without missing a single class. But that was just the beginning. I attended a major university seeking higher knowledge and learning. I was seeking to understand the higher Truth of this picture language. I studied agriculture, psychology, philosophy, anthropology, and economics. I was introduced to mythology and symbology. Yet still I never found all the answers I sought.

Then one night I had my first out of body experience. I was lying in bed, the lights out, at night. I was about to go to sleep when all of a sudden I felt a powerful vibration spreading throughout my body. The next thing I experienced was a golden ball of light exploding from my chest in the area of the heart and leaving my body with a tremendous "whish" sound. I found myself on the ceiling. I was looking down on my physical body which was still lying on the bed on its back, while I, the soul or essence that is me, was floating on the ceiling feeling light and tremendous freedom.

This was my first out of body experience or astral projection. I was able to identify what had occurred to me and consider it many times after I returned to my physical body for I had studied the types of astral projection and out of body experiences of others. The most important part of the whole event was that I discovered that most important key which would unlock the secrets of Bible interpretation as well as interpretation of other Holy Books and scriptures from all over the world. The key is that all Holy Works, including the Bible, are written from the *soul's* perspective and not from the physical body's limited awareness. This realization tied in directly with my past understandings and my soul's assignment for this lifetime.

The language of the Bible, the language of dreams, in fact the whole universal and sacred language of mind, is written from the soul's perspective and is therefore written from the vantage point of *function*. The question "what motion, if any, does a particular action and thought process create in the Self" is appropriate. "What *function* does it serve" is the key phrase or question to ask in understanding the images presented in the Bible. From that point forward I knew without a doubt and as a matter of fact that I was not a physical body; I was a soul. I knew from direct experience, my physical body was a vehicle that housed the essence which is my Self. I knew my Real Self as soul, inhabiting this physical body for a lifetime for a specific purpose. I also realized that a part of this lifetime's assignment was to give to mankind a service, a tool, and a technology, for increasing soul progression, spiritual awareness, and uplifting of consciousness. I understood my dreams as messages from my inner essence, soul, and subconscious mind, given for the purpose of aiding the conscious mind and physical body so the conscious mind could produce the experiences and learning necessary for soul progression.

I practiced remembering, writing down, and interpreting my dreams in this Universal Language of Mind using the soul's perspective and drawing upon my experiences. For years and years I remembered, wrote down, and interpreted my dreams six and seven times weekly. I also interpreted thousands of dreams of other people. I taught millions of people how to interpret their own dreams. I also solidified my understanding in my consciousness of the Universal Language of Mind as applied to the Bible.

One Saturday I read the entire *Book of Revelation* of the Bible from beginning to end, interpreting it in the language of the soul as I read it. I transferred the words to mental pictures in my own mind's eye using the keys of interpretation according to *function*. I was clarifying and acknowledging the coming together of my life's intuitions and experiences.

Many people have attempted Bible interpretation. Unfortunately they fell short, as the authors or writers only understood a few of the keys for understanding the Bible. The reason they had only a few of the keys is that they were not conversant in the Universal Language of Mind. The reason they were not conversant in the language of mind is they did not practice remembering, writing, and interpreting their nightly dreams in the language of mind let alone teach dream interpretation to others. Many had never had an out of body experience. Yet, if one is to really and truly understand the Holy Scriptures of the world including the Bible, one must have developed a thorough understanding of the Universal Language of Mind via dream interpretation using the universal symbols represented from subconscious mind to conscious mind every night and upon awakening. It is also very beneficial to learn to view the physical existence from the soul's perspective.

I know that many people will come to accept and use the Bible because of this book. Nothing in this book is based on faith. Rather this book depends on you; the reader's use of the information contained herein in order to *know* and prove to your Self (which is the only true proof) the Truth of the Universal Language of Mind. In addition, anyone can verify the Truth of this language by an in-depth study of their own night dreams, for dreams are communicated in this Universal Language of Mind every time we go to sleep. The ancients, through in-depth experience with the inner Self and inner levels of mind, understood this universal language and utilized it in writing Holy Books such as the Bible.

I have lectured to tens of thousands of people over the past 17 years, taught face to face thousands, and taught through the medium of radio and television millions of people about the mind. I have found and know through experience that every individual of mankind has a desire to know the meaning of life and who they really are as a soul, an immortal being akin to their Creator, God.

Over almost two decades of teaching spiritual teachers and students of the mind metaphysics and Universal Laws and Truths, I have found the individual who is serious and committed to knowing Self is invariably interested in the deeper symbology of the <u>Bible</u> as well as other Holy Books of the world.

Jesus was an avatar, an Enlightened individual, a Mahatma, a divine incarnation, as were others who have come before and since. It is not the purpose of this book, however, to rate the spiritual masters of mankind's history. Rather this book explains the inner secrets of the Universal Language of Mind which was used to write the <u>Bible</u> and other Holy Books of the world, and is the key to understanding the <u>Bible</u>.

Perhaps the most important Truth any student can realize is that thoughts have reality and therefore each person creates his or her life with all its situations and circumstances through Self's thoughts, attitudes, and consciousness. Thought is cause. One's consciousness determines the level of success and achievement one has in a lifetime. Therefore, it behooves all individuals to devote their lifetimes to the expansion of consciousness in order that they may transcend the limitations of the conscious mind and be transfigured into a being full of light and awareness, fully exhibiting a radiance that gives light to all the world.

Secret Keys to Understanding the <u>Bible</u>'s Symbolic Language and Spiritual Growth

The <u>Bible</u> has been called "Divinely Inspired" throughout the past 2000 years. The word inspire comes from a Latin word *inspirare* which means *to draw in* or *to breathe upon* as to draw in a breath of air. Divine means, "of God" or Creator. Divine is from the Latin *divinus* meaning *God*. Hence, our English word divinity meaning God or of God. The <u>Bible</u>, as presented in this book as having been written in the language of mind, indicates the ability to draw into the outer, conscious mind from the inner levels of subconscious and superconscious mind the understanding of creation and Creator.

Passages which show the Lord God as capable of anger and ready to destroy and to encourage the Israelites to destroy whole peoples other than the Israelites as in *Deuteronomy 9:14* can be seen as referring to aspects of Self that need to be changed; unproductive attitudes of the conscious mind that need to be eliminated in order that the productive and disciplined conscious mind can be effectively utilized in conjunction with the subconscious mind for the betterment of the whole Self. One's focus should always be on encouraging and facilitating the growth of the productive aspects and change of the unproductive or negative qualities in the Self.

The writers of most of the *Old Testament*, the four Gospels, and the *Book of Revelation*, were spiritually instructed and Enlightened people; advanced souls who gave their effort to creating and recording a textbook of mind for reasoning man to utilize. They thus offered a step by step manual for movement forward from reasoning man to intuitive or spiritual man. Man means mankind or thinker, whether male or female. The word man comes from the Sanskrit word *manu* which means *thinker*. The Sanskrit word *manu* descended to and was borrowed by Latin where it was used to mean the *thinker that used hands*. Hence, our word manual as to operate manually which means for a thinker to operate with his or her hands. For man is the toolmaker and has evolved the opposable thumb.

Scriptures and mythologies of the world are a combination of history, allegory, and symbology used to explain human life, mental and spiritual evolution, experiences and destiny. The scriptures reveal profound spiritual Truths and laws. Increasingly on behalf of the human race, a growing number of individuals have embarked upon the search for Truth, wisdom, knowledge, and an understanding of the Universal Laws of life and mind.

The Bible is a doctrine of individual responsibility. People need to learn how the mind works including not only the conscious mind but also the subconscious and superconscious minds so they know how to use their lives fully to gain the Self realization they so richly deserve.

One of the greatest secrets and most powerful keys to understanding the Bible on its deeper, interior level is imagination. The ability to engage the image making faculty is the beginning and essence of creation.

> *Genesis 1 *[26]*Then God said, Let us make man in our image, after our likeness: and let them have dominion over the fish of the sea, and over the birds of the air, and over the cattle, and over all the earth, and over all the creatures that crawl upon the earth.* [27] *So God created man in his image, in the divine image he created him; male and female he created them.*

The secret key to this passage is the word image. Image and likeness are two different qualities. Likeness means with similar attributes. In other words, since the creator creates and man is made in his likeness, with like or similar attributes, then man can create and has the potential to create on a level with the Creator. Image, however, has a different meaning than likeness. To image is to imagine. To image is to form a mental construct in the mind of what one desires to create. Imaging is the precursor and beginning of creation. In order to create anything, one must first image or imagine that creation. It is also interesting to note that God is referred to in the plural form, not one but several times. Our and us are both plural forms. This is because the English word for God comes from the German word for God which is *Gott* but the original word used in this passage of *Genesis* is *Elohim* which is the plural of *El*. Elohim is the Gods of the first chapter of *Genesis* and has within it both the male and female or aggressive and receptive qualities.

It is the imager or image making faculty which sets humans apart from animals. Animals have memory and animals have attention, but only humanity has developed the ability to effectively utilize the creative imagination for the progression of the soul. The directed imagination is the key to consciously and willfully quickening the soul growth of the individual. It is this process, this quality of imagining your desire to become Enlightened and the activity towards this desire, which produces caused, intentional learning and permanent understanding that normally would have required years or lifetimes. Thus learning and Self understanding can be compressed into one tenth, one hundredth, or one thousandth of the physical time required for Enlightenment.

People are here for the sake of others. It is through service to others that we create the climate and environment conducive to learning and therefore receive from experiences the learning we need.

Self surrender is another key of quickened evolutionary growth. One has to surrender the egoic conscious mind Self that is built on the limited memories of the past which produce stubbornness and replace them with the expansive power of the imager. The mind needs a direction in which to move. Memory causes the mind to move to the limited past. Imagination causes the mind to move to the expansive future. The highest spiritual law entails self surrender of the lower or conscious mind self to the High Self. This is accomplished by service to others conjoined with effective use of mental imagery of Enlightenment including but not limited to holding in mind the image of one's spiritual teacher as well as spiritual leaders throughout history.

The conscious mind Self needs to be taught systematic Self discipline through concentration, will power, meditation, dream interpretation, and visualization so one's consciousness can be raised as in yoga, the science of union with God through Self understanding. Upon union with God one is not to lose consciousness nor is one to be absorbed, losing all individual Self identity. Rather one becomes compatible to their maker, the creator, as a child becomes compatible with parents upon maturing and gaining an equivalent level of maturity. And without the self-imposed walls of isolating separateness experienced by the average person, such a one expands to fill the world and the universe. Love for all mankind is only possible to the degree that one has expanded one's consciousness to all of mankind.

The word Christ in the English version of the Bible comes from the Greek word *Cristos*. Cristos is a word used long before the time of Jesus of Nazareth. It was used to mean or indicate *an Enlightened individual*. The idea of the term Christ or Cristos being limited to one person would have been appalling to the ancient Greeks who owned or invented the word. In other words, the word *Christ* or *Cristos* was not invented by the Greeks for Jesus, but had been in continuous use hundreds of years prior to the time of Jesus.

The actual word from the original Hebrew or Syriac language from which Cristos or the English word Christ was loosely interpreted was *messiah*, which means *saviour*, and therefore has a different meaning from Christ which means Enlightened. One who is a Christ is Enlightened. Christ or Cristos is not a proper name. It is not a last name like Smith or Jones. Rather Christ is a title as is Doctor. Jesus is a proper name. Therefore, Jesus the Christ is more accurate as meaning Jesus the Enlightened One. In the one who has become the Christ, the kundalini or creative energy has reversed its downward flow and has risen up the spine and through the crown of the head, filling the body with light so the body and Self radiate light becoming Self radiant.

The individual embodiment of the powers of creation and superconscious, subconscious, and conscious minds, were called in Palestine by the Hebrews *Elohim* as the Elohim of the first chapter of the *Book of Gen-*

esis. In India they were called Devas, and in Egypt and Greece, gods. The ancients used these terms to explain, denote, teach and understand these living energies of creation and their interactions and cooperation with a developing mankind. The universe consists of energy and interrelationships of energy and space. Matter or physical substance as we know it by our five physical senses is made up of these energy interactions. The farther one progresses in Self awareness, the greater the ability to control and direct energy transformations on the subatomic level. There is no dead matter. There are only living dynamic energy exchanges available through the action of God the Creator for mankind to use in order to understand the creative process and develop as a creator.

As one progresses in Self awareness and understanding of creation the separative aspects of Self are understood and developed into a union or whole Self. As this process occurs and is caused by the individual, the walls of separation between Self and all of creation come down and one recognizes that all are connected and that everything Self thinks, says, and does affects all the rest of creation. Thus, the illusion of Self separateness is released and outgrown as one's consciousness expands to fill the entire universe.

Since there is this connectedness with all of creation, all sincere prayers and desires for Self growth, awareness, understanding and Enlightenment are fulfilled or given answer. Earnest efforts for the light of awareness are responded to or answered. All prayer for the benefit of others is effective.

The idea, that is the full use of the image making faculty, is more powerful than word and action. Whenever the person earnestly, willfully, and determinedly lives according to the highest ideals that are within Self, the opportunity for greater growth occurs.

Thoughts are creative, and thought ideas implemented and manifested into our physical life change the world. Every invention created by individuals in the history of humanity began as a thought, an idea of one or more individuals. Those moments of inspiration come from the subconscious and superconscious minds and are given to the receptively prepared conscious mind for the uplifting of mankind.

In order to explain further how thought transforms and acts on matter, use this Mind Chart diagram of the divisions of mind, the dimensions of consciousness.

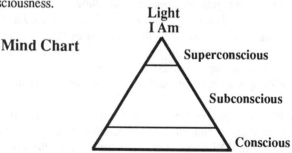

Mind Chart

Light
I Am

Superconscious

Subconscious

Conscious

The thoughts and attitudes created in your conscious mind affect your inner Self, the subconscious mind. In the subconscious mind, they combine, gathering substance until they become concentrated enough to "pop" back into existence at the subatomic level. The idea of particles popping into and out of existence has been recognized in modern physics for over 50 years.

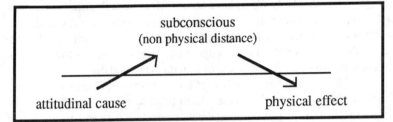

Jesus symbolizes the action and quality of *knowing* in the Bible. Therefore, I shall refer to him in this book as the knower. Knowing is the quality that proceeds from believing backed up with or complemented by activity and reasoning. Therefore, the direct, interior, spiritual, inner level, mental experience, and interpretive understanding of the Bible and other Holy Scriptures must replace blind faith. Doubt always follows blind faith. A study of Christian origins and the history of the Christian church reveals that much change and dilution has occurred in the understanding of the Bible, as well as the essentials of the original idea of the church.

Freedom is another key to spiritual growth because one must learn to exercise one's free will effectively and productively. Only then is there the possibility of spiritual development, mental evolution, and improving one's inner and outer Self. Change and growth must come from free will, will power, and reasoning. The earnest student will open Self up completely to the learning. Others can teach, stimulate, communicate with, and cajole you but the bottom line is Self must desire to grow and expand the consciousness of Self and must be willing to employ will, discipline, and activity. One must be willing to surrender one's lower, unconscious or egoic habits by opening Self to learning. Knowledge of the inner Self and the language of mind is based upon the mental will, discipline, and spiritual practices to produce interior experience and understanding.

The Scriptures or Holy Works of the World are a special and unique category of literature. Holy Scriptures are largely, but not entirely, symbolical or allegorical. They are constructed of symbols, analogies and parables. This symbolical language of mind preserves for posterity the profound spiritual Truths of Self and the inner levels of mind.

This method of writing referred to as the sacred or mystery language is actually the Universal Language of Mind. It was developed and used by the sages of old in order to reveal the timeless Truths to those who would quicken their spiritual progression. In ancient times these secrets were given out to the few who had reached a point in their spiritual progression and mental evolution to be able to utilize these powerful Truths. In our present time period, 2000 years later, many more of our race have progressed sufficiently to be able to understand and use, through a disciplined life, the ancient secrets and Truths that once were revealed to only the very few.

Although founded in general upon historical events, these stories of the Bible and other Holy Works have deeper scientific and spiritual meanings and in some cases have up to a sevenfold significance. However, all true spiritual works written in the language of mind have a threefold significance. Layer after layer of hidden knowledge waits to be revealed as the soul progression and spiritual development of Self quickens and deepens.

Those who possess the keys of interpretation are able to discover the Truths within the sacred language. Then practice and application of those Truths in one's daily life is required if one is to truly absorb and make a part of Self this knowledge and Truth. Otherwise, it becomes just brain food and an intellectual exercise devoid of spiritual enhancement or soul growth.

In order to successfully use the keys one must have developed the intuitive faculty and understand responsibility to Self and service to others.

Preparation and experience are needed in order to prepare and educate the mind to receive the inner Truths. The student's preparation must be not only intellectual, as in the memorization of symbols and their meanings, but spiritual as well. The student should take up and embrace the daily practice of meditation and dream interpretation as well as concentration and visualization or imaging.

For the authors of the Holy Books every material or physical happening and effect was filled with spiritual significance and mental cause.

The records of the history of the universe and of the earth as given in the Holy Books of the world, portray far more than events in time called "history." They reveal eternal Truths, ultimate reality, and consciousness itself. By using historical events as well as allegories, parables and symbols, the spiritual teachers of the ancient world were able to overcome the limitations of time. Thus, besides revealing universal Truths, the sacred or universal language of the Bible can be used successfully to solve difficult passages revealing the deeper Truths of creation. The Bible is less a literal history than it is a revelation of fundamental Truths by means of the Universal Language of Mind as presented through symbols.

True, various passages of the Bible have been mistranslated or more often translated poorly. Nowadays, however, due to the *Dead Sea Scrolls*, the *Nag Hammadi* texts of Egypt, the texts of the Eastern Christian Church and other sources not previously available, accurate translations are available. In addition, one can gain valuable insights by comparing texts and translations.

Selfless giving brings mental, spiritual, emotional and physical riches, and more abundant life. Desire for exclusive personal possessions and powers brings loss of the meaning of life and eventually death without awareness. This has been demonstrated throughout history by both nations and individuals. This law of sacred, selfless service is fundamental to the universe and in fact keeps the universe in existence. Giving is the initiator of life. Only after giving has been initiated repeatedly can receiving create the space and place to nourish the new life. To die, in the sense of separate egoic, possessive conscious mind Self, is to free Self to live life with unlimited freedom. One must surrender the walls of protection which the conscious mind and ego have created in an attempt to protect the self, and replace the wall of false security with an openness and willingness to receive the learning in each experience. This process of openness or surrendering the walls of protection and isolation in the self, also creates an opening for moving out beyond those walls of one's prison through giving and service. In this way one has a Self forgetfulness or a forgetting of all one's fear, reactions, and limitations. Self-lessness brings abundance.

When the outer self, the conscious mind self, becomes aware of the inner urge and the need to know the Real Self and surrenders to one's mission and assignment for a lifetime, then a great transformation occurs within Self. Wholeness, harmony, peace, and fulfillment are initiated and developed in Self. Then the inner master draws the disciple into union with Self. This process is assisted by the external teacher who increases the idealism; supporting use of the imager, will, and desire of the outer thinker in order to become responsive to the master, the Christ within.

When this occurs the kundalini energy flows up the spinal cord. It is concentrated first at the base of the spine. When fully roused, this serpent fire rises in a circular and upward moving spiral or serpentine motion within the spinal cord up to the head. This is referred to as the crown chakra located at the top of the head. The kundalini energy is symbolized by snakes, serpents, and dragons in the Bible and Holy Scriptures. The true inner secrets are known by those who ascend by the regular practice of meditation into an illumined state. Those who gain firsthand experience and achieve directly perceived spiritual knowledge are knowers. They were referred to as gnostics in early Christianity. *Gnosis* is a Greek word which means *to know*. Jesus the Christ was such a person. Hence, when the name Jesus is presented in the Bible, recognize this as the knower. Jesus is symbolical of the knower, the one who knows from direct experience and application of the universal Truths of creation. *Gnosis Cristos* = knower, Enlightenment = Jesus, the Christ.

The universality of the sacred books of the world reveals the Universal Truths contained in the original sayings of the world's greatest teachers. In fact, the Bible is a manual of meditation and a textbook of the mind. Man's capabilities include the ability to bring about the manifestation in the outer self of the purely Spiritual or inner Self which creates a full use of the learning process. The individual exists in creation as a part of Creator. The deity is not external to Self. Mankind was created out of Creator and can be reunited in divine eternal communion. This is Truth taught as an inner Secret.

The engrossed Self who is limited to brain consciousness suffers from spiritual amnesia. By directing into the brain the electro-vital power of kundalini, then aroused and directed into the heart, it heightens the speed of the vibratory frequency of the cells and electrifies the organs of the brain. The person thus sensitized becomes aware that he or she is spiritual and endowed with divine powers. This full awakening of the serpent or spiritual fire is the ultimate object of all spiritual endeavors. Then you will know the Truth given in the Bible, *"I and my Father are One."* (*John 10:30, 14:20.*)

The purpose of man's existence is spiritual and mental evolution until one becomes fully conscious and, in fact, consciousness itself. This is why all people incarn in a physical body with the loss of knowledge of divinity. The spiritual or mental Self is like a seed. The Self contains the potentiality of the parent that produced the seed, which is God.

The experience of life, when created as imaged through reasoning and will, creates an alignment of inner and outer minds which allows one to follow the interior evolutionary impulse thus fulfilling one's purpose for a lifetime. Gradually or quickly, depending on the will of the individual, the understanding within Self is increased and brought to fullness, becoming fully evident in the expression of Self. The intelligent thinker cooperates with the divine plan and thereby creates happiness and fulfillment within the life of Self. A lost soul is impossible, for the true Self is immortal, eternal and indestructible. However, a wasted lifetime occurs to those who deny the true lessons of life.

The evolutionary process is without beginning or end because creation is continual. Perfection is thus not a good word for the mental evolutionary process of spirituality since it suggests finality. God is not distant in a far off heaven but present in everything and everyone. God, the divine creative principle in nature and in each individual, is evolving together with the whole universe. All of creation moves forward and the thinker determines the pace at which he or she progresses.

Enlightenment is a result of evolutionary progress and is achieved by means of successive incarnations in material, physical body vehicles. Repeated incarnations in physical bodies provide the necessary time and opportunity for such attainment. All incarnations are connected with each other by the operation of the law of cause and effect. Self is the cause of one's life whether painful or pleasurable. Kindness brings happiness and health. Therefore, meditatively find the reality behind the physical shadow.

Successful interpretation, whether through the five senses or the Universal Language of Mind, is an experience in consciousness. Certain age old symbols have a constant meaning throughout time. This enables Enlightened sages from the remote past to speak to the mind of mankind today. The authors of the Bible utilized history to give symbolical presentation of everlasting Truths. When reading the Bible remember we are reading a special category of literature written in the Universal Language of Mind. The light of

Truth will illumine and radiate Self as the symbology and imagery of the <u>Bible</u> is revealed in its timeless Truths. The outer layer of the <u>Bible</u> is pseudo-history, sometimes totally accurate and in other cases only partially so; historically speaking it is local and temporary. The inner layers of the <u>Bible</u> consist of universal, eternal Truths. The life activities of people and groups of people such as nations provide clues as to their underlying use and meaning in the <u>Bible</u>.

Major historical events frequently occur at the convergence of cycles and sub-cycles. This is also true of crises in the lives of individuals. The human egoic cycle of prenatal attention on the physical body then incarnation in a physical body, the constricted and entrapped life therein, death, movement of attention into subconscious mind, and finally understanding and existence with one's source is the cycle of the human evolutionary drama. This cyclic progression is the central theme of all stories written in the Universal Language of Mind. Initiations are the earned movement from a lower to a higher level of consciousness, from a limited perception to an expanded consciousness.

The resistance to motion and inertia of physical matter is personified by enemies in the <u>Bible</u>. Battles between two opponents portray in symbols, the conflict and need for harmony between spirit and matter, life energy and physical form and structure, consciousness and its vehicles of Self expression. This is the eternal Armageddon, the Kurushetra of the <u>Bhagavad Gita</u>, the battle between the Kurus and the Pandus.

All the recorded, external, supposedly historical events of the <u>Bible</u> occur interiorly. Each recorded event is descriptive of a subjective experience of Self. That is, the event symbolizes the efforts of Self to learn while in the physical lifetime. By understanding this process, individuals may quicken their own evolution surpassing that of humanity as a whole. Thus early upon the path of swift unfoldment the student develops enhanced will power and mental and perceptual abilities.

Scriptures of the world must be read with an open mind and intuitively with responsibleness to the vaster consciousness which is waiting and willing to come through. The presence of Jesus the Christ on earth and his activities are mirrors of the interior awakening of the soul and its subsequent expansion of consciousness. The entire universe and all its parts is interconnected to make a single whole. Though the parts may seem to be separated by distance or space, still they are interrelated and connected with each part affecting the whole. Each story is a graphic description of the experiences and learning of the soul as it understands and moves through the phases and steps of its evolutionary journey to cosmic consciousness which is the ideal and summit of human attainment.

Different people figuring prominently in each story in the <u>Bible</u> represent abilities, qualities, and particular characteristics of every human being.

Times change, and as mankind progresses the hidden secrets of the mind become available to greater numbers of people. This is due to more people being more aware of themselves as soul instead of thinking they are just a physical body. The soul's messages of progress and forward moving growth and evolution are received by the conscious mind which has prepared through mental discipline, meditation, and dream interpretation. Stillness of the mind is essential to Self illumination.

People in the Bible represent a condition of consciousness and a quality of one's character. People symbolize personifications of aspects of human nature. They represent attributes, principles, powers, faculties, limitations, weaknesses, and errors of Self. Average people in the Bible represent the normal stage of development of the average person and aspect. When the person portrayed in the Bible is moving forward successfully in God's cause, the image is of the Self progressing towards Self understanding. When the central figure is Enlightened, his experiences narrate the later phases of the evolution of Self into Christ or Buddha consciousness. The deity or Father in heaven refers to the highest spiritual essence in Self.

To unveil the hidden Truth in the Bible one needs knowledge of creation, evolution, and most importantly the Universal Language of Mind. A person needs knowledge of the symbolical language, its purposes, structure, and composition as well as the highly developed skill, art, science, mental faculty, and ability to interpret the stories, history, and parables. Then the person desirous of understanding the deeper meanings of the Bible and other Holy Books can form a complete, clear, and concise image of the development of each individual as a mental and spiritual being.

The Bible can be read from many different viewpoints.

1. The Bible can be read literally, as if everything reported in the Bible physically occurred. This is a physical way to go about using the Bible and will keep the reader physically entrapped. Using this physical type of reading, the Bible can be read as a historical or pseudo-historical book. Reading the Bible physically can impart value to the individual by using the Bible to create ethics and morals within the Self.

2. The Bible can be read as a group of separate parts with each part having relevance to the individual today. Using this method, one can pull verses out of the Bible to back up one's point of view or to give understanding and meaning to one's present situation and circumstances in life. Using this method, one can read a passage in the *Book of Matthew* today, one in the *Book of Genesis* tomorrow, and one in the *Book of Revelation* the day after tomorrow and believe each passage is relevant to Self right now.

3. The <u>Bible</u> can be read as a step by step textbook of the use of the mind. Using this method one utilizes the Universal Language of Mind which is the use of mental images or pictures to convey ideas. This method of <u>Bible</u> interpretation using the Universal Language of Mind, to convey not only one's current state of awareness but also where one has evolved from and what one is evolving to become, will reveal the step by step process of man's evolution as a thinker. Humanity has been evolving not only physically, but also mentally and spiritually since long before recorded history. The anthropologists of the world are attempting to discover humanity's physical evolution through digging up the bones of the physical ancestors of Homo sapiens. These ancient skeletons reveal the evolution of the physical body through such forms as Homo habilis, Homo erectus, and Neanderthal, who was probably or possibly a side branch of present humanity's evolution. For every physical production there is a mental production preceding it. The mental evolution of the soul used the more advanced forms of the physical body to develop the capability to reason.

Genesis provides instruction in the beginning of creation and the movement of evolution, mentally and physically, in order to reach the stage of mankind as a reasoning being. The first chapter of *Genesis* provides the plan, the blueprint, for the rest of the <u>Bible</u>. Today mankind is fully involved in the fifth day of creation called reasoning. Some individuals exist in the infancy or adolescence of reasoning while others who have gained a degree of enlightenment exist in the adulthood of reasoning. It is at this stage that humanity finds itself today. Humanity is knocking on the door of the next day, the sixth day of creation, called Intuitive Man.

This mental interpretation using the Universal Language of Mind is the process used in this book. It is the same language used by each person's subconscious mind every night to deliver messages in the form of dreams to the waking conscious mind. I have spent over two decades studying and investigating the Universal Language of Mind. This is the language of *function*. Whereas the languages of physical life and the conscious mind are the languages of *form*. The use of the Universal Language of Mind, verified by dreams of myself and the millions of others I have taught to interpret their dreams, is what makes this book unique in the history of the world concerning the understanding of the deeper meaning of the <u>Bible</u> and other world scriptures.

<u>Bible</u> interpretation is also tied closely to the process of initiation. As long as one thinks physically, which is to believe the cause for your life is outside of yourself, then one will see in the <u>Bible</u> only a record of physical

events. However, when one begins to accept responsibility for one's life and ceases to blame the environment and other people for the conditions and circumstances in the life, then the freedom to cause one's life to be as desired and imagined is created within the life.

The inner secrets of the Universal Language of Mind were known to a few in ancient times. Those who understood the veiled language were called adepts, priests, priest-kings, keepers of the secrets and spiritual masters. These initiates of the higher Enlightenment were the authors of the world's Holy Works. The Bible was written by people, albeit highly evolved souls with expanded consciousness, as a way to pass on to future generations the understanding of evolution, creation, Universal Laws, soul progression, spiritual Truth and the inner secrets for using the whole mind; that being conscious, subconscious, and superconscious minds.

Many early writing systems used individual pictures to represent ideas and concepts. This method of writing is called hieroglyphics and was practiced in Egypt, the Mayan civilization, and other civilizations of the ancient world. The Chinese system of writing has every letter in the Chinese language representing a whole word. Thus, every proper name in the Bible has a mental picture or image behind it. It is in combining the symbols of a chapter or book of the Bible into a coherent whole which provides the greatest challenge and requires the skills of a person practiced in this subtle art and science.

I am sometimes asked if I believe everything or certain events written in the Bible actually happened as a physical event or as factual history. Where the writers of the Bible found historical events that could be used to describe the inner Self, the evolution and development of the mind, and the secrets of quickened evolution, they were used. Thus, the physically minded person would read the narrative as a physical event while the initiated thinker, the one who had delved into the inner parts of Self, could therefore discover the inner Truths within its pages.

In situations where physical events did not present the factors needed for the portrayal of the correct symbolic meaning, or only partially so, the spiritual writers and authors adjusted the recording of events accordingly so the complete mental image of that portion of the evolution of the soul could be explained and presented.

For example, few people today believe the story of Adam and Eve in *Genesis* of the Bible is a story of physical history; even though it may well turn out that genetically all mankind is descended from one woman in Africa. If it were physically so, then the children of Adam and Eve would have engaged in incest and inbreeding in order to expand the population. Whatever remains to be revealed about physical evolution, the story of Adam and Eve is a cryptic code written in the Universal Language of Mind. Adam represents the subconscious mind from which the conscious mind (woman) was formed. The rib which Adam unconsciously "donated" in order that the Lord might create the woman, represents the emotional level of consciousness. The emotions or the emotional level of consciousness binds the conscious and subconscious minds together. Its function is to move thought from the inner levels of mind out into one's physical life and reality.

No one believes that Jesus is saying someone should cannibalistically eat his physical flesh when in the *Book of John* Chapter 6 he says, *"He who feeds on my flesh and drinks my blood has life eternal."* Jesus, representing the quality and action of knowing, is here speaking symbolically in allegory and metaphor of the need to receive and assimilate the highest spiritual Truth and knowledge into one's conscious mind and soul.

Jesus, the knower, even admits in the *Book of Matthew* Chapter 13, Verse 10, that he presents knowledge on more than one level of awareness. He calls this type of speaking parables. *"The disciples came, and said to him, Why do you speak to them (the common people) in parables? He answered and said to them, Because it is given to you to know the mysteries of the kingdom of heaven but to them it is not given. For whoever has, to him will be given, and he will have more abundance; but whoever has not, from him will be taken away even that he has. Therefore I (Jesus) speak to them in parables: because they look but do not see; they hear but they do not listen, neither do they understand."* Verse 16 *"But blessed are your eyes, for they see; and your ears, for they hear."*

When the Bible is read in only a physical sense, one finds the Bible contradicts itself over and over. When the Bible is interpreted in the symbolical Language of Mind, the Bible never contradicts itself.

Compare the promises of physical prosperity and divine protection by the Lord to Abraham and his successors with the subsequent defeats at the hands of the invaders including the Babylonian exile and the lost ten tribes.

The strong divergence and contradiction between the promises and divine assurances and what actually happened as portrayed later in the Bible give strong reasons and needs for interpreting the Bible on a deeper level of symbolical meaning where the information can be universally applied on a day to day basis to cause a quickening of one's soul growth.

Numbers as a Symbolical Representation of the Form and Structure of Creation

What could be more important than a new beginning? Without a beginning there is no middle or ending. Without a beginning there is no opportunity for experience, for the experience never begins. To begin is to initiate. To initiate is to set into motion certain actions. These actions, when directed by a willful, goal-minded thinker, will move to and towards the chosen goal or ideal.

Thus, the beginning or first step of motion and life is represented by the beginning or first number which we call, One.

The first point from which all creation proceeds is a point; that is *everything* must have a start or a starting point. This is symbolized by a dot or point which has neither length nor height nor width. Since the point has none of these dimensions it is symbolized in the western culture by zero. Zero indicates naught or no-thing. Zero also has the valuable symbolical function of indicating placement. Thus, the number one is indicated as different from the number 10 because the digit one in the number ten has been moved one space to the left by the insertion of a zero.

1
10

Zero, used to indicate or symbolize placement, therefore represents powers of 10. One multiplied by 10 is 10. Ten multiplied by ten equals 100. One hundred multiplied by 10 equals 1000 and so on.

1 — one
10 — ten
100 — one hundred
1000 — one thousand
10,000 — ten thousand
100,000 — one hundred thousand
1,000,000 — one million

0

Zero represents power. Zero indicates the power of understanding when used in the <u>Bible</u>. Zero symbolizes the power that is created from understanding the present stage, level, or cycle of learning one is in and incorporating that learning fully into the whole Self where it becomes a part of one's storehouse of permanent learning called understanding. When the individual has completed one level of learning and awareness that person is prepared to move to the next higher threshold of the expansion of one's consciousness. All this is symbolized by the factor zero.

1

Moving out from a point to another point and connecting the two, we form a line.

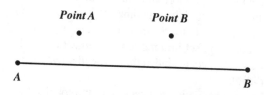

A line, unlike a zero or point, has a dimension. A line has the one dimension of length. Length is the ability to move from one place or situation to another. This movement is called the aggressive factor or quality. The aggressive quality is the ability to initiate activity towards one's desired goal or ideal.

2

To continue producing the steps necessary for creation, the factor of height is added to length as a second dimension. This second line added to the first may be pictured as a second line moving out from the first line.

Thus, one line moves forward and the second line receives or is receptive to the first line thereby moving to a higher or more complex form of existence. Receptivity is the symbolic meaning of the number two. For any initiative action to produce in abundance or more expansive quality than its present condition, a receiving or receptive unit, or receptacle, is needed for the directed motion. With the joining of the aggressive and receptive qualities a third mutation or creation occurs which is symbolized by the number three. Through the process of adding a third line to the first two a self-enclosed figure is formed. This dimension of space is referred to as width.

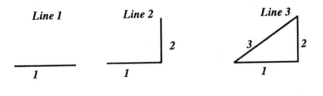

3

Notice the figure created through the addition of a third line or dimension is a triangle, a three-sided figure. Notice also, that for the first time, the figure (3) is Self enclosed while figures one and two are open. From the coming together or union of the aggressive and receptive qualities is created a third unit with expanded possibilities. The Self enclosed form indicates the beginning of an autonomous unit or individual capable of independence with the future possibility and capability of non-separative function with others. This produces, through cooperation with others, greater opportunities for learning, growth, change, transformation, and soul growth.

The two coming together as aggressive and receptive to create through unity or union a third form is symbolized in the <u>Bible</u> as Adam, the aggressive and subconscious mind, forming a union with Eve, the receptive conscious mind, in order to form a new, aggressive vehicle or aspect for higher awareness called Cain, Abel, and Seth.

The aggressive quality is also symbolized by Joseph of the *Old Testament*. Joseph symbolizes the ability to perceive and utilize subconscious mind, marrying (union of commitment) Mary, receptive nurturing quality of love in the conscious mind, to form or create through the action or intervention of the Holy Spirit (whole mind) a mutation called Yeshua, Yoshua, Jesus, or IM-man-u-el = I Am manu El. I Am Manu El may be interpreted as; I Am resides in the thinker which is a creator made in the image and likeness of his Creator-God, El. The plural name of the Creator-God, El is Elohim. Elohim is the name of God used originally in the book of *Genesis* in its original language of Hebrew. Later, as *Genesis* was translated to English the name of the Creator in *Genesis* Chapter one was changed to God.

From this point forward in soul evolution, each structure, each form, will be Self enclosed. Each individual entrapped in a physical body is Self enclosed. The ideal is to use our individualized identity of I AM to develop, understand, and become completely aware of universal consciousness that is consciousness itself. This is accomplished by moving beyond the separatism of the enclosed Self through serving others to gain fulfillment in life and to increase in awareness.

4

The number 4 is represented by a Self enclosed figure called a square or rectangle.

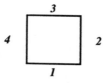

The quality added to our progression in understanding creation and form symbolized by the number four is stability. The square or rectangle is four-sided. Consider that most chairs and tables have at least 4 legs. A pyramid has four sides plus its base. When the number four is presented in the <u>Bible</u> you can be sure a level of stability has been achieved so that a firm foundation has been built on which to erect the next level of creation. A tetrahedron has four sides including its base and is stable.

When Jesus spent 40 days and nights in the desert he gained stability within Self as all experiences, learning, and knowledge of the past was processed and assimilated. All that was found lacking or without further value was left behind. This is why at the end of the forty days Jesus was able to resist the temptation of the devil (conscious ego) and remain true to the ideal of living the whole lifetime for the Enlightenment of Self and others.

The stability gained from leaving the past behind and moving beyond the past and its limited memories is also symbolized by Noah and his voyage of 40 days and nights in the ark. During the forty days and nights everyone and everything perished (the past and its limitations) except for what Noah brought on his Ark (the productive body vehicle of the thinker).

The stability of 4 is also symbolized by the 40 years Moses and the Israelites spent in the wilderness or desert during which all of the generation except for two men (Joshua [the knower] and Hur) died, symbolizing the change in all aspects that identify with limitations. These people (aspects) without slavery consciousness that applied reasoning and having free will consciousness were able to enter and conquer the promised land which symbolizes physical existence. The Israelites (keepers of the secrets) were slaves in Egypt but were free people in the desert and there learned to wield their will under the direction of first Moses and then Joshua the greatest general or military leader the Israelites ever had.

5

The number 5 builds on the qualities and structure of the previous four numbers. As the number one is the number for gases and unformed substances which have the quality of motion, so the number two is the number of minerals and solid objects. Three is the number of plants and includes the qualities of one and two but adds the factor of reproduction and sensitivity to the environment, ie: the beginnings of a nervous system. The number four is the number of animals. Animals add the quality of directed motion to the understanding mentioned in the previous three root races which are gases, minerals, and plants. Animals incorporate both memory and attention into their cognitive and learning faculties but are short on the factor of imagination. It is this factor of imagination that is added and symbolized by the number five. The addition of the image making capability *(Genesis 1:26, and God said, let us make man in our image)* to the previously developed memory and attention provide for modern humanity the three factors necessary for reasoning. Thus, five is the number of reasoning man, or the thinker. The word man comes from the Sanskrit word manu and means thinker.

Consider that the shape of a square or rectangle may be used to indicate the number four. By adding an extra line the number five can be illustrated graphically.

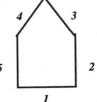

The number five in this case, takes on the form of a house with a slanting roof. This is understandable as the number five represents reasoning or the reasoning faculty and a house in the universal language represents the mind. The first floor of a house represents the conscious mind, the second floor the subconscious mind and the third floor symbolizes the superconscious mind. A pyramid has five sides including its base.

The numbers one through four indicate operation and activity under the law of compulsion. Reasoning, symbolized by the number 5 provides a means and opportunity for free will to exert itself in the individual through one's life and experience in the physical existence.

Through the use of reasoning and free will or will power, humanity progresses and moves forward in their evolutionary growth. Reasoning is the faculty that enables the individual to draw upon memory of previous experience gained through undivided attention in order to build a better future through utilization of the imaginative faculty.

6

Six is the number of service for it is through service to the whole Self and others that real, intentionally caused, soul progression occurs. The number 6 may be represented as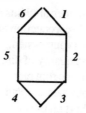

but more clearly the symbolic representation is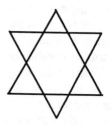

A fascinating creation occurs when one extra line is added to the previous five. Now instead of one enclosed form we may form two enclosed forms--triangles which are joined to form a six-pointed star.

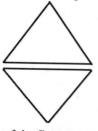

Each point represents one of the five senses, touch, taste, smell, hearing and sight. The 6th or upward directing triangle point represents the combination of all the five senses through the action of undivided attention to form direct mind perception and full use of the intuitive faculty. The sixth day of creation, called intuitive man, man meaning thinker, is the intuitive age for humanity. The key for causing enhanced and quickened soul progression in Self is service. The mind directed beyond the isolated Self to service to others expands past its narrow confines of reasoning to encounter the higher mind functions of the subconscious mind and thereby expands in consciousness to higher awareness. A cube has six sides.

The triangle contains a total of 180° A right angle used to show the two lines equals 90° double the 90° when forming a triangle. 180° is one half the number of degrees in a circle. A circle contains 360°. A triangle is equal to one half of a circle in that 180° is one half of 360°.

7

Seven is the number of control. The number seven indicates the connecting of the energies of Self such as the seven major chakras and the seven levels of mind so that the individual may use all energies of creation. To control is to use effectively. As new and greater learning and Self awareness dawns in the individual he or she must utilize the information effectively and consistently in order to progress and grow in one's spiritual evolution.

The structure or form of seven may be illustrated pictorially as a triangle on top of a square.

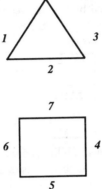

By merging the two forms, a seven pointed form is created.

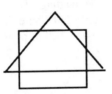

What are the characteristics of a seven-sided figure? Two enclosed figures are contained within it as within the six-pointed star which symbolizes the Universal Truth, "as above, so below".

Control of one's life and physical existence through the use of creation factors of three, is symbolized by the triangle over the stability of the four-sided figure which symbolizes the stability or inertia of physical existence. The result is controlled direction and use of one's physical lifetime for maximum benefit.

It is through full controlled and directed use of one's mind and life that Self moves first to gaining the full value of the physical experience (symbolized by the number 8) and following that the completion of a stage and cycle of learning symbolized by the number nine.

8

The number eight symbolizes value. This is the value added to Self of adding the inner energies (symbolized by the second 4) to the outer energies. The symbol for 8 may be formed by two squares to form an eight-pointed star.

In fact, the number 8 is formed by placing one square on top of the other. Gradually, over time, the rough edges of the two squares have been rounded to form the modern figure (picture) 8.

Remember, 4 represents stability and the figure eight is made up of two fours or two squares as the number six is made of two triangles or two threes.

Stability of existence in the physical life is indicated by the number four. The greater value of a higher mental or spiritual stability is encompassed in the figure eight. Eight symbolizes a mental being who is causing permanent learning and Self understanding. Thus, 8 indicates value. Where the number eight appears in the <u>Bible</u> be sure that the full value of a new understanding is being added to one's Self as permanent memory.

9

Nine is the number of completion. Nine shows the inner energies of the Self more fully connected to the outer energies with conscious awareness and use. The form and structure of nine may be formed by interlacing three triangles. The number 9 is formed from the addition of three threes. Each three may be symbolized by a triangle. Nine is thus the first number that is or can be made up of three interlocking structures.

The figure nine may also be represented by a square and pentagram interconnected, showing stability (4) with reasoning (5).

The three threes indicate a completion of the previous form and structures as form moves to create greater complexity.

Three symbolizes the unity of the aggressive and receptive qualities coming together to create and 6 (3 plus 3) symbolizes service used to expand one's consciousness. Nine represents the culmination of three as the creative factor in the learning process.

The numbers ten, eleven, twelve, and thirteen are referred to as Master Numbers.

10

Ten symbolizes completion with understanding, which is power. The number ten shows the completion of a cycle with the power that comes from understanding that cycle. The number ten indicates the power and understanding that comes from teaching others how to connect inner and outer energies with consciousness and conscious awareness. Ten shows completion with understanding which is power. Zero always symbolizes power. Refer to the discussion on the meaning of zero given earlier.

11

Eleven symbolizes the initiation of a new cycle with understanding from the previous cycle. The number 11 indicates one who is aggressively initiating the new cycle of creation. Eleven shows mastery of the keys and secrets of creating in the physical environment and from that understanding causing forward motion in the life as a spiritual teacher teaching others to master creation. Eleven symbolizes understanding of the aggressive quality of creation within Self and initiation of a new cycle on a higher level with expanded consciousness.

12

Twelve symbolizes the understanding of the aggressive and receptive qualities within the Self. Twelve is a master number indicating that there has been mastery of the basic cycle of human physical evolution and understanding gained of creation. The number twelve shows the ability and need to teach to others both the aggressive and receptive factors of creation as a prelude to final mastery of the creative energies.

13

Thirteen symbolizes the full understanding and use of the aggressive and receptive principles of creation utilized to create Enlightenment and divine understanding within Self. Thirteen is the number of one who has attained the Christhood or Christ consciousness. Therefore, Jesus is seen to have had twelve disciples, himself making the thirteenth of the group. Thirteen represents the leadership, consolidation and understanding of the previous twelve stages of mastery of creation. The aggressive and receptive qualities have been mastered and used to create completely, including full Christ consciousness within Self. Full awareness of Self and creation and compatibility to one's Creator is known. The meaning of *Genesis 1:26* is understood. *Let us make man in our image after our* (plural) *likeness.*

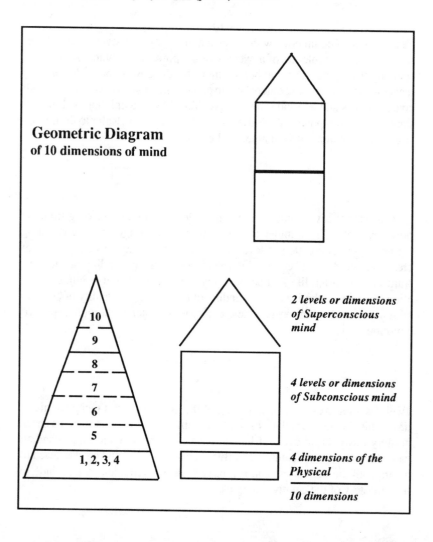

Geometric Diagram
of 10 dimensions of mind

10
9
8
7
6
5
1, 2, 3, 4

2 levels or dimensions of Superconscious mind

4 levels or dimensions of Subconscious mind

4 dimensions of the Physical

10 dimensions

The Essence of
The Book of Matthew
in the
Universal Language of Mind

Few Word Essence
of Each Chapter of the *Book of Matthew*

1
Evolution

2
Entrapment of Awareness

3
Believing

4
Ego-discipline

5
Attitudes

6
Desire

7
Karma - Cause and Effect

8
Faith - Healing

9
Life - Motion

10
Aspects

24
Son of Man - Thinker

25
Commitment to the Inner Self

26
Motivation

27
Alignment

28
Enlightenment - Divine Radiance

Brief and More Expanded Essence
of Each Chapter of the *Book of Matthew*

1
The steps of mutation and mental evolution in the development of the thinker.

2
The knower, the one capable of Enlightenment, is entrapped in a physical body.

3
Believing, though powerful and useful, must precede knowing.

4
The conscious ego is I AM, in the physical body, and is responsible for motivation.

5
The attitudes of productive being — be-attitudes — versus attitudes that cause dis-ease and pain.

6
Communicating with the inner Self and mind; and assimilating the knowledge from experiences.

7
Karma's cause, the power of thought, and the benefits of the application of universal Truth.

8
The ability to cause permanent healing by applying more expansive imaging to change attitudes of hate and resentment to those of creation and purpose.

9

The ability is gained to produce motion in Self where it was previously absent, to gain greater discipline of Self, and to change and transform the Self at will to remove stagnancy and increase motion.

10

Awareness of the twelve major aspects of Self is gained through discipline of Self and mind.

11

The steps of developing faith into believing are identified. Believing is a step beyond goal setting.

12

The knower consistently assimilates knowledge from experience, without lag time between the two. The knower has descended into the physical existence yet will fulfill the commitment to gain Enlightenment while in the body.

13

Symbolic instruction utilizing the Universal Language of Mind.

14

The time has arrived to supplant believing with knowing.

15

Hypocrisy in Self is confronted. The lies called dishonesty in the conscious mind are identified. Productive thoughts and ideas will be matched with action and application.

16

Will power must be employed to build the foundation for knowing the whole mind. The knower understands the goal for physical existence and the ideal of Enlightenment.

17

The connection and importance of the effective use of the image making faculty, transforms limitations in consciousness to an elevated pinnacle of Self Realization.

18

The ability to change by embracing new learning with the quality of infancy is the key to fulfilling the plan for Enlightenment held in superconscious mind. The plan for enlightenment is the steps of developing and becoming a creator. The minds must be united.

19

Build and enhance the commitment to the inner Self. Engrossment in sensory stimulation and physical possession must not distract and overpower Self.

20

Knowledge produced from experience and reasoning is matured into wisdom. Understanding built in the present lifetime must be used to draw from the inner levels of mind into the conscious mind all one's permanent memory.

21

The knower moves the full consciousness forward to completely connect conscious and superconscious minds. The mind is cleansed of dishonesty, and limited sense of value.

22

Self is connected to all others and all of creation. Develop connection and relationship with I AM and all aspects of Self.

23

Self observation and Self honesty through consistent vigilance by the thinker must be applied. Security derives from that which is permanent — understanding.

24

Full commitment to Self understanding for all time will create awareness of the inner thinker.

25

Constant awareness is needed in the conscious mind to build the marriage made in heaven, the commitment to the subconscious mind, the soul. Use the understandings gained and more will be developed.

26

The disciplined ego ensures motivation is available to the knower in order to gain the full Enlightenment. The conscious ego is thus transformed.

27

The knower produces consistent and constant growth, learning, and transformation in Self and is therefore guilty of no sin. The full understanding and connection between horizontal time and vertical time is completed.

28

Physical limitations do not limit the Enlightened One. Understanding of mind, Self, and Creation is gained. All aspects will be disciplined, strengthened and brought into alignment with I AM.

Summaries of the Inner Meanings
of Each Chapter of the *Book of Matthew* as Given
in the Symbolic and Universal Language of Mind

1

The steps and stages of evolution described and explained. These steps of
forward motion, uplift, and progression produces ultimately the knower; then
the Christ or Enlightened One.

As the earned ability to perceive the next stage in evolution combined with
the nurturing, receptive ability and desire to surrender one's limitations in the
conscious mind, provide fertile ground for the mutation known as Immanuel
= I-AM-manu-El or Jesus, the knowing quality to be created.

2

The new awareness of the possibility and infancy of Enlightenment disturbs
the conscious ego and its egoic limitations which were constructed in an effort to survive (fight or flight syndrome) rather than with the intention of
growing.

The limited conscious mind and egoic Self then attempts to destroy or
get rid of or to change the new mutation which is based in expansion and
movement beyond limitation.

The egoic Self is threatened by change and therefore strikes out attempting to destroy everything in any way associated with this expansion which
threatens its false sense of security based on a deteriorating structure of non-
change.

3

The believing quality must be cultivated and nurtured in the thinker as the
knower matures.

As the stage of believing is completed by the maturing knower then the
quality of believing gives its all to the knower. This is the commitment to use
the physical life totally and completely to produce Enlightenment and transformation of consciousness.

Believing, when understood and used as a full commitment in the context of a stage of life and evolution, is more powerful than information storage in the brain which is termed memory.

The superconscious mind is fulfilled by one committed to awareness of the God Self or creator within.

4

The developing, emerging and expanding conscious mind which is reaching beyond the physical existence, the world of effects and its limitations, encounters the conscious ego, the egoic part of Self which has used physical desires as a motivator up to the present time.

The accumulation of physical desires no longer serves to motivate the one who understands the nature of the physical with its constant death, physical decay, and temporary sensory gratification. The thinker, the one producing greater knowing in Self, will not be fooled by the temporary pleasures of physical existence knowing the pairs of opposites rule the physical. Therefore, when there is pleasure there is also pain.

Rather, the thinker strives for awareness of creation and mind that lies beyond and transcends physical existence to that which is permanent. When stability is achieved in permanency then full commitment to use the lifetime of physical existence to produce permanent memory stored in subconscious mind is achieved. Discipline is needed to cause consistent forward motion.

5

Thoughts have reality and thoughts are things. An attitude is a thought process practiced repeatedly until it becomes a habitual way or manner of thinking. These attitudes can, over time, become limiting unless aligned with the Universal Laws and Truths.

One who is blessed is one who will gain and prosper. The Be-attitudes, or attitudes productive to be-ing and existence, provide the insight and framework for full use of physical existence in order to gain understanding of Self and creation.

Self discipline provides the structure where awareness can exist and expand. All Universal Laws, Truths, and principles must be fulfilled by the one who would be Enlightened. The thinker must nurture every productive aspect of Self into existence.

6

Intention causes Karma. Understanding relieves Karma.

The knower will learn to move the attention into superconscious mind. The Self must assimilate the experiences in order to produce permanent memory and Self understanding.

That which is permanent (understandings) are the true riches.

Enlightenment is greater than wisdom.

7

That which you react to in the environment and which you see in others can be a starting point for understanding the areas of learning needed in Self.

You really can have anything you desire. The subconscious mind's duty is to fulfill the conscious mind's desires. The subconscious mind will accomplish this when allowed to do so by a conscious mind that is utilizing cooperation.

Those who desire to progress spiritually and through mental evolution to gain Enlightenment, will find it is possible and the opportunity is available.

All creation begins with thought. Thought is cause, everything else is subcause.

8

All limitations can be overcome and transcended by the one who exercises the qualities of believing and knowing.

The power of numbers and the power of understanding is available to the one who exercises a clear mental image and allows no doubt to enter.

That which is of the past, is over. It no longer exists except as memory, and memory is a part and function of the animal brain. Therefore, do not allow the compulsive, habitual, or animal part of you to control Self. Rather, place security in attention and in the effective use of the imaging faculty (imagination) so the whole Self may move forward.

9

The knower has authority to cause motion when he or she wills it. This is because the knower understands and teaches mental discipline.

The knower continually creates new opportunities for learning. One who creates purpose for the actions of the life, gradually and surely, aligns and identifies with Truth. The improvement and development of perception is a product of continually imaging what one productively desires to occur within Self.

It is the duty of the 12 major aspects of Self to educate and enlighten all minor or lesser aspects of Self. The minor or lesser aspects of Self are the 144,000 referred to in the *Book of Revelation*, Chapters 7 and 14.

10

The 12 major aspects of Self must be used and understood in order for Enlightenment to occur.

The mission of the knower is to root out all limitation, all restriction and constriction until the light of awareness shines into the depths of one's being.

11

Faith mutates and develops the higher understanding of believing. The one who desires to learn, grow, and build permanent understanding must be willing to receive and absorb new learning without restriction through the use of the infancy stage of learning.

12

Understandings are the desire of the subconscious mind, not restriction or limitations. The one who causes continual forward motion has no need of stopping to assimilate learning for learning is continual.

To become a knower, to heal any aspect of Self, one must develop or gain purpose.

The thinker must be willing to change.

13

The Universal Language of Mind is understood by the knower at the stage of growth described in this chapter. Every time Self identifies with memory, the animal part of the brain-self, little learning is possible.

14

As the knower progresses, the quality of believing holds less power in the life of the thinker. Knowing, built from repeated mental successes added to teaching this to others, produces permanent understanding. Believing is transformed into higher awareness.

Ability to expand knowledge and have full control over one's life is gained by the knower at this stage of forward growth and Self awareness.

15

Information stored in the brain as limited memory and brain pathways will never give Enlightenment and will, if allowed, keep Self engrossed in the physical experiences and limitations. All aspects of Self need to be healed for the full progression of Self and transcendence of the physical, conscious mind Self. Self understanding is the heart. The heart symbolizes Self understanding, and eventually, Self transformation.

16

Faith and believing, matched with will, gains knowing first, then the keys to the superconscious mind. The limitations of the physical self and conscious mind are transcended as one identifies with the Real Self which is not physical and is unlimited.

17

To be trans-figured is to change and expand beyond one's limited form or figure, mind, and Self to a higher, more evolved and greatly expanded consciousness.

The transfigured Self exists in greater and fuller relationship to God. The ideal of the Enlightened Soul and the full use of the Universal Laws is fulfilled in the knower who is preparing for Christhood. Ideal, purpose, and activity are the keys to knowing Self. Therefore, use the physical and its myriad of experiences to build Self understanding.

18

The one who is willing to accept the qualities of infancy (which are trust, absorbing information, openness and desire to receive, learning without the restriction of doubt and fear, constant action, love, and desire to learn) into the Self shall gain superconscious awareness. The greatest is the one who fully surrenders to the will and direction of the divine consciousness of Christ consciousness.

19

The conscious mind is separative, alone, and isolated due to its dependency on the five physical senses and their limitations for communication and information. The Real Self is in its essence and origin, divine and all inclusive. Therefore, the separative conscious mind self must mold itself and reform or refigure to the model and will of I AM.

Attachment leads to engrossment as does avoidance. Full use and engagement of experiences leads to the opportunity for full and complete learning and awareness.

20

The plan of creation held in superconscious mind is to be fulfilled and will be fulfilled. The one aligned in action with the ideal of producing permanent Self understanding will fulfill that plan in Self.

The divine Self serves the conscious mind which is limited. The knower serves Self and others and gives the gift of grace, bliss, learning, and consciousness itself.

21

The conscious mind must be cleansed or purified of its limitations, restrictions, constrictions, negativity, doubt, and fear in order to serve the whole Self. Only then is the process of Self transformation possible. Those activities and thought patterns of Self that do not produce permanent learning will be released or changed. The only one who understands authority is the one who possesses authority. Such a one images greater Self understanding and through this gains greater understanding of creation and the creative process.

22

The one who persists in commitment to Self understanding for a whole lifetime, is one among millions. Respect and give to physical existence for it provides Self with a vehicle for needed experience. Death and life are not stagnant and non-changing forms. Rather life and awareness is permanent and all pervasive. The heart of understanding is the seat of consciousness.

23

The conscious mind self must find, discover, listen and come to know the teacher within, which is one's soul. Then one can begin to be saved from entrapment in the physical body and engrossment in physical experience.

Attachment to the past via memory may seem to be fulfilling but it is actually Self contraction and restriction. The only true, real, and permanent movement is forward. Be honest with Self.

24

I Am is the messiah, the anointed One, the savior, the Enlightened One. Change is the nature of physical existence. Therefore, embrace and cause change, growth, and transformation instead of avoiding it.

The chosen are those aspects of Self committed to Enlightenment. Enlightenment is their uppermost priority and everything else in life revolves around this imaged ideal.

The aggressive thinker learns to control all parts of mind and all levels or planes of existence and consciousness.

25

Every minute of every day and every unit of time in one's full lifetime is to be used to increase one's awareness of Self and consciousness. Life is an investment. One can squander the investment by pursuing physical attachments and by attempting to hide behind the false sense of security of physical possessions or one can give the whole lifetime to Self understanding and the expansion of consciousness.

26

The thought aligned with the highest ideals of Enlightenment are to be treasured, respected and nurtured. This is of the greatest value. The conscious ego motivates as long as one exists in a physical body. However, the conscious ego only thinks physically as it is aligned with the conscious mind.

The Universal Language of Mind is given in pictures or symbols. Therefore, choose that which symbolizes the highest ideals of Enlightenment to fix the attention upon and constantly hold the attention on the image, ideal, or symbol.

27

The conscious ego is changed and transformed as the divine radiance of Self outpours and envelops the body and consciousness of the thinker. The Son of the superconscious mind continues to exist and experience. Inner communication and awareness guides the thinker to the completion of one's assignment for a lifetime. The knower with Christ consciousness has full control and authority over all doubts and indecision. The knower overcomes all physical limitations.

28

The nurturing aspects of Self are the first to have awareness of divine transformation. When this occurs Self has full awareness with or without a physical body. Divine radiance is the essence of such a one. Such a one is omnipresent and has full Self understanding. Full and complete consciousness in relationship to Creator-God and creation is compatibility and divine, omnipresent consciousness.

The Book of Matthew

Interpreted in the

Universal Language of Mind

Symbols of *Book of Matthew*
new symbols added, chapter by chapter

Symbols and Their Interpretation

Chapter One

1.   Jesus - the Knower
2.   David - reasoning
3.   Abraham - honest conscious mind
4.   Isaac - subconscious mind
5.   Jacob - who became Israel - superconscious mind
6.   Joseph - perception
7.   virgin - one without sensory engrossment
8.   Immanuel - the thinker within
9.   Mary - nurturing factor of love in the conscious mind

Chapter One

The first book of the *New Testament* builds on the knowledge previously presented in the *Old Testament* and shows, in fact, a *New Testament*. This is to say, it reveals a new covenant between God and mankind that is a new, quickened way of evolutionary living and new effort of moving to Enlightenment. The true word of God and the Universal Laws were presented in the *Old Testament*. Because mankind's evolution had advanced thousands of years since the time of the beginning of the *Old Testament* there was a need for a new presentation, a new way to relate to a more evolved humanity. This is called the *New Testament* or the New Gospel or the New Covenant in the Bible. Abraham was given a covenant from God or Jehovah. Noah was given a covenant from Yahweh-Jehovah-God. Now there is a new covenant given by Jesus.

The first chapter of *Book of Matthew* begins by presenting the coming of a Saviour through the genealogy of Jesus. Verse one says, *"A family record of Jesus Christ, son of David, son of Abraham. Abraham was the father of Isaac, Isaac the father of Jacob, Jacob the father of Judah and his brothers."* This is the Judah connection from which all people called Jews or Ju's (plural of Ju) say they are descendents. Jew or Ju comes from the word Ju-dah.

> [1] *The book of the generation of Jesus the Christ, the son of David, the son of Abraham.* [2] *Abraham begat Isaac; and Isaac begat Jacob; and Jacob begat Judah and his brother;* [3] *And Judah begat Phares and Zara of Thamar; and Phares begat Esrom; and Esrom begat Aram;* [4] *And Aram begat Aminadab; and Aminadab begat Naasson; and Naasson begat Salmon;* [5] *And Salmon begat Boaz of Rachab; and Boaz begat Obed of Ruth; and Obed begat Jesse;* [6] *And Jesse begat David the king; and David the king begat Solomon of her who had been the wife of Uriah;*

Judah is the Greek form of the Hebrew name Judas. Both indicate the same quality of mind energy in the context of the motivating ego. King David represents the reasoning capability. David represents another mutation as was also the case with Abraham, Isaac, Jacob. All of these symbolize mutations in mankind's evolution. Humanity at this point in its evolution needed to develop in a new direction which would provide an appropriate body-vehicle for the thinker, man, or mankind. Before the point represented by Noah in *Genesis,* the way we mutated was to wipe everybody out on the planet (symbolized by the flood) to enable the correct mutation to flourish without being overcome by the older peoples. Later, by separating Abraham or Abram from Ur of the Chaldeans and bringing him to a new land, he could flourish and the new mutation could be nurtured without the factors found in Ur which would tend to dilute and harm the new mutation found in Abram.

Forward evolution occurs through a new aspect or new mutation. This new development in the thinker demonstrated by reasoning man will become the ruler of all the people. People symbolize aspects of Self. The soul-thinkers learned to control the rate of mutation; to cause and quicken that evolution by building on previous capability. They not only lived in harmony with the physical environment, which an animal can do, but began to control the environment. King in the Bible symbolizes a controlling factor. The king is authority. A king is a director of many people which shows that reasoning has come of age in mankind being able to control the environment. This shows the development, as indicated in the *New Testament,* of the Homo sapiens body. Saul who was the King immediately preceding David (reasoning) represents Neanderthal. David represents Cro-Magnon or Homo sapiens. This shows the movement into the current state of development in the anthropological lineage of modern man or protomodern human man. Accompanying this physical evolution is the mental evolution of the soul into and through the stages of reasoning to the sixth day of creation called Intuitive Man.

The lineage continues with Solomon. Solomon we recognize as representing wisdom. Wisdom is the next step following David (reasoning) and is symbolized in the *Old Testament* by Solomon. Wisdom peaked with Solomon for the Bible states that none who came after him were as wise. Then there is a seeming decline of evolution because after Solomon's reign came lesser kings until the time of the next mutation called Jesus or Immanuel. Then Enlightenment begins to supersede wisdom, for wisdom is a product of reasoning applied in the conscious mind.

> *7 And Solomon begat Roboam; and Roboam begat Abia; and Abia begat Asa; 8 And Asa begat Josaphat; and Josaphat begat Joram; and Joram begat Ozias; 9 And Ozias begat Joatham; and Joatham begat Achaz; and Achaz begat Hezekiah; 10 And Hezekiah begat Manasses; and Manasses begat Amon; and Amon begat Josias; 11 And Josias begat Jechonias and his brother, about the time they were carried away to Babylon:*

The weakening of Israel and movement away from the One Living God represent the personal entrapment of the individual. Adam and Eve indicate movement away from God so that the point of attention moves out (from 1st level to 7th level) into the physical. Egypt represents entrapment and Moses indicates the building of the faculty of imagination required to overcome and transcend entrapment. Babylonian captivity represents one's personal entrapment, as two tribes of Israel came back and ten tribes did not come back to the promised land from the Babylonian captivity. This entrapment of the individual souls occurred at the time of the beginning of Homo sapiens sometimes called the time of the Cro-Magnon. Joseph the great grandson of Abraham went to Egypt indicating movement of the soul's attention into the physical and recognizing the slavery of being trapped in a physical body. In a similar manner, the final captivity or the final entrapment of the individual occurs with the full emergence of Homo sapiens. At this point we were and are to develop reasoning fully in the physical environment and the physical body by the development of the imaginative faculty. Through our physical activities, action, and reasoning we build permanent memory called understandings. It is this process that produces and creates Enlightenment.

The *Book of Matthew* Chapter 1 then goes on to describe the lineage of Jesus.

> *12 After they were brought to Babylon, Jechonias begat Salathiel; and Salathiel begat Zerubbabel; 13 And Zerubbabel begat Abiud; and Abiud begat Eliakim; and Eliakim begat Azor; 14 And Azor begat Sadoc; and Sadoc begat Achim; and Achim begat Eliud; 15 And Eliud begat Eleazar; and Eleazar begat Matthan; and Matthan begat Jacob; 16 And Jacob begat Joseph the husband of Mary, of whom was born Jesus, who is called the Christ. 17 So all the generations from Abraham to David are fourteen gen-*

> *erations; and from David until the Babylonian captivity fourteen generations; and from the Babylonian captivity to the Messiah, time of Christ, are fourteen generations.*

The last half of the name Zerubbabel is the same as the Babel of the *Old Testament*. This presents a picture of the final point of entrapment. This is the time when the telepathic abilities and mind-to-mind communication was lost. For, as the Bible says, everyone spoke a different language. Contrast Eliakim with the prophet Eli in the *Old Testament*. Contrast that and compare Matthan with Matthew. Next in the lineage is Jacob, then Joseph. Compare this Jacob and Joseph with the *Old Testament* Jacob who was also the father of Joseph as related in *Genesis* of the *Old Testament*.

This lineage is completed with this statement, *"Joseph was the husband of Mary, of whom Jesus who was called the Messiah was born. So all the generations of Abraham to David are fourteen generations, from David to the Babylonian captivity fourteen generations, from the Babylonian captivity to the Messiah, time of Christ, fourteen generations."* One plus four (14) = 5 which is the number of reasoning.

Recognize that Jesus is the Greek form of the Hebrew name Joshua or Jeshua. Now Joshua was the greatest war leader, the greatest general the Israelites ever had. He took over when Moses died. Moses led the Israelites out of Egypt but died before they entered into the promised land. Moses never made it to the promised land but Joshua did. Moses was allowed by the Lord to view the promised land from afar, that is from a distance. Moses shows the effective utilization of the imagination to create an ideal and begin the movement toward the imaged ideal. Joshua symbolizes the effective use of activity to produce the manifestation of the illumined ideal thereby creating knowing in Self. This describes in precise terms exactly how the imagination functions. The imagination is effectively utilized to direct the creative mind to that which is to come and what can be achieved. The imagination, effectively used, will always be out in front of the thinker's present conditions, circumstances, and activity. This is the way creation works for humanity in our entrapped condition.

Joshua led the Israelites into the promised land. Joshua never lost a battle for the Israelites. As long as he was alive, and as long as the Israelites obeyed the Lord's commands, the Israelites never lost a battle. Jesus represents the same quality of never losing a battle. However, instead of physical battles, Jesus represents the battle of the commitment to the Whole Self which is the commitment to causing enhanced learning, growth, and inner awareness so the conditional, animal or physical Self is transcended. For such a one, the whole life is committed to Enlightenment. The physical environment never controls or causes the true reasoner to become limited, distracted and engrossed again.

This genealogy is divided into three sections of fourteen generations each. Adding the numbers one and four of fourteen together equals five and five symbolically represents the reasoning quality. In each of these generations there is a certain quality of reasoning built within Self. The faculty of imagination is improved with each step. Attention and memory have already been gained and understood in the previous animal man and animal stages of evolution. Abraham to David represents the infancy of reasoning moving into adolescence of reasoning. From David to the Babylonian captivity represents adolescence in reasoning. The Babylonian captivity to the Messiah symbolizes the moving towards the understanding of adulthood of reasoning through the physical entrapment in the human body and the desire to be like the Creator. The achievement of full understanding and use of imagination is necessary in order that one can prepare the foundation for the coming of the Messiah, which is commitment to knowing the inner, real Self. Creating Intuitive Man and the sixth day of creation within Self is Enlightenment and follows the complete development of reasoning and the imaginative faculty.

> *18 Now the birth of Jesus Christ occurred in this way: When his mother Mary was engaged to Joseph, before they came together, she was found with child of the Holy Spirit. 19 Then Joseph her husband, being a just man and not willing to make her a public example, decided to put her away privately. 20 But while he thought on these things, behold, the angel of the Lord appeared to him in a dream, saying, Joseph, son of David, fear not to take unto you Mary your wife: for that which is conceived in her is of the Holy Spirit.*

Joseph in the *Old Testament* had dreams. *Genesis 37* presents a dream that predicted Joseph's future. It was these dreams symbolizing Joseph's elevation over his eleven brothers that influenced them to sell Joseph into slavery in Egypt. Joseph of the *Old Testament* interpreted people's dreams including the Pharaoh's dream. Pharaoh was priest king of Egypt.

Genesis 40 [1] *And it came to pass after these things, that the butler of the king of Egypt and his baker had offended their lord the king of Egypt.* [2] *Pharaoh was against two of his officers, against the chief of the butlers and against the chief of the bakers.* [3] *He put them in ward in the house of the captain of the guard, into the prison, the place where Joseph was bound.* [4] *The captain of the guard charged Joseph with them, and he served them: and they continued a season in ward.* [5] *And they dreamed a dream both of them, each man his dream in one night, each man according to the interpretation of his dream, the butler and the baker of the king of Egypt, which were bound in the prison.* [6] *Joseph came in unto them in the morning, and looked upon them, and, behold, they were sad.* [7] *He asked Pharaoh's officers that were with him in the ward of his lords house, saying, Why do you look so sad today?* [8] *And they said unto him, We have dreamed a dream, and there is no interpreter of it. And Joseph said unto them, Do not interpretations belong to God? tell me them, I pray you.* [9] *And the chief butler told his dream to Joseph, and said to him, In my dream, behold, a vine was before me;* [10] *In the vine were three branches: and it was as though it budded, and her blossoms shot forth; and the clusters brought forth ripe grapes:* [11] *And Pharaoh's cup was in my hand: and I took the grapes, and pressed them into Pharaoh's cup, and I gave the cup into Pharaoh's hand.* [12] *And Joseph said unto him, This is the interpretation of the dream: The three branches are three days:* [13] *Within three days will Pharaoh lift up thine head, and restore you to your place: and you shalt deliver Pharaoh's cup into his hand, after the former manner when you were his butler.* [14] *Think of me when it will be well with you , and show kindness, I pray you, unto me, and make mention of me unto Pharaoh, and bring me out of this house:* [15] *For indeed I was stolen away out of the land of the Hebrews: and here also have I done nothing that they should put me into prison.* [16] *When the chief baker saw that the interpretation was good, he said unto Joseph, I also was in my dream, and, behold, I had three white baskets on my head:* [17] *In the uppermost basket there were bakemeats for Pharaoh; and the birds ate them out of the basket upon my head.* [18] *And Joseph answered and said, This is the interpretation thereof: The three baskets are three days:* [19] *Yet within three days will Pharaoh lift up your head from off you, and will hang you on a tree; and the birds will eat your flesh .* [20] *And it came to pass the third day, which was Pharaoh's birthday, that he made a feast unto all his servants: and he lifted up the head of the chief butler and of the chief baker among his servants.* [21] *And he restored the chief butler unto his butlership again; and he gave the cup into Pharaoh's hand:* [22] *But he hanged the chief baker: as Joseph had interpreted.* [23] *Yet chief butler did not remember Joseph, but forgot him.*

Genesis 41 [1] *And it came to pass at the end of two full years, that Pharaoh dreamed: and, behold, he stood by the river.* [2] *And, behold, there came up out of the river seven well favored cows and fatfleshed; and they fed in a meadow.* [3] *And, behold, seven other cows came up after them out of the river, ill favored and leanfleshed; and stood by the other cows upon the brink of the river.* [4] *And the ill favored and leanfleshed cows did eat the seven well favored and fat cows. So Pharaoh awoke.* [5] *He slept and dreamed a second time: and, behold, seven ears of grain came up upon one stalk, fat and healthy.* [6] *And, behold, seven thin ears and blasted with the east wind sprung up after them.* [7] *And the seven thin ears devoured the seven healthy and full ears. And Pharaoh awoke, and, behold, it was a dream.* [8] *And it came to pass in the morning that his spirit was troubled; and he sent and called for all the magicians of Egypt, and all the wise men thereof: and Pharaoh told them his dreams; but there was none that could interpret them unto Pharaoh.* [9] *Then spoke the chief butler unto Pharaoh, saying, I do remember my faults this day:* [10] *Pharaoh was angry with his servants, and put me in ward in the captain of the guards house, both me and the chief baker:* [11] *And we dreamed a dream in one night, I and he; we dreamed each man according to the interpretation of his dream.* [12] *And there was there with us a young man, a Hebrew, servant to the captain of the guard; and we told him, and he interpreted our dreams; to each man according to his dream he did interpret.* [13] *And it came to pass, as he interpreted to us, so it was; me he restored unto mine office, and him he hanged.* [14] *Then Pharaoh sent and called Joseph, and they brought him hastily out of prison: and he shaved himself, and changed his garments, and came to Pharaoh.* [15] *And Pharaoh said to Joseph, I*

Notes:

have dreamed a dream, and there is none that can interpret it: and I have heard said of you, that you can
understand a dream to interpret it. [16] And Joseph answered Pharaoh, saying, It is not in me: God will give
Pharaoh an answer of peace. [17] And Pharaoh said
unto Joseph, In my dream, behold, I stood upon the
bank of the river: [18] And, behold, there came up out of
the river seven cows, fatfleshed and fat; and they fed in
a meadow: [19] And, behold, seven other cows came up
after them, poor and very gaunt and leanfleshed, such
as I never saw in all the land of Egypt for badness: [20]
And the lean and the gaunt cows did eat up the first
seven fat cows: [21] And when they had eaten them, it
could not be known that they had eaten them for they
were still gaunt, as at the beginning. So I awoke. [22] I
saw in my second dream, behold, seven ears came up
in one stalk, full and healthy: [23] And, behold, seven
ears, withered, thin, and blasted with the east wind,
sprung up after them: [24] And the thin ears devoured
the seven good ears: and I told this unto the magicians;
but there was none that could interpret it for me. [25]
And Joseph said unto Pharaoh, The dream of Pharaoh
is one: God has shown Pharaoh what he is about to
do. [26] The seven healthy cows are seven years; and the
seven good ears are seven years: the dream is one. [27]
And the seven thin and gaunt cows that came up after
them are seven years; and the seven empty ears blasted
with the east wind will be seven years of famine. [28]
This is the thing which I have spoken unto Pharaoh:
What God is about to do he showed unto Pharaoh. [29]
Behold, there come seven years of great plenty throughout all the land of Egypt: [30] And there will arise after
them seven years of famine; and all the plenty will be
forgotten in the land of Egypt; and the famine will con-
sume the land; [31] And the plenty will not be known in
the land by reason of that famine following; for it will
be very grievous. [32] For that the dream was doubled
unto Pharaoh twice; it is because the thing is established by God, and God will shortly bring it to pass. [33]
Now therefore let Pharaoh seek a man discreet and
wise, and set him over the land of Egypt. [34] Let Pharaoh do this, and let him appoint officers over the land,
and take up the fifth part of the land of Egypt in the
seven plentiful years. [35] And let them gather all the

food of those good years, and lay up corn under the hand of Pharaoh, and let them store food in the cities. ³⁶ *That food will be kept for the seven years of famine, which will come in the land of Egypt; that the land perish not through the famine.* ³⁷ *This was good in the eyes of Pharaoh, and in the eyes of all his servants.* ³⁸ *And Pharaoh said to his servants, Can we find such a one as this, a man in whom the Spirit of God is?* ³⁹ *And Pharaoh said unto Joseph, Forasmuch as God has shown you all this, there is none so discreet and wise as you:* ⁴⁰ *You will be over my house, and according unto your word will all my people be ruled: only in the throne will I be greater than you.* ⁴¹ *And Pharaoh said unto Joseph, See, I have set you over all the land of Egypt.* ⁴² *And Pharaoh took his ring from his hand, and put it upon Joseph's hand, and arrayed him in vestures of fine linen, and put a gold chain about his neck;* ⁴³ *He made him to ride in the second chariot; and they cried before him, Bow the knee: and he made him ruler over all the land of Egypt.* ⁴⁴ *And Pharaoh said unto Joseph, I am Pharaoh, and without you no man will lift up his hand or foot in all the land of Egypt.* ⁴⁵ *And Pharaoh called Joseph's name Zaphnath-paaneah; and he gave him to wife Asenath the daughter of Potim-herah priest of On. And Joseph went out over all the land of Egypt.* ⁴⁶ *Joseph was thirty years old when he stood before Pharaoh king of Egypt. Joseph went out from the presence of Pharaoh, and throughout all the land of Egypt.* ⁴⁷ *In the seven plentiful years the earth brought forth by handfuls.* ⁴⁸ *He gathered all the food of the seven years which were in the land of Egypt, and stored the food in the cities: the food of the field which was round about every city, he stored in the same manner.* ⁴⁹ *Joseph gathered grain as the sand of the sea, so vast that at last he stopped measuring the grain; for it was beyond measure.* ⁵⁰ *And unto Joseph were born two sons before the years of famine came, which Asenath the daughter of Poti-pherah priest of On bore unto him.* ⁵¹ *Joseph called the name of the firstborn Manasseh: For God, said he, has made me forget all my toil, and all my fathers house.* ⁵² *And the name of the second called he Ephraim: For God has caused me to be fruitful in the land of my affliction.* ⁵³ *The seven years of plenty in the land of Egypt ended.* ⁵⁴ *And the seven years of famine began as Joseph had said: the famine was in all lands but in the land of Egypt there was bread.* ⁵⁵ *When all the land of Egypt was famished, the people cried to Pha-*

Notes:

> raoh for bread: and Pharaoh said unto all the Egyptians, Go unto Joseph; what he says to you, do. [56] The famine was over all the face of the earth: Joseph opened all the storehouses and sold to the Egyptians since the famine had gripped the land of Egypt. [57] All countries came into Egypt to Joseph to buy grain because the famine had gripped all lands.

To interpret dreams accurately one must understand the Universal Language of the Mind and this requires reasoning and perception. Joseph represents the power of perception, the use of the inner mind and inner teacher, which is the final building block of mind prior to the knowing quality of Jesus. Judah and Joseph of the *Old Testament* were brothers showing the connection of imagination aligned with perception used by the reasoner to build permanent memory (knowing) aligned with perception. Perception must always be developed before knowing occurs. The reasoner must heed the inner Self through meditation and dream interpretation. This is why at first Joseph and the tribes of Joseph (Ephraim and Manasseh) are dominant, but later the tribe of Judah through his descendant David became the most important and powerful tribe. Judah, David, Solomon, and Jesus are of the lineage that wins out in the drive to produce the Christ, the Enlightened being. The Holy Spirit represents the whole mind. The word spirit translated from the Greek can be translated equally spirit or mind. It is by the power of the whole mind that Mary could conceive this child destined to achieve Enlightenment, the Christ Consciousness. This birth of Immanuel, I-AM-MANU-EL, symbolizes the opportunity to realize and understand the whole Self. I AM, which is the whole identity, uses the reasoning faculty (MAN, manu, the thinker) to know the God within called EL. *El* (plural Elohim) is the name of Creator in the first Chapter of *Genesis* in the *Old Testament* of the <u>Bible</u> that has been translated into German as *Gott* and from German Gott to our English God.

This is a repeat of the prophet *Isaiah's* statement in Chapter 7, Verse 14 where it is said, *"There-*

fore the Lord himself will give you this sign: the virgin will conceive and bear a son, and will call his name Immanuel." Immanuel a name which means, 'God is with us.' This means God is within each of us. I Am is the thinker, like God (made in the image and likeness). The El is a God. Man symbolizes the thinker who can know the God within us. Joseph had no relations with his wife Mary at any time before she bore a son whom he named Jesus. Joseph named the boy Jesus, even though the Holy Spirit or the Angel said they will call him Immanuel. Joshua is the conqueror of every battle. Joshua, Jeshua that is, Jesus will win the greatest battle of the High Self over the low conscious mind Self in order that Enlightenment may occur. Thus, the inner Self will know I Am = Immanuel and the outer Self Jesus will conquer every obstacle in the conscious mind until full Christ consciousness is a part of the outer Self and one attains full divine or God consciousness.

> *21 And she will bring forth a son, and you will call his name Jesus: for he will save his people from their sins. 22 Now all this was done that it might be fulfilled which was spoken of the Lord by the prophet, saying, 23 Behold, a virgin will be with child, and will bring forth a son, and they will call his name Immanuel, which being interpreted is, God with us. 24 Then Joseph being raised from sleep did as the angel of the Lord had bidden him, and received her into his home as his wife. 25 And he did not have relations with her until she had brought forth her firstborn son: and he called his name Jesus.*

Home or house is where you live and symbolizes in the Universal Language of Mind, the whole mind. The first floor of a house symbolizes the conscious mind. The second floor of a house symbolizes the subconscious mind. And the third floor or attic of a house symbolizes the superconscious mind. Joseph's home in verse 24 symbolizes the mind of Joseph which is the quality of perception willing to cooperate fully with the reasoning power of the conscious mind to nurture the knowing quality into Enlightenment. The nurturing and love quality of the conscious mind is symbolized by Mary. For any new idea, quality, or mutation to grow and develop into adulthood requires nurturing. Abraham was removed from Ur of the Chaldes to Canaan where the mutation could be developed without being diluted or destroyed by the old mental and physical genetic structure. The mutation represented by Noah was able to thrive because Noah's competition was wiped out in the flood. The word Jesus means "the Lord is salvation."

Symbols and Their Interpretation

Chapter Two

1. King Herod - the authority of conscious ego.
2. Astrologers (wise men) - new awareness in conscious mind
3. Scribes - brain pathways, information and mental images stored in the brain
4. High or Chief Priests - aspects who attempt to serve God in a physical manner
5. Messiah - one who is to release aspects from the mistakes of entrapment by moving the awareness forward.
6. Judah - steps ego takes to produce the knower
7. Gold, Frankincense, and Myrrh - value
8. Egypt - entrapment in the physical body
9. Prophet - goal setter, one who creates the ideal of Enlightenment within Self
10. Nazarene - commitment to know the whole Self

Chapter Two

[1] When Jesus was born in Bethlehem of Judea in the days of Herod the king, behold, there came astrologers from the east to Jerusalem, [2] Saying, Where is he that is born King of the Jews? for we have seen his star in the east, and have come to worship him. [3] When Herod the king heard these things, he was troubled, and all Jerusalem with him. [4] He had gathered all the chief priests and scribes of the people together and demanded of them where the messiah was to be born. [5] And they said unto him, In Bethlehem of Judea: for thus it is written by the prophet, [6] And you Bethlehem, in the land of Judah, are not the least among the princes of Judah: for out of you will come a Ruler, that will shepherd my people Israel. [7] Then Herod, called the astrologers aside and inquired of them diligently the exact time of the star's appearance. [8] And he sent them to Bethlehem, saying, Go and search diligently for the young child; and when you have found him, bring me word again that I may come and worship him also. [9] When they had heard the king, they departed; and, lo, the star, which they saw in the east rose till it came and stood over where the young child was. [10] When they saw the star, they rejoiced with exceeding great joy. [11] And when they were come into the house, they saw the young child with Mary his mother, and prostrated themselves and worshipped him: and when they had opened their treasures, they presented unto him gifts; gold, and frankincense, and myrrh. [12] And receiving a message in a dream that they should not return to Herod, they departed into their own country by another route.

Chapter two begins with a presentation by the astrologers, sometimes called the wise men. King Herod represents the ego, the conscious ego that is motivating Self to produce motion. This is the ego motivating Self for security's sake. This motion can then be translated into opportunities for new experiences and increased learning. The wise men or astrologers represent aspects of Self who have wisdom and Self awareness. They have value and influence and are gaining awareness of the stars, which symbolizes new awareness in the conscious mind. The quality of Judah as represented in the phrase, *"and you Bethlehem, in the Land of Judah,"* is a factor in building a productive use of the conscious ego. Judah represents the productive use of the ego, hence, later in the *New Testament* we find the word Judas which is just the Greek form of the Hebrew word Judah. Judas and Judah are the exact same word, with the same symbolic meaning but from two different languages. *Judas* is the Greek translation of the word *Judah* which is Hebrew. They both represent the motivating ego creating or attempting to create forward motion and therefore the opportunity to learn. Herod represents the quality of the ego, also. Herod represents a special quality of the conscious ego because he was a Roman. Romans symbolize discipline in the conscious mind which has united many aspects. This part of the conscious mind is still entrapped. Herod is an entrapped, yet disciplined, part of the ego. Herod is not a part of the lineage of Jesus, nor is Jesus related to Herod. Herod represents that part of the disciplined ego that reacts to change in the environment by stimulating movement. King Herod has a type of physical authority.

Mary and Joseph go to Egypt as did Abraham and Sarah in the *Old Testament*. This represents the recognition by the conscious mind that the soul of Self is entrapped in the physical. The soul who is to produce Enlightenment grows up entrapped in a physical body until the soul, existing in the body, begins to be aware of Self as independent or separate from others in the conscious mind.

Herod desired to learn from the astrologers the exact time of the star's appearance. Time as a symbol in the Universal Language of Mind represents a measurement of the soul's progression just as time in the physical environment is measured by a progression of events such as sunrise to sunrise or the rotation of the hands of a clock or the progression and change of the seasons. As events progress in the physical existence they always change. The nature of the physical is to always change. The conscious mind that has yet to embrace growthful change supports a dishonest conscious ego. Therefore, this ego will react to any new situation, mutation, or opportunity for advancement with insecurity. This insecurity will attempt to stifle change as a means of protecting itself and its position of physical power, misguided as this may be. The astrologers arrived in Jerusalem, the city where Herod, the conscious ego resided. This was also the city of David of the tribe of Judah in the *Old Testament*. The astrologers inquired, *"Where is the newborn king of the Jews?"* King Herod was greatly disturbed at this news for there can be only one King in a country. This baby Jesus was a threat to Herod, the insecure conscious ego's authority. When one embraces change as a part of life and harnesses change as a step to transcending the limited physical Self then spiritual progression is rapid as limitation is vanquished.

The lineage and tribe of Judah is by no means least among Israel for Jesus, symbolizing the knower, is of the tribe of Judah. Bethlehem is not the least of Judah for from this city of Judah comes Jesus. *John 7:42* states this as a prophesy saying, *"does not scripture say that the Messiah, being of David's family is to come from the village of Bethlehem."* The gifts of gold, frankincense and myrrh represent value recognized and appreciated in the conscious mind. In this case, value is recognized in the mutative quality called knowing. This is the quality of being able to consciously cause one's own mental and spiritual evolution to quicken and progress at a rate faster than those given under the laws of compulsion from which plants, animals, and non-reasoners operate. Frankincense is a gum resin that was burned as incense in the time of Jesus, as was myrrh. Myrrh was an Arabian ointment used as a pain killer, representing the ability to free the attention from the finite, physical existence. Both of these had great value at the time. Incense was offered to God via smoke rising off an altar. The ancient Israelites offered animal sacrifices to God, whom they called Yahweh, translated as *Lord* in the <u>Bible</u>, and also sometimes mis-translated as *Jehovah*, all of which symbolizes I Am. The use of dreams is again a factor as presented in verse twelve. This indicates the mental perception is being used to perceive and receive that which is beyond the five senses and thereby avoid the destructive habits of the conscious ego and the limited conscious mind.

> *13 When they were departed, behold, the angel of the Lord appeared to Joseph in a dream, saying, Arise, and take the young child and his mother, and flee into Egypt, and stay there until I bring you word: for Herod will seek the young child to destroy him. 14 When Joseph arose, he took the young child and his mother by night, and departed into Egypt: 15 They remained there until the death of Herod: that it might be fulfilled which was spoken of the Lord by the prophet, saying, Out of Egypt have I called my son. 16 Herod, when he saw that he was mocked of the wise men, was exceedingly angry, and sent forth, and killed all the*

> *children that were in Bethlehem, and in all the coasts thereof, from two years old and under, according to the time which he had diligently inquired of the wise men, the astrologers. [17] Then was fulfilled that which was spoken by Jeremiah the prophet, saying, [18] In Ramah was there a voice heard, lamentation, and weeping, and great mourning, Rachel weeping for her children, and would not be comforted, because they are not. [19] But when Herod was dead, behold, an angel of the Lord appeared in a dream to Joseph in Egypt. [20] Saying, Arise, and take the young child and his mother, and go into the land of Israel: for they are dead who wanted the young child's life. [21] He arose, and took the young child and his mother, and came into the land of Israel. [22] But when he heard that Archelaus did reign in Judea in the room of his father Herod, he was afraid to go there: notwithstanding, being warned of God in a dream, he turned aside into the region of Galilee: [23] He came and dwelled in a city called Nazareth: that it might be fulfilled which was said by the prophets, He will be called a Nazarene.*

The physical has limitations. It is temporary. Each person needs to recognize these and understand them. When the individual begins to be dissatisfied with physical life, he or she begins to move out of Egypt to enter the promised land which symbolizes Self using the physical environment to cause permanent learning. Self will fully utilize the physical life sooner or later. Yes, there are limitations in the physical, however, the developing, learning and growing individual will not allow those limitations to restrict or constrict Self. One needs to learn to create the inner urge to gain Enlightenment. The gifts of gold, frankincense, and myrrh show the value for the new mutation because Jesus is the new mutation for Intuitive Man.

The prophet says, *"Out of Egypt I will call my son"*, meaning, out of entrapment the aggressive, forward moving Self will develop to master all of mind. The aggressive action of Self moves into the inner levels of mind to create the new Self.

Herod ordered the massacre of all boys age two years and under. The number two symbolizes the aggressive and receptive qualities. Anytime a new factor is introduced there exists the possibility for the new mutation to be diluted or crowded out by the old. The killing of all boys two years old and younger left no boys alive of Jesus' age. This mutation of Jesus the Knower was able to thrive because his influence was the *only* influence of that age group and quality.

This is the way of any new mutation if it is to exist and thrive and build. This is an alternate solution to how the mutation of Abraham, Isaac and Jacob was caused to survive and prosper. In Abraham's case the mutation was removed from the diluting influence of Ur of Chaldees. In Jesus' case the diluting influence was removed from the mutation by killing off all boys Jesus' age. Just like when the dinosaurs possibly were killed by a giant meteor striking the earth, then the mammals were able to thrive as the predominant species of animals on the planet and move into the dominant ecological niche. The one who intends to build Enlightenment this lifetime needs to be in an environment conducive to learning.

After Herod's death an angel appeared to Joseph in a dream. The dream indicates once again perception in the form of the conscious mind listening to its inner guidance is guiding one to become Enlightened as he listens to the inner urge. They returned to a region in Galilee and settled in a town called Nazareth. In this way what was said through the prophets was fulfilled. *"He will be called a Nazarene"*.

> *I Samuel 1:22 states, But Hannah (the mother of Samuel) went not up; for she said unto her husband, I will not go up until the child be weaned, and then I will bring him, that he may appear before the Lord, and there abide for ever. I will offer him as a perpetual Nazarite.*

A Nazarene is one who is committed to God. A Nazarene or Nazarite never shaved meaning the conscious thoughts are focused on learning creation.

Notes:

Symbols and Their Interpretation

Chapter Three

1. John - the disciplined action of believing (believing with mental discipline)
2. Baptist - one who makes a commitment to Self
3. Reform - change, re-form
4. Reign of God - responsibility to High Self to gain Self awareness and Enlightenment
5. Garment of camels hair and leather belt - physical body
6. Grasshoppers - habits, compulsion
7. Honey - knowledge
8. Tree - subconscious experience or existence
9. Feet - spiritual foundation such as meditation, concentration, and directed imagery
10. Fire - expansion of consciousness
11. Stones - will
12. Holy spirit - whole mind
13. Barn - mind
14. Hand - purpose
15. Grain - knowledge
16. Chaff - information and experience which does not add to total subconscious existence
17. Spirit of God - the mind of creation; conscious, subconscious, and superconscious
18. Dove - subconscious thoughts
19. Son - initiatory quality, initiating action to produce knowing

Chapter Three

[1] In those days John the Baptist appeared, preaching in the desert of Judea, [2] This was his theme, reform your lives: for the reign of God is at hand. [3] For this is he that was spoken of by the prophet Isaiah saying, The voice of one crying in the wilderness, Prepare the way of the Lord, make his paths straight. [4] John was clothed in a garment of camel's hair and a leather belt about his loins; and his food was grasshoppers and wild honey. [5] They went out to him Jerusalem, and all Judea, and all the region round about Jordan, [6] And were baptized of him in Jordan, admitting their mistakes. [7] But when he saw many of the Pharisees and Sadducees come to his baptism, he said to them, O generation of vipers, who has warned you to flee from the wrath to come? [8] Bring forth some evidence that you intend to reform. [9] And think not to say within yourselves, We have Abraham to our father: for I say unto you, that God is able of these stones to raise up children unto Abraham. [10] And now also the axe is laid unto the root of the trees: therefore every tree which is not fruitful will be cut down and cast into the fire.

Jesus represents the knowing quality, and John represents the action of believing. Believing must precede knowing and the birth of John preceded the birth of Jesus. In order to build the knowing quality, one must first have enough belief or faith in Self to begin motion through Self initiative. Belief is the stimulus provided by someone or something outside Self. Belief or faith occurs when Self images one's own stimulus for forward motion. Instead of allowing doubts and fears to get in the way of mental pictures, one can create what is wanted mentally. Image the ideal and begin movement toward the desired ideal with belief. This is the productive process of expanding consciousness. Belief stimulates motion toward the goal or ideal. After the movement toward the ideal begins, knowing can then be developed through reasoning with the new, more expanded field of experience.

Reform your life, was John the Baptist's admonition. Re-form means to change. To change is to gain a greater and more productive form. *"The reign of God is at hand"* means that the time for making the commitment to learning, growing, and developing the inner awareness of one's purpose in life is now. John was clothed in a garment of camel's hair and wore a leather belt around his waist which symbolizes the soul's entrapment in a physical body. Leather is produced from the skin of animals. The human body which is an evolved type of animal body is covered with skin. Camel's skin has hair on it. Leather is made out of skin. Hair was a predominant characteristic of Esau in *Genesis*. Esau was a son of Isaac. Hair indicates the conscious thoughts of one entrapped in a physical body. Even though mankind is moving toward Enlightenment, we are still in an animal body, the skin or hide of which is used to make leather. Grasshoppers and wild honey that were John the Baptist's food present an image of assimilating habits and not letting them control Self. Grasshoppers and bees symbolize habits. The Believer, John, uses the brain pathways of the animal body to nourish Self so that brain pathways do not limit Self. In this way, he can move forward in growthful learning. The wild honey shows that using knowledge produced from compulsion is John's main theme. The entrapped soul's forward evolution is produced in this manner from the point of evolution symbolized by John to the present time in evolution. At the current stage of our evolution, mankind individually has progressed to the level of causing quickened evolution. The thinker can use the knowledge and experience available to produce permanent understandings. At that time of John, Jerusalem and all Judea were going out to him. Jerusalem symbolizes the commitment in the physical to the superconscious mind. It shows the willingness on the part of the conscious mind to use the full lifetime and all its activities to bring about the full use of the inner mind while physically incarned by giving all energies to the High Self which is the New Jerusalem.

Genesis 14 [18] *And Melchizedek king of Salem brought bread and wine: he was the priest of the most high God.*

[19] And he blessed him, saying, Blessed be Abram of the most high God, possessor of heaven and earth: [20] And blessed be the most high God, which has delivered your enemies into your hand. Then Abram gave him a tenth of everything.

Salem is one half of the word Jeru-salem and shows the ideal of superconscious awareness in the conscious mind.

The Jordan River, being comprised of water, represents all the physical experiences. The people being baptized in the Jordan River symbolize making a commitment to use the physical for learning, growth, and Self awareness. John never liked the Pharisees and Sadducees. He called them a brood of vipers because they were only intellectuals. They read and preached the *Old Testament* and Universal Law without practice, so there was never any change, movement or growth in their inner Self, and they restricted other people's growth by making them follow rules with no inner purpose. The phrase, God can raise up children to Abraham from these very stones symbolizes the ability on the part of the disciplined reasoner to employ will (stones) to cause the development of immature aspects of Self which are progressing. Trees represent subconscious experience. A tree that is not fruitful symbolizes any aspect or thought pattern of Self that is producing nothing for the soul or inner Self. Throwing these unproductive trees into the fire symbolizes the thinker's willingness to release all limitation, giving energy up rapidly to a higher cause thus creating rapid expansion in Self.

Matthew 3 [11] I indeed baptize you with water to change hearts, but he that comes after me is mightier than I, whose shoes I am not worthy to bear. He will baptize you with the Holy Spirit, and fire: [12] His winnowing fan is in his hand. He will clear the threshing floor and gather his grain into the barn; but he will burn up the chaff with unquenchable fire. [13] Then came Jesus from Galilee to Jordan unto John, to be baptized of him. [14] But John forbade him, saying, I have need to be baptized of you, and yet you come to me? [15] And Jesus answering said unto him, Give in for now: for thus it becomes us to fulfill all of God's demands. So John gave in.

The commitment will be not only to use the physical productively but to use the whole mind, and to use physical experience together with reasoning to cause expansion and give to the inner Self. Hand symbolizes purpose. The verse *"his winnowing fan in his hand"* shows that purpose is the catalyst for causing expansion (fire) in the life. To clear the threshing floor is the preparation to receive knowledge into the Self. Gathering the grain represents accumulating the knowledge gained from experiencing in the physical, learning from those experiences and teaching them to others. In this way the permanent knowledge storage capacity of one's subconscious mind is filled and there is no longer any need to reincarn. The purpose of the physical existence is fulfilled. The Self can move expansively forward to greater fields of learning. One must be fully committed to using the believing quality in order to have this firm foundation from which to employ knowing. So John gave in and did as Jesus requested.

The essence of service is to give wholly and freely. This John, the action of believing, accomplished. He did this by giving to someone greater than himself. The person who gives to someone and something greater than Self gains the opportunity to receive a greater awareness of Self and expansion of consciousness which creates a fulfilling, satisfying, and abundant life.

The experience of giving freely and completely will cause to achieve the greatest fulfillment. Each individual needs to expand their consciousness between Self and all of humanity. By changing the way one relates to others, one changes their consciousness.

> [16] *And Jesus, when he was baptized, immediately came out of the water: and, lo, the heavens were opened unto him, and he saw the Spirit of God descending like a dove, and lighting upon him:* [17] *And lo a voice from heaven, saying, This is my beloved Son, in whom I am well pleased.*

The spirit of God descending and hovering over Jesus shows that the aggressive conscious mind, committed to gaining Enlightenment, understands the plan of creation held in superconscious mind, the mind of God. The plan of creation is the mind of God. The whole mind, conscious, subconscious and superconscious, is the spirit of God. The thoughts of inner Self (dove), the subconscious mind, and the plan of God, unified and moving together in unison, are symbolized in this image. Heaven or skies are metaphors for superconscious mind. A voice from the heavens is one's own superconscious mind communicating directly to the conscious mind as one's whole Self is aligned and moving in harmony and unison. The beloved son is the person causing continual forward motion toward learning, growth, and Self awareness. He is beloved because an alignment of the minds and therefore a union of Self has been created for I Am existing in the three divisions of mind.

Symbols and Their Interpretation

Chapter Four

1. Desert (wilderness) - untamed, uncontrolled or unproductive part of conscious mind
2. Spirit - mind
3. 40 - stability plus the power of understanding
4. Bread - knowledge
5. Mouth of God - medulla oblongata
6. Holy city - whole mind devoted and committed to Enlightenment
7. Pinnacle of temple - crown chakra
8. Devil - conscious ego
9. Angels - messengers from I AM
10. By the sea - emotional level of consciousness
11. Darkness - need for awareness
12. Light - awareness
13. Simon Peter - will
14. Andrew - imagination
15. Fish - spiritual awareness
16. Men - physically engrossed aspects of Self. Physical aspects associated with physical body.
17. Disciples - disciplined aspects of Self
18. James - disciplined effort to know
19. 10 - completion of a cycle with understanding that produces power

Chapter Four

*¹ Then was Jesus guided by the Spirit into the wilderness to
be tempted of the devil. ² He fasted forty days and forty
nights, and afterwards was hungry. ³ When the tempter came
to him, he said, If you are the Son of God, command that
these stones be made into bread. ⁴ But he answered and
said, It is written, Man will not live by bread alone, but by
every word that proceeds out of the mouth of God. ⁵ Then
the devil took him up into the holy city, and sat him on a
pinnacle of the temple,*

The devil is the conscious ego. Jesus fasted for forty days and forty
nights. This compares to the forty days and forty nights of Noah in the ark.
The number forty was also identified with the forty years the Israelites, under
Moses' direction, dwelt in the wilderness or desert before moving into the
Promised Land, Canaan, the land of milk and honey.

*Genesis 7:12 And the rain was upon the earth forty days
and forty nights.*

The number four symbolizes the quality of stability. Zero symbolizes the power of completing a cycle and beginning a new stage of life. The
thinker desirous of promoting full spiritual Enlightenment must understand
and master the conscious ego; then the ego can be directed as a motivator to
Self awareness. The mouth of God is the medulla oblongata. It is the ana-
tomical point where life force enters the body. To be truly spiritual, one must
learn to live on life force and to bring life force into the body willfully through
the medulla oblongata so that Self is not distracted by the body. Then the
individual can go into the inner levels of the mind and not be trapped in the
body. Because the breath binds the soul to the physical body, the attention
can only be freed when breath is slowed and the body can be sustained by life
force. The pinnacle of the temple is the crown chakra.

Notes:

> ^{6} And said unto him, If you are the
> Son of God, cast yourself down: for
> it is written, He will give his angels
> charge concerning you: and in their
> hands they will support you, that you
> may never stumble on a stone. ^{7} Jesus
> said unto him, It is written again, You
> will not tempt the Lord your God.

Jesus is quoting what is stated in *Deuteronomy*
6:16: "*You will not tempt the Lord your God, as you
tempted him in Massah.*"

Every activity is not just for fun and games,
although life can be very entertaining. Life is for gaining blissful Enlightenment. All the action of Self should
be towards that which is permanent and lasting. Action needs to profit the Self permanently so that one
will have the benefit of the learning as a permanent
part of Self at the end of this lifetime and forever. Distractions and actions that will not add permanently to
Self are a very poor investment. No one can cause
Enlightenment in the thinker except the Self. Yet everyone needs a teacher. Anyone has the capability of
progressing spiritually by using a lifetime efficiently.

> ^{8} Again, the devil took him up into an
> exceeding high mountain, and
> showed him all the kingdoms of the
> world, and the glory of them; ^{9} And
> said unto him, All these things will I
> give you, if you will fall down and
> worship me. ^{10} Then said Jesus unto
> him, Get behind me, Satan: for it is
> written, You will worship the Lord
> your God, and him only will you
> adore.

Jesus' response is a direct quote from
Deuteronomy 6:16. One who gives the whole lifetime
for the sole motivation of accumulating physical possessions or physical security, is worshipping the conscious ego. Homage to the Lord your God (Yahweh-
Jehovah) is to give the full attention and effort to knowing I AM. The statement "*him only will you adore*" is

a command to give the number one priority in one's life to knowing the whole Self, the Real Self. Do not worship and give all of your attention to the conscious ego, rather give your full effort to knowing I Am = EGO which is the Real Self.

> *11 Then the devil left him, and, behold, angels came and ministered unto him.*

Thought forms from I Am and superconscious mind come to the service of the knower to nourish and aid one who is committed to knowing the inner Self and gaining Enlightenment.

> *12 When Jesus heard that John was put into prison, he departed to Galilee; 13 Leaving Nazareth, he came and dwelled in Capernaum, which is by the sea in the borders of Zebulun and Naphtali: 14 That it might be fulfilled which was said by Isaiah the prophet, 15 The land of Zebulun, and the land of Naphtali, by the way of the sea, beyond Jordan, Galilee of the Gentiles: 16 The people living in darkness have seen a great light; and to them which sat in the region and shadow of death, light is sprung up. 17 From that time on Jesus began to preach, and to say, Reform your lives: The kingdom of heaven is at hand.*

When Jesus heard that John was arrested he withdrew to Galilee. This indicates believing is relied on less and less as the knowing quality becomes stronger and stronger. It is time to move from believing into knowing. And he went down to live in Capernaum, by the sea in the land of Zebulun and Naphtali. Land, which represents subconscious mind substance, and sea (water), which represents conscious experience, come together at the shoreline which represents the sixth level of mind, the emotional level of consciousness where the conscious and subconscious minds are joined. People living in darkness have seen a great light. The great light is knowing, which is the movement towards en-light-en-ment. From that time on Jesus began to proclaim the theme: re-form (change) your lives. The kingdom of heaven is at hand. This is the same proclamation that John had made which was to reform your lives. *"The kingdom of heaven is at hand."* To re-form is to change. It is to refocus the structure of one's life around knowing the whole mind and becoming Enlightened.

> *18 And Jesus, walking by the sea of Galilee, saw two brothers, Simon called Peter, and Andrew his brother, casting a net into the sea for they were fishermen. 19 He said unto them, Follow me and I will make you fishers of men. 20 And*

> *they immediately left their nets and*
> *followed him.* [21] *Going on from*
> *there, he saw two other brothers,*
> *James the son of Zebedee and John*
> *his brother, in a ship with Zebedee*
> *their father, mending their nets; and*
> *he called them.* [22] *They immediately*
> *left the ship and their father, and fol-*
> *lowed him.*

The word disciple and the word discipline
come from the same root. Disciples represent disciplined aspects. To grow and mature, one must discipline the mind. One needs to discipline and strengthen
the will. Self needs to teach the physical body that the
individual, not the body, is the master. One must discipline the very Self in order to sit in meditation for an
hour or longer and so that one can keep attention on
knowing God, so that one can keep the attention on
knowing the Self, so that everything done can be for
illumination.

Peter represents the quality of will. Andrew
represents the quality of imagination. These two factors are the basic foundation upon which the reasoner
causes the quickening of the evolutionary development
of Self. Fish symbolize spiritual awareness. Peter and
Andrew being fishermen indicate spiritual awareness
has been gained in the use of will and imagination. The
highest use of will and imagination is to move to the
ideal of an Enlightened whole functioning Self.

Just as John the Baptist represented the action of believing so also does John the disciple symbolize the quality of believing. John the Baptist preceded Jesus in his ministry symbolizing the need for
believing to precede knowing in the construction of
the framework and structure of the thinker's ability to
move to Christhood or Enlightenment. John the Baptist being thrown into prison shows that believing has
tremendous value. When Self begins to move into an
understanding of the knowing quality and how to produce knowing in the Self and life, then one is aware of
the limitations of believing. This does not mean, however, that believing is no longer of any use to the thinker.
Rather, the development of the knowing quality takes

top priority in all areas of life and believing is used as a much needed step towards this. The difference in the knower is the realization that believing is a temporary step to be used in building the permanency of knowing called Self understanding. Thus, even though Jesus symbolizes the awareness in Self of the highest value given to completing permanent learning through each experience, there is still the recognition of the need for further learning to occur on the road to Enlightenment. This further learning is presented throughout the *Book of Matthew* as the experiences — teaching, learning, and finally full acceptance of God's will. This learning fulfills the plan of creation held in Superconscious mind, culminating in the crucifixion and resurrection of Jesus the Christ (anointed). Fish represent spiritual awareness. Jesus called two brothers, James, Zebedee's son, and his brother John, to be his disciples. John represents the believing factor as did John the Baptist. Even though John the Baptist is in prison, still Jesus, the Knower, is always going to use the believing quality and it is going to be disciplined. Believing will be a disciple, a disciplined aspect of Self.

> ²³ *Jesus journeyed throughout Galilee, teaching in their synagogues, preaching the gospel of the kingdom, and healing all manner of sickness and all manner of disease among the people.* ²⁴ *And his fame went throughout all Syria: they brought to him all sick people that were taken with many kinds of diseases and torments, and those who were possessed with devils, and those who were lunatic, and those who were paralyzed; and he cured them all.* ²⁵ *Great multitudes of people followed him: from Galilee, and from the ten cities, and from Jerusalem, and from Judea, and from beyond Jordan.*

"He cured them all." This indicates Jesus taught people to change from unproductive attitudes which cause an illness, to productive thoughts which cause wholeness. Therefore he was teaching permanent healing. Since people represent aspects of Self in the Bible, through his teaching and through his giving and healing, he is learning about Self. The knower is learning about the unproductive, limiting parts of Self. Jesus is changing aspects of Self to ones which are productive and therefore permanent in the Self. The various diseases represent the various qualities of the unproductive attitudes. Paralyzed people represent areas where there is a need to cause forward motion in the life. Lunatics are the aspects of Self who need to cause undivided attention and reasoning. The great crowd that followed him came from the sea of Galilee to Jerusalem and Judea, and from across the Jordan, representing all the different parts of mind and Self. The ten cities represent using power to know Self for zero symbolizes the power and understanding gained from completing a cycle and from completing the learning one starts.

Symbols and Their Interpretation

Chapter Five

1. Beatitudes - attitudes of being - Be-Attitudes
2. Single-hearted - singular ideal and purpose
3. Peacemakers - one who aligns many aspects of Self
4. Salt - preserving knowledge as permanent memory
5. Bushel basket - limited container for knowledge
6. Law - structure to produce Enlightenment
7. Murder - destroying learning opportunities
8. Judgement - karma
9. Anger - Sustained misunderstanding. Incomplete understanding.
10. Gehenna - unused experience expanded
11. Altar - attention
12. Prison - Self imposed limitations
13. Adultery - Breaking the commitment of conscious to subconscious minds
14. Lust - sensory engrossment
15. Eye - perception
16. Divorce - withdrawal of attention from the physical body and conscious mind by the soul or subconscious mind
17. Oaths - need to make thoughts, words and actions match
18. Love - giving to Self and others without restriction and receiving freely, non-separation
19. Tax collectors - aspects that place value outside of Self and need to recognize Self value
20. Pagans - aspects that worship the physical which includes possessions and sensory engrossment

Chapter Five

¹ And seeing the multitudes, he went up into a mountain: and when he was set, his disciples came unto him: ² And he opened his mouth, and taught them, saying, ³ Blessed are the poor in spirit: for theirs is the kingdom of heaven.

Lamsa translates this as, *"Blest are the humble, for theirs is the Kingdom of Heaven."* To be blessed is to gain the understanding which was not previously possessed. To receive a blessing is to gain something valuable from a higher source, energy, or soul that one previously had not possessed. To bless is to make Holy which is to make whole. A person causes Self or an aspect of Self to be whole by gaining new awareness and, following this, a new and greater understanding of Self. The disciples accepted the knower Jesus as their spiritual teacher. The seeking and acceptance of guidance from a spiritual teacher, one greater than the Self, is necessary in order to have rapid spiritual growth. The one who is secure within the Self, having neither a Self inflated nor a Self depreciating ego attitude thus aligning their conscious ego with the I Am-Ego, will fulfill the plan of creation to gain Enlightenment which is held in the Superconscious mind. Spirit is mind. When one is poor in spirit, they haven't acknowledged and overcome doubts and fears. The person poor in spirit is innocent, as a newborn baby. Such a one has never learned doubts and fears. One can create things through that very innocence. Since there are few or no doubts one seems to have beginner's luck and can create things the first time. They are blessed because they can begin without any Self imposed limitations. They haven't been taught doubts therefore thoughts manifest as reality rapidly. The Lamsa <u>Bible</u> interprets poor in spirit as *humble* which in Aramaic literally means *poor in pride; unassuming.* One who is not abundant in prideful boasting and does not need to prove their egoic worth can therefore receive learning and knowledge without restriction, and is therefore blessed. Kingdom of heaven can be interpreted literally as "kingdom of the skies." Both skies and kingdom symbolize the superconscious mind in the Universal Language of Mind.

Notes:

^{4} *Blessed too are the sorrowing: they will be consoled.*

Lamsa; "*Blessed are they who mourn, for they will be comforted.*" Blessed are those who recognize the Truth of Gautama the Buddha's statement, one of his four noble Truths, "*the nature of the physical is pain.*" It is our duty to evolve from the pain of stagnancy and into the joy of creation. When Self recognizes the physical life is temporary then Self is ready to move to a life more permanent, lasting, and less painful. This is the movement to know the inner Self. They will be consoled means elevating the inner Self. These aspects will learn to create and produce growthful change more rapidly than the physical environment and world changes around them, therefore, they will have the Self direction and understanding to gain Enlightenment.

^{5} *Blessed are the lowly: for they will inherit the earth.*

Lamsa; "*Blest are the meek, for they will inherit the earth.*" The lowest place for experiencing is the physical body in the physical environment. The lowest place in mind is the physical experience. The divisions of mind are superconscious, subconscious, and conscious mind. The conscious mind functions with the brain in our waking, physical existence. When a person hits bottom, when a person hits rock bottom, and sees that the physical is not where the happiness is, then one is ready to hear the Truth. Know that when the physical life alone no longer fulfills, then there is a readiness to use the experiences productively. One who is meek endures the nature of the physical, which is change or pain, with patience and without resentment. Resentment only impedes learning and is therefore the enemy of learning. One who is resentful or hateful does not receive this blessing. The one who is lowly, that is, the one who identifies that they are a soul not a physical body and that the physical existence is to be used as a vehicle for gaining permanent Self understanding, receives this blessing. One who is learning from each experience has no resentment. Such a one does not have time to be resentful or unproductive in thoughts or action for there exists recognition that one's physical lifetime is a temporary school-room of learning to be used to add permanent memory to the soul. The word "lowly" can also be translated as gentle.

> *⁶ Blessed are they which do hunger and thirst for holiness: for they will be filled.*

Lamsa translates holiness as justice, and filled as satisfied. Hunger represents desire for knowledge or learning which adds to the soul. Food symbolizes knowledge. Thirst represents desire for physical experience that Self will use to add to the soul. Trying to fulfill all physical desires for taste, sensation, and other sense gratification will not fulfill the real hunger within. Use the experiences to add to the real Self or soul so that Self will be whole and complete. Know the whole Self. Such a one is blessed. They will have their fill means they will gain fulfillment. To obtain justice is to fulfill one's karma which is to complete one's indebtedness to the Self. The debt one owes to Self is learning and understanding Self in order to be Enlightened. We call this process, building permanent understandings. When one receives justice one has obtained the just returns upon actions taken, that is, all the learning they have earned. Avoidance is the root of loneliness. Those aspects of Self that desire to be open to receive life to the fullest instead of putting up walls of isolation around themselves will experience union and not the loneliness resulting from separation.

> *⁷ Blessed are the merciful: for they will obtain mercy.*

Mercy represents the factor of making a mistake and being willing to admit it was a mistake, then causing the learning which will ensure the mistake is never made again because one has transcended, through learning, the limitations previously accepted. Recognizing and looking to see the learning which took place in the mistake so that the same mistake is not repeated, is a step in gaining greater awareness. At that point, one can cause something permanent instead of temporary. Mercy is understanding karma. Mercy is also understanding cause and effect. Mercy is caused by understanding and wielding the Universal Laws, so that which fails to produce learning can be changed and learning produced.

> *⁸ Blessed are the single-hearted: for they will see God.*

Lamsa; translates single-hearted as pure in heart. The single hearted is any person who utilizes singular attention consistently for the purpose of producing permanent understanding. Heart symbolizes understanding. The thinker practices undivided attention and concentration so the mind is fo-

Notes:

cused. The attention can then be directed fully on meditation, for listening to the inner Self, to knowing all of
creation, and to gaining the full and ultimate from each
and every experience. Singular attention, focused on
the desire and need to achieve Enlightenment or the
next level of evolution is necessary and required to see
God which is to gain cosmic awareness of creation
through transcending the conscious mind and mind itself.

> *⁹ Blessed are the peacemakers: for
> they will be called the sons of God.*

A peacemaker is one who causes peace. This
could be a president of a country, this could be a general, this could be one who causes a war to come to an
end. This could be a Spiritual Teacher or leader. Anyone who creates a situation where people work together,
instead of existing as separate beings, fighting each
other, is a peacemaker. The individual needs significant understandings in order to associate with, form
friendships with, and learn from those different from
the Self. This understanding draws people who are
abundant in awareness and Self understanding so Self
can give abundantly to others. When all aspects are
unified and the whole attention is being focused toward one goal, one ideal, and one purpose, then one
becomes whole or Holy. Self can aggressively move
toward gaining that highest purpose which is knowing
the whole Self. Jesus is referred to as a Son of God,
and he is a peacemaker. Peace created by union of all
aspects of Self produces the freedom to actively pursue the full awareness of Self as a Creator.

> *¹⁰ Blessed are they which are perse-
> cuted for holiness' sake: for the reign
> of God is theirs.*

Lamsa; *"Blest are those who are persecuted
for the sake of justice, for theirs is the kingdom of
heaven."* The reign of God is awareness of the Whole
Self, the whole mind, and the complete, full, Enlightenment. The kingdom of heaven is the superconscious

mind. At first, the environment may not always cooperate because the environment is moving slower than the creative thinker who is causing a greater forward motion at a higher rate. Therefore, the creative thinker will teach others and aid them along the way to cause their motion to be quickened in order that they do not allow the restriction or the slow motion of the physical to slow their progress. Self increases the motion of the physical. Persecution for the sake of justice is one's willingness to pursue Self understanding no matter what insecurity, doubt, fear, or limitation may arise.

> *11 Blessed are you, when men will revile you and persecute you, and will say all manner of evil lies against you falsely, for my sake. 12 Rejoice, and be exceeding glad: for your reward is great in heaven: for so persecuted they the prophets which were before you.*

Lamsa translates *"your reward is great in heaven"* as *"your reward in heaven is increased"*. The limitations of the physical become a way for Self to recognize and identify restrictions and constrictions, to admit them, to transcend them, and to create a more expansive consciousness. Be glad and rejoice, for your reward is great in Heaven because you are fulfilling the plan and will move beyond any previously accepted limitation. The prophets related the goal and the plan to mankind. They were the goal setters. The prophets recognized the limitations that one encounters in the physical. When the Self moves beyond limitations soul rejoices. That is a time of great happiness. One's reward in heaven is increased means to raise one's consciousness until it encompasses all of creation. Going against the group consciousness, engrossed in the physical senses to pursue life beyond and more expansive than the physical, will add to Self and ensure the transcendence of the physical conscious mind Self.

> *13 You are the salt of the earth: but if the salt has lost its savor, how will it be salted? It is therefore good for nothing, but to be cast out, and to be trodden under foot of men.*

Salt is used as a preservative, also as a flavor enhancer. Salt is also a necessary nutrient for the human body's survival. Food, in the Universal Language of Mind, represents knowledge. This shows the ability to see the value of Self knowledge and to gain the most benefit from it. This is an injunction to preserve the knowledge that is available from temporary experiences and to transform it into permanent knowledge which is the ultimate preservation. This is knowledge called understandings that are stored within Self for all time. Therefore, use the experiences now, in the present, while the learning is available, rather than procrastinating by waiting for the perfect situation to act. Feet symbolize one's spiritual foundation. To trample underfoot is to refuse to use situations for the growth of Self.

> *[14] You are the light of the world. A city that is set on a hill cannot be hid. [15] Neither do men light a lamp and put it under a bushel basket, but on a lampstand; and it gives light unto all that are in the house. [16] Let your light so shine before men, that they may see your good works, and glorify your Father which is in heaven.*

Light represents awareness. When Self gains awareness, one can share, teach, and pass on that awareness to others. Until one is willing to give at anytime, to anyone, one will still live within their limits that are Self imposed. Awareness in one area of life can be used to gain greater awareness in other areas of Self. Lamsa translates city set on a hill as *"a city that is built upon a mountain cannot be hidden"*. A city is a place where many people reside and as such symbolizes many aspects of the mind. A mountain symbolizes a challenge or obstacle. To build a city on a mountain is to construct one's own understanding of thousands of aspects of the Self. A lamp symbolizes awareness. Compare the lampstand of verse fifteen with the lampstands of the *Book of Revelation* Chapter One.

> *[17] Think not that I am come to abolish the law, or the prophets: I am not come to abolish them, but to fulfill them.*

Lamsa translates abolish as weaken. The *New Testament* presents the completion of the evolution of mankind that was begun eons before. Jesus represents the knower. He is the culmination of all the prophets and their prophesies. All the goal setters and imagers are symbolized by the prophets. Jesus is the construction of awareness to complete what the prophets had not yet completed which is full knowing and awareness of the Self as an Enlightened being, as a Buddha, a Zarathustra, a Pythagoras, or an Enlightened Christ.

18 For verily I say unto you, Till heaven and earth pass, one letter or punctuation mark will in no way pass from the law, until all is fulfilled. 19 Whoever therefore breaks one of these least commandments and teaches men to do so will be called the least in the kingdom of heaven: but whoever will do and teach them, he will be called great in the kingdom of heaven. 20 For I say unto you, That except your holiness will exceed the holiness of the scribes and Pharisees, you will in no case enter into the kingdom of heaven.

The Universal Laws will remain universal and will continue to form the framework and structure of creation as long as there are individual souls who continue to use them. These souls are any person who has yet to gain Enlightenment and therefore needs the structure of conscious and subconscious minds to operate within. Anyone who breaks or weakens the commands or ten commandments that God gave to Moses, who then gave them to the Israelites, will be least in the kingdom of God or heaven. This is because such a one will remain entrapped in the physical existence, continually reincarning and going through similar experiences without learning the lesson of these experiences. This is similar to a child in school who refuses to learn the lessons of a particular grade and therefore needs to repeat that grade before progressing to the next higher level. Your Holiness indicates the whole learning must be greater than that of the scribes, who represent brain pathways, and the Pharisees, who symbolize intellectual learning. Brain pathways, habits, or intellectual learning and memorizing information, will not give the awareness that is needed to be a whole functioning Self. These are only steps in learning to reason so a foundation can be built for producing illumination.

21 You have heard that it was said by them of old time, You will not kill; and whoever will murder will be in danger of the judgment:

Jesus is referring to one of the ten commandments given in *Exodus 20:13* of the *Old Testament*. Murder symbolizes forcing a physical change prematurely instead of causing a mental progressive change within Self. Murder is the destruction of a learning opportunity. A forced physical change does not bloom and blossom. The worst result of physical murder is that you cut short a person's learning. That murdered person must then reincarn, going through infancy and adolescence to once again reach a similar opportunity for learning that was untimely terminated in the past life. To reincarn and to go through all those years of life just to get to the point where the same lesson can be learned, could set a soul back fifty or one hundred years in soul growth. Every opportunity to progress that remains unused or misused will leave the thinker with the same debt of learning yet to be paid to I Am.

> [22] *But I say unto you, That whoever is angry with his brother without a cause will be in danger of the judgment: and whoever uses abusive language toward his brother will be answerable to the Sanhedrin: but whoever will say, You fool, will be in danger of hell fire.* [23] *Therefore if you bring your gift to the altar, and there remember that your brother holds something against you;* [24] *Leave your gift before the altar and go your way; first be reconciled to your brother, and then come and offer your gift.* [25] *Agree with your adversary quickly, while you are in the way with him; lest at any time the adversary deliver you to the judge, and the judge deliver you to the officer, and you be cast into prison.* [26] *Verily I say unto you, You will by no means come out there, till you have paid every last penny.*

Emotional anger is a reaction to negative thinking, or unproductive thought. Thought is cause. Therefore, when thought is not productive and under the control of the thinker, there will be little or no learning created. Be reconciled with your thoughts and with your neighbor. Lose no time settling with your brother on the way to court because the longer you allow unproductive thoughts to continue, the longer your actions become unproductive; the more they gain strength and energy as habit and the harder it is to correct the situation. The time for learning and gaining in spirituality and Self awareness is now. The easiest time to create spiritual awareness is between the ages of sixteen and thirty. The easiest time to learn is the first few years of life. The older one becomes the more habits are accumulated and the more one becomes set in their ways; the more undisciplined or restricted in the thinking one becomes so there is more difficulty in changing. I have however seen people who are sixty years old and seventy who have changed more than those who are one-half or one-third their age, but these are exceptional cases. Prison symbolizes restriction and limitation in one's conscious mind. As a compulsive habitual brain pathway is practiced it becomes more limiting and more overpowering. Gradually such a person loses all ability to change. To reconcile is to restore to friendship, harmony, and communion. People are there for you to: 1] give to, and 2] receive from; in that order. Therefore, replace habits and constrictions with love and respect for all aspects of Self, nurturing them to grow. Harmonize all aspects of Self in order that "*nations* (groups of similar aspects) *you knew not will run to you*" as *Isaiah* 55 says. As all aspects move together in harmony, communion with one's superconscious mind is achieved.

> [27] *You have heard that it was said by them of old time, You will not commit adultery:* [28] *But I say unto you, That whoever looks on a woman to lust after her has committed adultery with her already in his heart.*

Thought is cause. The essence of Chapter Five is thought is cause. Everyone must learn this. In order to gain control of thought, Self must discipline the mind and exercise the will. In order to have control, one must direct thoughts productively so one leads a productive life. Direct all of the attention to learning, Self growth, and Self awareness. Woman symbolizes the conscious mind. To commit adultery is to break or destroy the commitment one has created between conscious and subconscious minds symbolized by marriage. The breaking of commitment to Self begins with one's thoughts, not with one's senses, such as sight.

> [29] *And if your right eye offend you, pluck it out, and cast it from you: it is better for you to lose part of your body than to have your whole body cast into Gehenna.* [30] *And if your right hand offend you, cut it off, and cast it from you: it is better for you to lose part of your body than to have your whole body cast into the Gehenna fire.*

Eye symbolizes perception. If your perception is unproductive then focus in a different way, in a new light. Do not continue trying to rely on the same old inaccurate perception. Hand represents purpose. There is no learning and growth unless a purpose is developed. Change a little every day. Develop a new purpose. A purpose that is productive for learning and growth and that adds to one's soul growth. Divorce represents breaking or destroying one's commitment to the inner Self. This commitment is illustrated in *Genesis 2:21-24*.

Notes:

Genesis 2 ^{21} *And the Lord God caused a deep sleep to fall upon Adam, and he slept: and he took one of his ribs, and closed up the flesh instead thereof;* ^{22} *And the rib, which the Lord God had taken from man, made he a woman, and brought her unto the man.* ^{23} *And Adam said, This is now bone of my bones, and flesh of my flesh: she will be called Woman, because she was taken out of Man.* ^{24} *Therefore will a man leave his father and his mother, and will cleave unto his wife: and they will be one flesh.*

Adam symbolizes the inner subconscious soul Self. Eve is the outer conscious mind Self. If a man, the subconscious mind, divorces a woman, the conscious mind, then there can be no learning in that lifetime. In such an instance, the conscious mind commits adultery because there is no commitment from the outer physical, conscious mind to the inner soul Self. The commitment always must be developed and reinforced on the part of the conscious mind to give learning to the inner Self. The inner Self, for its part, is always committed to learning. As concerns the inner Self, the only reality is forward motion.

^{31} *It has been said, Whoever will put away his wife, let him give her a decree of divorcement:* ^{32} *But I say unto you, That whoever will put away his wife, saving for the cause of fornication, causes her to commit adultery: and whoever will marry her that is divorced commits adultery.* ^{33} *Again, you have heard that it has been said by them of old time, You will not foreswear yourself, but will perform unto the Lord your oaths:* ^{34} *But I say unto you, Swear not at all; neither by heaven; for it is Gods throne:* ^{35} *Nor by the earth; for it is his footstool:*

*neither by Jerusalem; for it is the city of the great King. [36]
Neither will you swear by your head, because you cannot
make one hair white or black. [37] But let your communication be, Yes and no; for whatever is more than these comes
of evil.*

Make your thoughts and your words match. Make sure that your
words and actions match. Make sure that the thoughts and actions of Self
match. In this manner, there is the full alignment from the inner to the outer
to the physical, and the inner and the outer match or are harmoniously aligned
and productive. This produces Self trust, and then trust for others. Then one
has honesty, productivity, and growth in the awareness of Self. If the two
don't match, then there is dishonesty and distrust and there is unproductivity
or nonproductivity.

*[38] You have heard that it has been said, An eye for an eye,
and a tooth for a tooth: [39] But I say unto you, offer no
resistance to injury but whoever will smite you on your right
cheek, turn to him the other also. [40] If anyone wants to go
to law over your shirt, hand him your coat as well.*

An eye for an eye and a tooth for a tooth was not one of the ten
commandments. It was a commandment that the Lord, I AM, gave to Moses
and the Israelites while in the desert in order to enforce discipline. Do not
become distracted by outside influences. When you fight an influence that is
affecting you then it has distracted you. Keep your attention on your inner
urge. When *"anyone wants to go to law over your shirt, hand him your coat
as well"*. Then release the experience and let him go by returning your attention to your ideal. But do not be distracted. You can fight outwardly with
others, be beaten and take a month to heal, or a year, or a lifetime. You could
fight over the shirt and tear it up. You could make an enemy for life. Instead,
claim your abundance from the universe and keep attention on learning and
growth. Move forward instead of holding onto the past. When discipline has
been achieved mentally, emotionally, and physically then the next step to add
is intention and purpose. The intention for each experience needs to be to
promote Soul growth.

*[41] Whoever will compel you to go a mile, go with him two.
[42] Give to him that asks you, and from him that would bor-
row of you turn not you away.*

Give, give, give. And when you give then release completely so that
you can have your attention on receiving and giving and giving and receiving.
There is no release without giving. Allow no distraction of taking, forcing,

bullying, or other reactions to dilute the physical and opportunities for forward motion of spiritual evolution. The true nature of service is identifying the creative potential within Self as well as any other human being and offering what will cause the greatest growth in the creative potential.

> [43] *You have heard that it has been said, You will love your neighbor, and hate your enemy.* [44] *But I say unto you, Love your enemies and pray for your persecutors; do good to them that hate you and pray for them which despitefully use you;* [45] *That you may be the children of your Father which is in heaven: for he makes his sun to rise on the evil and on the good, and sends rain on the just and on the unjust.* [46] *For if you love them which love you, what reward have you? The tax collectors do as much.* [47] *If you salute your brother only, what is so praiseworthy about that? The pagans do as much.*

That which works and produces in infancy will not suffice in adulthood for they are different levels of responsibility and freedom. If one is always trying to "get even" with anything that pains the Self there will never be any time for learning and growth for all the attention will be spent on hate, resentment, and seeking revenge. One who constantly attempts to "get even" will never even "break even" let alone progress. This kind of discipline is necessary for training an army, which Moses was attempting to do for the Israelites when he was preparing them to conquer the promised land Canaan, to wrestle control of a land from the inhabitants. However, when one is tired of fighting, then one can practice peace; the peace of Self understanding. As one loves all of creation, including Self, one can nurture, harmonize and add to one's storehouse of permanent memory stored in subconscious mind. Tax collectors represent those who steal value from Self. Pagans symbolize aspects of Self who worship the physical existence as their God. Learn to love each and every physical experience, and love the Self in that experience, so much that learning occurs in each and every experience. In this manner there is no need to repeat an experience one thousand times or more before the lesson of life is learned. Then there is always forward motion.

48 Be made perfect, even as your heavenly Father is perfect.

View every experience in life as an opportunity to learn about Self as a creative being. Learn to determine the course of your life by choosing experiences that will be abundant in learning opportunities rather than taking whatever comes along. Use every experience to cause creation to occur. Create each experience as an experience to become compatible with the Creator. This is the ideal.

Notes:

Symbols and Their Interpretation

Chapter Six

1. Alms - giving to the universe
2. Prayer - sending the conscious mind's desires and thoughts to subconscious mind
3. Father - aspect of superconscious mind
4. Fast - to assimilate knowledge
5. Treasures upon earth - physical possessions
6. Moth - habits
7. Rust - temporariness of physical possessions
8. Face - identity
9. Body's lamp - awareness of perception
10. Mammon (money) - value
11. Clothing - outer expression and presentation
12. Food - knowledge
13. Birds - subconscious thoughts
14. Solomon - wisdom, the extension of reasoning

Chapter Six

[1] Take heed that you do not put your virtue in front of people to get their attention. If you do, you can expect no reward from your heavenly Father. [2] Therefore when you contribute to charity, do not sound a trumpet before you, as the hypocrites do in the synagogues and in the streets, that they may have glory of men. I say to you, They already have their reward. [3] But when you give to charity, let not your left hand know what your right hand does: [4] That your alms may be in secret: and your Father which sees in secret will reward you openly. [5] When you pray, you will not be as the hypocrites are: for they love to pray standing in the synagogues and in the corners of the streets, that they may be seen of men. I say unto you, They have their reward.

People, interpreted utilizing the Universal Language of Mind, symbolize aspects of Self. Heaven symbolizes superconscious mind. One's acts, actions, or activity are to be accomplished with the purpose and intention of adding to the inner Self. One who lives the whole life trying to please others will often find themselves missing the opportunity for learning available for that one's soul. Hand symbolizes purpose. Right hand symbolizes a righteous purpose, one given to the real inner Self. Left hand symbolizes a purpose for life given to physical sense gratification and Self aggrandizement. By causing the full attention to consistently rest on expanding awareness there is no opportunity for one's attention to go to the left hand purpose of entrapment. One's activities are to be for learning and growth, and this is the reward. You can only appreciate someone else's growth when you yourSelf are growing. Trying to impress others indicates the Self has not gained Self contained value, because one is always trying to do things for temporary gratification. Somebody gives a pat on the back and says you did really good; this gives only temporary satisfaction.

[6] But you, when you pray, enter into your storeroom, and when you have shut your door, pray to your Father which is in secret; and your Father which sees in secret will reward

Notes:

> *you openly. [7] But when you pray, use not vain repetitions, as the pagans do: for they think that they will be heard because of their multiplicity of words. [8] Do not imitate them: for your Father knows what things you have need of, before you ask him.*

Your storeroom is your subconscious mind. Shutting the door behind you symbolizes moving your attention inward so the attention is no longer outward in the conscious mind. Pagans symbolize those aspects who worship the physical as their God. Your intention should be to aid others so your learning and growth will be fulfilled. Anything else is temporary. Learning and growth is to be the number one priority. Don't try to impress others outwardly, but rather direct your thoughts in private because the full attention is to go within, not upon the physical body, and not engrossed in the physical environment. By placing the full attention within, distractions are eliminated. Then the whole attention can be directed to listening to one's inner Self, and listening to one's Creator. Through listening to God, one comes to the inner Self.

> [9] *After this manner therefore pray you: Our Father which art in heaven, Hallowed be your name.*

Our Father, the superconscious mind, our High Self in the superconscious mind, is hallowed. Holy, whole and complete, is one's identity symbolized by the word name. The complete plan for creation is in superconscious mind.

> [10] *Your kingdom come. Your will be done in earth, as it is in heaven.*

Live the full plan of becoming Enlightened while still in the physical existence of a lifetime. The individual choice-making faculty called free will is directed to becoming Enlightened; to know the One living God. To know one's own spirituality is to be aligned with the inner soul plan of Self. The kingdom of heaven symbolizes superconscious mind which comes into the awareness of the disciplined thinker while consciously existing in the physical body.

> *11 Give us this day our daily bread.*

Give us the knowledge. Bread represents knowledge. Through the act and action of giving, Self creates and receives experiences, gaining knowledge for growth and maturity to become a spiritual, mental evolving creator.

> *12 And forgive us our debts, as we forgive our debtors.*

Lamsa translates debts as offenses and offenders. One who offends or commits offenses is one who disrespects others' space and therefore does not respect Self. Forgive is a combination of two words, for and give. Release the past through giving fully in the present. Without forgiveness of Self or others one is always distracted by pain, error, or mistakes. Learn from mistakes by giving and forgiving Self and move on rapidly. One who is ruled by regrets in the past and shoulds in the future needs to direct the full attention of Self into the now.

> *13 Subject us not to the trial, but deliver us from evil: For yours is the kingdom, and the power, and the glory, forever. Amen.*

Lamsa translates; *"And do not let us enter into temptation, but deliver us from evil. For thine is the kingdom and the power and the glory forever and ever. Amen."* God would not lead one into temptation. However, maintaining one's mind and attention on one's goal, and aligning the inner and outer minds, will deliver one that will move the Self from evil, unproductive activity. For the kingdom of heaven, which is superconscious awareness, is the power and ability to create at will and with desire under the laws of creation. The glory forever is the praise, honor, and distinction which creation deserves, and which Self needs, to move to developing the Enlightened creator Self.

> *14 For if you forgive men their trespasses, your heavenly Father will also forgive you: 15 But if you forgive not men their trespasses, neither will your Father forgive your trespasses. 16 When you fast, do not be like the hypocrites, of a sad countenance, for they disfigure their faces that they may appear unto men to fast. I say unto you, They have their reward. 17 But you, when you fast, anoint your head and wash your face; 18 That you appear not unto men to fast, but unto your Father which is in secret: and your Father*

Notes:

which sees in secret will reward you openly.

As one gives to the Self one can gain relief from (forgive) the hurts or mistakes one has made in the past. As one gives to the Self and thus discharges (forgives) the pain in the conscious mind — that is, in one's waking, day-to-day thoughts — one has gained the freedom to give to the inner Self (for-give to one's heavenly father) in the form of permanent understanding. Fasting symbolizes assimilating knowledge within Self. Hair symbolizes conscious thoughts and face represents one's identity. As one uses, applies, and teaches the knowledge one has gained the thoughts need to be focused, the mind stilled, and the identity of Self associated with the learning of the experience rather than entrapment in the experience itself. Self will be repaid with awareness, steps to Enlightenment, and permanent understanding. Remove the attention from the ego reactions, for the evil one is the devil (d-evil), the uncontrolled conscious ego. Maintain attention on the imaged ideal of Enlightenment. Impressions come and go. Remain established in the image of the great Enlightened One. When you forgive the faults of others, your Heavenly Father will forgive you yours. Give for the purpose of adding to the whole Self; then one will always move forward and the conscious mind Self can release the past and be happy in the eternal present. Live in the eternal present, which is the only place that learning exists. If you do not forgive others then neither will your Father forgive you. Give to the inner Self and to the inner Self of others, and you will receive.

[19] Do not lay up for yourselves treasures upon earth, where moth and rust does corrupt, and where thieves break through and steal: [20] But lay up for yourselves treasures in heaven, where neither moth nor rust corrupts, and where thieves do not break through nor steal: [21] For where your treasure is, there will your heart be also.

Heavenly treasure is that which is eternal and no one can destroy. Heavenly treasure is the permanent learning, permanent knowledge, permanent awareness, the understandings. Meditate daily and consistently. Meditation heightens one's awareness of one's reason for existence. The wisdom that has been made a complete part of Self in day-to-day life is in turn given to the inner Self. This permanent understanding cannot be destroyed. It belongs to Self forever, for this lifetime, and between lifetimes, and future lifetimes if needed. Moths connote habits.

> 22 *The light of the body is the eye: if therefore your eye is single, your whole body will be full of light.* 23 *But if your eye is evil, your whole body will be full of darkness. If therefore the light that is in you is dark, how great is that darkness* 24 *No man can serve two masters: for either he will hate the one, and love the other; or else he will be attentive to the one, and despise the other. You cannot serve God and mammon.*

Lamsa translates; *"The eye is the lamp of the body: if therefore your eye be bright, your whole body is also lighted."* The word eye used here is referring to the eye of attention and must be singular for the energy transformers or chakras to be fully directed to transform the Self until divine radiance outshines any outward source of light. Direct the singular attention to the goal of Self awareness, and Self awareness one will gain. Then one will be full of awareness, and will have the awareness of the Enlightened. One will be a light being. You cannot give yourself to God and to money. One whose attention is allowed to dwell on physical sense attachments and distractions cannot give to the inner Self that which is physical. One can either give Self to knowing the true inner Self or one can have the attention on the physical and the transient. It cannot be done half way. One of the two will be the master. So choose. The intelligent choice is to choose the permanent, to be committed to the whole Self. "Mammon," the Syrian God of riches, was a word the Jews used to describe the paganistic worship of money. Jesus the Knower, here presents a reoccurring theme of his teaching: it is not money but making money your god that turns people away from God. The love or lust for money brings one into further entrapment.

> 25 *Therefore I say unto you, Take no thought for your life, what you will eat, or what you will drink; nor yet for your body or what you will put on. Is not the life more than food, and the body more valuable than clothes?*

Worry occurs when one is imagining what one does not want to occur. It is important to always imagine what you <u>want</u> to occur. As you image and move toward that image, so you become. Tomorrow's life is being created by today's thoughts and mental images. As you think, so you become.

> [26] *Look at the birds in the sky: for they sow not, neither do they reap, nor gather into barns; yet your heavenly Father feeds them. Are you not much better than they?* [27] *Which of you by worrying can add one inch to his stature?* [28] *And why be concerned for clothes? Consider the lilies of the field, how they grow; they toil not, neither do they spin:* [29] *Yet I say unto you, That even Solomon in all his glory was not arrayed like one of these.* [30] *If God so clothes the grass of the field as it is today, and tomorrow it is cast into the oven, will he not much more cloth you, O you of little faith?* [31] *Therefore take no thought, saying, What will we eat? or, What will we drink? or, How will we be clothed?* [32] *All these things do the Gentiles seek: your heavenly Father knows that you have need of all these things.*

Subconscious thoughts (birds) will always exist because each individual exists in subconscious mind as soul. Solomon, representing wisdom developed in the conscious mind, can never match the total understandings of one's own soul stored in subconscious mind. The superconscious mind holding the plan of creation is constantly supplying life force to the conscious mind.

> [33] *But seek you first the kingdom of God, and his righteousness; and all these things will be added unto you.* [34] *Enough, then, of worrying about tomorrow. Let tomorrow take care of itself. Today has troubles enough of its own.*

Worry proceeds from an undisciplined mind which then leads to fear which then grows into terror of the unknown. When the full attention is on knowing the whole Self the individual will have everything needed mentally, emotionally, and physically. Not just needs, but all things including desires of the physical will be given unto you. Give your full attention to the eternal now, the present, and you will gain the full benefits of using the present as you move to the desired future of bliss and happiness.

Symbols and Their Interpretation

Chapter Seven

1. Dogs - habits
2. Pearls - value gained from conscious experience
3. Swine - habits
4. Snake - kundalini energy, creative energy or conscious ego
5. Gate - doorway to the inner levels of mind
6. Sheep - aspects of Self who are following the plan of creation to gain Enlightenment
7. Thorns - doubts
8. Figs - knowledge
9. Grapes - knowledge that can produce wisdom
10. Thistles - indecision
11. Miracles - use of inner levels of mind
12. Devils - unproductive thoughts and attitudes
13. Evil - unproductive thoughts and actions
14. House - mind
15. Wind - thought in motion
16. Floods - out of control conscious (physical) experiences
17. Water - life/physical experiences

Chapter Seven

The *Book of Matthew* is a presentation of the reasoner during the stage of evolution that mankind finds itself today. The first chapter of the *Book of Matthew* presents the genealogy, which is the physical and mental evolution needed in order to produce the body and the mind, and the experience to reach the point of reasoning man which mankind exists in presently. Chapter 2, the appearance of Herod and the movement into Egypt show the activity of the ego to motivate Self to move out of entrapment. Chapter 3 presents the value of believing and how believing has been used productively to aid us to master the physical existence. Believing is showcased as a tool for imagining goals and creating expectations of achieving them to move forward in life and learning. Chapter 4 shows it is time to use the ego (symbolized by the devil) on a higher level of development in order to bring about the development of the whole Self. Discipline will be required as shown in Chapter 5. Discipline is a must if we are to know the whole Self and become a knower which is one who dwells in understanding. Chapter 6 shows the importance of placing the attention within, where the true riches and value exist, through prayer, fasting, and meditation. Place the full attention on knowing the whole Self and building permanent memory or understandings rather than worshipping the physical as a god such as making money or possessions. It is the choice between the metaphysical and physical. Spiritual or material. God or money. God or manna.

In each of these chapters, the first sentence is always important because it gives an overview of what is going to happen in that chapter and Chapter 7 is no exception. Chapter 7 presents the importance of understanding that cause begins with Self rather than blaming the environment for one's problems.

[1] Do not judge, so that you will not be judged.

You can be sure that most people who point the finger at others declaring them to be wrong all the time and having faults will usually have faults within themselves which they are unwilling to admit. If you want to avoid being judged guilty by Self and others then stop passing all kinds of judgements on others and your environment. The environment is essentially neutral. When you criticize yourself you will be critical of others also. You may be criticizing your Self on the inside but not doing anything to change it. If you want to avoid judgment in the physical which are the painful experiences, then stop producing painful thoughts and attitudes, such as, guilt, doubt, worry, fear, condemnation, hate, and resentment. These are limiting, unproductive attitudes.

> *[2] Your verdict on others will be the verdict passed on you. The standard with which you measure will be used to measure you.*

Lamsa translates verdict as judgment. The attitudes one holds affect one's environment and the world. Those attitudes return to Self in like kind.

> *[3] Why behold you the speck that is in your brother's eye, but consider not the log that is in your own eye? [4] Or how will you say to your brother, Let me pull the speck out of your eye; and, behold, a log is in your own eye? [5] You hypocrite, first remove the log from your own eye; and then will you see clearly to remove the speck from your brothers eye.*

Lamsa translates speck as splinter. This passage illustrates the importance of the correct use of the symbolic language of mind. When perception is blocked or cloudy, it shows that one views the world and one's environment based on one's own thoughts, limitations, and attitudes. Stop blaming the world for your unhappiness. The physical world cannot supply permanent happiness because the physical world is not permanent, it is temporary. The nature of matter is change. Therefore look to Self to change in order to cause happiness and peace within.

> *⁶ Give not that which is holy unto the dogs, neither cast your pearls before swine, lest they trample them under their feet, and turn against you and tear you to shreds.*

Swine and dogs indicate habits. What is Holy is whole and therefore complete. The dogs represent compulsive tendencies, brain pathways called habits, that are temporary and therefore incomplete. That which is Holy is complete and permanent. Do not waste permanent awareness on temporary sense gratifications. Rather, what you know to be permanently true, continue to practice and apply. You are soul, a spirit inhabiting a physical body. Give your whole time and attention to building that awareness.

> *⁷ Ask, and you will receive; look, and you will find; knock, and it will be opened unto you: ⁸ For the one who asks always receives; and he that looks finds; and to him who knocks it will be opened. ⁹ Or what man is there of you, that if his son asks for bread, you would give him a stone? ¹⁰ Or if he asks a fish, you would give him a poisonous snake? ¹¹ If you then, being evil, know how to give good gifts unto your children, how much more will your Father which is in heaven give good things to them that ask him?*

The Truth is, you really can have anything you desire. The Universal Laws and mind are designed in such a way that it is the subconscious mind's duty to aid the conscious mind Self to fulfill all desires. Referring to *Genesis 1, "God created man in his image and likeness"*. As one images a desire and keeps it Holy in mind and then moves toward and into that image, the image becomes part of one's life and Self. One becomes a greater and more expansive person because a more expansive Self has been imaged. Self has moved toward and into the expansive image. In order to ask for anything, one first needs to create a mental image of the desire. Then seek and you will find the exact activity that opens the door of opportunity. Knock and it will be opened to you means there must be a willingness to move forward through new doorways in one's thinking, to more expansive areas in Self and mind. In the process one automatically removes limitations. The one who asks; receives, the one who seeks; finds, the one who knocks; enters. There is no such thing as an insurmountable obstacle to Self awareness. All higher levels of consciousness are available to one who can image them, and cause the changes and transformations given in the *Book of Matthew* and the Bible.

> *¹² Do unto others as you would have others do unto to you: for this sums up the law and the prophets.*

In all the great Holy Books of the world which record what the great spiritual masters have said and taught, the Golden Rule is invariably taught in one form or another. *"Do unto others as you would have others do unto you"* is the Golden Rule. Another way to state this is: everything you want people to do for you, do the same for the people. This is because of several factors. One factor is Karma. The intention with which you give something is the manner in which it returns. This refers not just to the physical effect, but the mental attitude behind the giving or the action. When the attention is fully on growth and developing spiritual awareness, then one will encounter others who are also on the Holy path, the path to Enlightenment. They will have much to offer to aid one in growth. One may receive from them because they have gained an awareness, also. But if one is constantly putting others down and pushing people away because of one's limitations, constrictions, and fears then he will constantly push away those who will help him the most.

> [13] *Enter through the narrow gate: for wide is the gate and broad is the way that leads to destruction, and many there are which go in there:* [14] *Because how narrow is the gate and rough is the road which leads unto life, and few there are that find it.*

Lamsa translates rough as difficult. There is only one way to enter the kingdom of heaven and to know the whole mind and that is singular ideal and purpose. Singular ideal begins with undivided attention. Singular ideal and purpose is the narrow gate. When you go through the narrow gate, you see what is in front and before you, and you will move toward the ideal of full Enlightenment. This leaves no space for distractions. The road to Enlightenment is difficult because discipline, reasoning, and will power are required. Therefore, the path to Enlightenment is infinitely more rewarding and fulfilling than the slow path of humanity which is suffering and pain due to the slow progress of physical evolution.

15 Beware of false prophets which come to you in sheep's clothing but inwardly they are ravening wolves. 16 You will know them by their fruits. Do men gather grapes from thorn bushes, or figs from thistle plants?

A prophet is a goal setter but a false prophet is one who only sets physical goals. Physical goals are temporary. Spiritual and mental ideals of consciousness expansion are permanent. Wolves are habits that destroy and take from their prey everything, including life. The grapes of knowledge never proceed from the thornbushes of doubt. Thorns and thistles symbolize doubt and indecision. Self knowledge and understanding comes from the confidence to image what one desires to occur and most importantly what one desires to be and become.

17 Even so every good tree brings forth good fruit; but a corrupt tree brings forth evil fruit. 18 A good tree cannot bring forth evil fruit, neither can a corrupt tree bring forth good fruit. 19 Every tree that brings not forth good fruit is hewn down, and cast into the fire. 20 Wherefore by their fruits you will know them. 21 Not every one that says unto me, Lord, Lord, will enter into the kingdom of heaven; but he that does the will of my Father which is in heaven.

This whole statement of fruit trees is an example of knowing a person by their deeds. One's accomplishments are not dependent solely on one's actions but are intimately tied to one's thoughts and attitudes. When one's thoughts and attitudes are expansive and giving, one will experience expansion and growth in the life and in one's consciousness. When one holds doubt, condemnation, or resentment in the mind's eye then little will occur in one's life beyond what was previously accomplished. You can tell a good tree by its fruit means you can always discern a productive, expansive person moving toward greater soul awareness from one who lacks imagination or refuses to leave the old worn out memory pictures behind. The productive consciousness-increasing individual will produce extra in their life. The diseased tree type person will live life operating mainly from old limited memory pictures of their childhood and adolescence and will produce little if any growth or expansion. The one who does the will of my Father in heaven is the one who exercises the strongly developed will power with discipline to follow and fulfill the plan for one's Enlightenment contained in superconscious mind. Such a one comes to be like, that is with like attributes of creatorship, the Creator or heavenly Father.

22 Many will say to me in that day, Lord, Lord, have we not prophesied in your name? and in your name have cast out

Notes:

> *devils? and in your name done many miracles? ²³ Then will I profess to them, I never knew you: out of my sight, you evildoers.*

By a person's actions, and more importantly their accomplishments, are they known. People can spend much of their time talking of how great a person they are and all the great things they are going to do. However, words without actions are empty, and ideas without the will and discipline to hold them constantly in mind to apply them every day are also "evil". That is destructive. By a man's (thinker's) works — accomplishments, successes, and expansion — will he be known. An evildoer is any person and any aspect of a person who devotes their time and attention to temporary, restrictive, or limited pursuits. It signifies one who destroys rather than builds and expands. Self needs to identify and understand the permanent and expansive qualities of character that add to the whole Self.

> *²⁴ Therefore whoever hears these sayings of mine and does them, I will liken him unto a wise man who built his house upon a rock: ²⁵ And the rain descended and the floods came and the winds blew, beating upon that house; but it did not collapse for it was founded upon a rock. ²⁶ Every one that hears these sayings of mine, and does them not, will be likened unto a foolish man, who built his house upon the sand: ²⁷ And the rain descended and the floods came and the winds blew; beating upon that house; and it collapsed, and great was the fall. ²⁸ It came to pass when Jesus had ended these sayings, the people were astonished at his doctrine: ²⁹ For he taught them with authority, unlike the scribes.*

House symbolizes mind. The one who practices and applies the universal Truths everyday is building their house on solid rock and therefore their creations, their manifestations, will increase and magnify. The one who lives in the memory of the limited past will be ineffectual in constructing an expanded mind capable of consciousness expansion and ever enlarging manifestations of Enlightenment in the physical world. The one who is consistently expanding consciousness and creating greater and more enlightening physical manifestations is the one whose house (mind) is built on solid rock and is therefore stable, secure, and lasting. Such a one speaks from the authority of knowing how to create and being willing to make the necessary changes and transformations to do so.

In reading Holy Books, they must be applied with practice in daily life to build discipline, will power, attention, commitment to the Self, divine and spiritual love, devotion, and full service to others. Like the wise man who built his house upon a rock. The rock represents the spiritual foundation of Self. The spiritual foundation is built in the physical by the discipline of the conscious mind! Concentration and meditation are the most important factors. Dream interpretation is also of benefit. Imaging and learning to still the mind are also included.

At the end of this chapter Jesus finished his discourse and held the crowd spellbound at his teaching. The reason they were spellbound was that he taught with authority and not like their scribes. The scribes represent brain pathways. Consider anytime you have read a book, if you have found something good in that book and thought the book contained stimulating information, then this stimulating information is stored in the brain, but it doesn't permanently add to soul growth. When the information is used and applied, as in verse twenty-four *"put it into practice"*, then the information becomes personal experience and personal knowing. Therefore, from personal experience one knows what produces success and can teach it to others. This is the ability to produce spiritual success, mental success, Self awareness and Self realization and add to the permanent, whole Self; rather than merely engaging in that which is temporary, not lasting and painful. The nature of the physical is change and therefore painful unless one changes, grows, and evolves at a more rapid rate than the physical environment changes.

Symbols and Their Interpretation

Chapter Eight

1. Leper - Self destructive attitude of hate
2. Mountain - challenge or obstacles. Ascent to the summit of a mountain symbolizes the attainment of a higher level of mind or consciousness.
3. Proof - One's own experience
4. Centurion - disciplined aspect that is understood and therefore can be wielded with power
5. Servants - Universal Laws
6. Faith - The ability to hear Truth and an expanded image of creation and to accept it into oneself. The beginning of the effective use of imagination.
7. East and West - levels of subconscious mind
8. Mother - receptive aspect of superconscious mind
9. Isaiah - a goal setter. Understanding of the ideal of Enlightenment.
10. Foxes - habits
11. Head - identity
12. Disciple - disciplined aspect
13. Dead - stagnancy, no motion
14. Storm - thoughts out of control in the conscious experience
15. Tombs - a part of mind that is stagnant and without motion
16. Sea - conscious, physical life experiences

Chapter Eight

Chapter Eight presents a new capability of the thinker, represented symbolically as Jesus, who is developing the understanding of knowing. Healing the sick is the new capability being practiced, employed, and applied that was not demonstrated in earlier chapters. These healings are a prelude to the ultimate healing, raising from the dead, which Jesus accomplishes in the final chapters of the *Book of Matthew*. Healing of the sick represents changing an unproductive thought, an unproductive attitude, into a productive attitude that contributes to the whole Self. Healing the body shows that limitations held in one's conscious mind have been changed and transcended since thoughts and attitudes cause physical disease and disorder. By changing the thought and the attitude, one discovers how to create a greater state of Self improvement and mobility in the body. When we have a disease or illness, it creates immobility in the body. The point being revealed here is that having productive thoughts gives rise to mental efficiency. Mental efficiency translates into the ability mentally, emotionally, and physically to operate more productively in order to create greater learning, growth, spiritual or soul awareness within the Self. This causes greater forward motion in the life of the learner.

> [1] *When he descended the mountain, great multitudes followed him.* [2] *Behold, there came a leper and worshipped him, saying, Lord, if you will, you can heal me.* [3] *Jesus put forth his hand, and touched him, saying, I will; be healed. And immediately his leprosy disappeared.* [4] *Jesus said unto him, See you tell no man; but go your way, show yourself to the priest, and offer the gift that Moses commanded, that should be the proof they need.*

Mountain represents an obstacle, a challenge. Jesus descending the mountain shows a challenge has been completed and an obstacle overcome in which a lesson in life has been learned and completed. People represent aspects of Self when presented in the Bible, as they do in dreams. Giving to more aspects of Self creates new awareness, new understandings of life, and expansion of consciousness in Self. It is this willingness, often referred to in the Bible as having faith, that heals Self. Faith is accepting another person's mental picture of a more expansive life that moves the Self from a condition of non-motion to motion. When Self believes expansively, where doubts had existed previously, the mental picture is changed. A doubt creates a mental picture of, "I can't; I shouldn't; I won't." Fear limits Self in a similar manner. These doubts and fears all create limitations; mentally, emotionally, physically, and spiritually. When the mental picture changes to belief — that is, believing one can be healed, which is to accept a more expansive thought form which overcomes the limiting attitude — then no more does one dwell in the doubt or fear of negative limitations. Create a picture of what is wanted and desired. Hold nothing in the mind but that desire of improvement, development, gain, adding to, and building. It is this change in the mental picture that then must be reflected in the physical life.

The mental attitude causing leprosy is similar to what causes cancer. Hate, extreme hate, held in the mind creates leprosy. The person often blames others or conditions in the life as the source of their hardship, but really the hate is for the Self. Leprosy eats away at the body. Hate eats at the Self in the conscious mind. Hate eats at the Self as does leprosy. It consumes one's life, body, mind; destroying everything and rendering experience useless to the inner mind.

The word centurion comes from the same root as the Latin word *century* which means *a hundred years.* A centurion works with a hundred men. He leads the hundred soldiers which are under his command. A centurion was a leader of Roman soldiers, and soldiers represent the quality of discipline in the conscious mind that is founded on physical desire achievement and physical possession accumulation. Romans represent that part of the physical Self which will exert the will with discipline to accumulate possessions and a physical security which is temporary.

> [5] *When Jesus entered Capernaum,*
> *there came to him a centurion, be-*

seeching him, ⁶ Saying, Lord, my servant lies at home sick
of the palsy, terribly tormented. ⁷ Jesus said to him, I will
come and heal him. ⁸ The centurion answered and said,
Lord, I am not worthy that you should come under my roof:
but speak the word only, and my servant will be healed. ⁹
For I am a man under authority, having soldiers under me:
and I say to this man, Go, and he goes; and to another,
Come, and he comes; and to my servant, Do this, and he
does it. ¹⁰ When Jesus heard it, he marveled, and said to
them that followed, Verily I say unto you, I have not found
this great faith in all Israel.

When the centurion, the leader of a hundred men, gave an order to any of his soldiers he expected the order to be carried out. He knew his commands would be carried out or fulfilled. He was a leader and he had trained his men to follow his orders. In the same way, when a person has that much believing and knowing in Self then one will initiate the activity to fulfill desires. Doubt keeps us from moving forward. Doubts and fear keep us from changing. When we have mastery of believing, we create good, clear pictures of what we want to occur. Then we can create what we desire. The paralyzed servant who is lying in bed indicates very little ability to produce any type of motion in life. When the body is paralyzed, one experiences physical immobility. Opportunities for motion continue to present themselves but the individual is incapable of responding to them. Through the power of knowing what you desire — having a clear ideal, a direction to move in, and believing in Self enough to initiate action on your desires immediately — you overcome immobility; moving beyond and moving through that paralyzed and restricted condition. Not knowing which way to go, what to do next, how to go and feeling depressed, will immobilize you. The authority within the Self, the ability to know that there is much more that one can produce and to image it so clearly one believes the Self created image can be achieved, will move Self forward. Nothing is impossible when there is a clear ideal or picture within the mind's eye of what is desired to be accomplished and there is the will to move toward it with activity. Learn during the process, which is the purpose.

> *¹¹ I say unto you, That many will come from the east and*
> *west, and will sit down with Abraham, and Isaac, and Jacob,*
> *in the kingdom of heaven. ¹² But the children of the king-*
> *dom will be cast out into outer darkness: there will be weep-*
> *ing and grinding of teeth. ¹³ Jesus said to the centurion, Go*
> *your way; and as you have believed, so be it done unto you.*
> *And his servant was healed at that very moment.*

Abraham symbolizes the beginning of a commitment in the conscious mind to use reasoning consistently. Isaac symbolizes one beginning to use reasoning in the conscious mind to build permanent understandings in subconscious mind. Isaac's son Jacob became Israel, IS-RA-EL, representing the superconscious mind or more specifically the conscious mind committed to completely fulfilling the plan, the blueprint of creation for man the thinker to become Enlightened and compatible with the Creator. The word Israel is a combination of the names of the Gods Isis and Ra of Egypt and El (plural Elohim) of *Genesis Chapter 1*. The natural heirs of the kingdom refer to anyone incarned in the physical body including the conscious mind and brain. Therefore, all incarned entities have the capability of reasoning in the conscious mind. Yet, just because one has a physical body and conscious mind does not by itself guarantee the Enlightenment or higher awareness as symbolized by Isaac and Jacob. Those aspects who gain the knowledge of superconscious mind (heaven) are those that realize the physical owes them nothing. Instead, the physical life and world are a temporary and fleeting opportunity to gain Enlightenment through discipline, will, higher reasoning, and commitment to the whole Self. With the doubt removed there is nothing to keep one from moving forward again.

> *[14] When Jesus entered Peter's house, he saw his wife's mother in bed with a fever. [15] He touched her hand, and the fever left her: and she arose, and served them.*

The keys in this passage are hand, fever, and Peter. Peter represents the will; the ability to discriminate and to understand what choices are the best, most correct, decisions. The fever represents the desire for expansion because heat represents expansion. Yet, the expansion of the mind is to be directed productively. The hand represents purpose. Aligning with purpose, Self discovers the reason for being in the physical. Once the purpose has been discovered then the important mission of a lifetime becomes evident. The excess energy, caused by unfulfilled spiritual desires, has a place to move productively. The fever, the excess promoting the expansion, is no longer restricted so the body returns to health.

> *16 As evening came, they brought unto him many that were possessed with devils: and he expelled the spirits with his word, and healed all that were sick: 17 That it might be fulfilled which was spoken by Isaiah the prophet, saying, It was our infirmities he bore, and our sicknesses he endured.*

This is a direct quote from *Isaiah 53:1-12*. That chapter gives an exact description of Jesus' assignment for his lifetime.

> *Isaiah 53 1 Who has believed our report and to whom is the arm of the Lord revealed? 2 For he will grow up before him as a tender plant, and as a root out of a dry ground: he has no form nor comeliness; and when we will see him, there is no beauty that we should desire him. 3 He is despised and rejected of men; a man of sorrows and acquainted with grief. We hid our faces from him; he was despised and we esteemed him not. 4 Surely he has borne our griefs and carried our sorrows, yet we did esteem him stricken, smitten of God, and afflicted. 5 But he was wounded for our transgressions, he was bruised for our iniquities: the chastisement of our peace was upon him; and with his stripes we are healed. 6 All we like sheep have gone astray; we have turned every one to his own way; and the Lord has laid on him the iniquity of us all. 7 He was oppressed and he was afflicted, yet he opened not his mouth: he is brought as a lamb to the slaughter and as a sheep before her shearers is dumb, so he opened not his mouth. 8 He was taken from prison and from judgment, and who will declare his generation? For he was cut off out of the land of the living, for the transgression of my people was he stricken. 9 He made his grave with the wicked and with the rich in his death; because he had done no violence, neither was any deceit in his mouth. 10 Yet it pleased the Lord to bruise him; he had put him to grief: when you will make his soul an offering for sin, he will see his seed, he will prolong his days, and the pleasure of the Lord will prosper in his hand. 11 He will see of the travail of his soul, and will be satisfied: by his knowledge will my righteous servant justify many; for he will bear their iniquities. 12 Therefore will I divide him a portion with the great, and he will divide the spoil with the strong; because he has poured*

*out his soul unto death. He was num-
bered with the transgressors: and he
bore the sin of many and made inter-
cession for the transgressors.*

The *New Testament* of the <u>Bible</u> was translated from Aramaic to Greek, from Greek to Latin, and
then into the various other languages, such as English.
In the ancient Greek language the word for spirit can
also be translated as mind. This indicates that Jesus,
the knower, expelled the unproductive thoughts or attitudes from the conscious mind. The possession with
devils shows a habit, a compulsion, an unproductive
way of thinking practiced for a long time that gives the
illusion that it is a part of Self. The conscious mind is
not the real you, the essence, the I Am. The unproductive or limiting thoughts have been created and learned
this lifetime. Expelling of these d-evil spirits shows
the ability to release any unproductive thoughts, mainly
habits and compulsions, in the conscious mind Self.

*[18] When Jesus saw great multitudes
about him, he gave commandment to
depart to his own town. [19] And a certain scribe came, and said unto him,
Master, I will follow you wherever
you go. [20] Jesus said unto him, The
foxes have holes, and the birds of the
air have nests; but the Son of man
has nowhere to lay his head. [21] Another of his disciples said unto him,
Lord, let me first to go and bury my
father. [22] But Jesus said unto him,
Follow me; and let the dead bury
their dead.*

When a person fears loss, he or she needs to
examine what they are afraid of losing. It will be of
benefit then to give to life and others the qualities and
genuine expression of Self that one fears will be taken
away. The more one gives of Self, the more secure one
will become. The individual will discover the great
beauty and value one has within Self as well as discovering that Self grows and becomes stronger with every

action of giving. The person desiring full utilization of life will form a clear image of what he or she wants to move toward, so there can be the withdrawal of attention from the past. The secret of existence is in being able to imagine what one wants to become.

To be a son of man as Jesus was — to be a knower, to be a full reasoner, to know the inner Self — means in part to no longer live in the past. The past has already occurred. The only place to cause change and growth, expansion of consciousness and greater awareness, is in the present. Living in the past will never produce growth or awareness or improvement in Self. The past is to be used only to observe what occurred in memory so Self can correlate the past to the present and prepare for the future. Drawing on the past in the form of memory is to be used to produce change in the Self in the present. By itself, memory has no worth for the inner soul. It is best to place attention fully in the present and create a greater Self. Prove the limitations or the falsity of the past unpleasant experiences. The real identity, I AM, of the one who is aware of the inner Self realizes one's true home and security is not in the physical existence; *"nowhere to lay his head."* True permanent security is found by following the knowing aspects of Self.

> ²³ *When he entered into a ship, his disciples followed him.* ²⁴ *Behold, a violent storm came up in the sea, inasmuch that the ship was covered with the waves: but he was asleep.* ²⁵ *His disciples came to him, awaking him, saying, Lord, save us: we perish.* ²⁶ *He said unto them, Why are you fearful, You have such little faith. Where is your courage? Then he arose, and rebuked the winds and the sea; and there was a great calm.* ²⁷ *But the men marveled, saying, What manner of man is this, that even the winds and the sea obey him?*

The disciples were visualizing what they did *not* want to occur. The disciples were visualizing death; being swamped overboard, their ship being destroyed. Fear produces unproductive, limited thought pictures that Self does *not* want to create. Self needs to create the mental pictures of what one *wants* to occur. So Jesus says, *"Where is your courage?"* The knower images what is desired to occur, which is the wind and sea calming, instead of what one does not want to occur. His words matched his thoughts showing the ability to move thought from the inner subconscious mind into the physical life. Wind symbolizes thought in the conscious mind. Sea represents the conscious life experiences. One who disciplines the conscious mind with concentration and meditation and is committed to knowing the whole Self, will control and direct their thoughts in the conscious mind productively, stilling the winds of those conscious mind thoughts. Every person must learn to still their mind and stop the busy thoughts from intruding upon one's consciousness. As long as one is busy in the mind, one will react emotionally for the emotions reflect one's mental state or condition. In every motion Self can attain a point of quiet, stability, and steadiness. Constant motion and static in the mental system leaves one out of control and a victim of fear.

> [28] *As he approached the country of the Gadarenes, he met two men possessed with devils, coming out of the tombs, they were violent so that no man might pass by that way.* [29] *Behold, they cried out, saying, What have we to do with you, Jesus, you Son of God? Have you come here to torment us before the time?* [30] *Some distance from them a herd of swine were feeding.* [31] *So the devils besought him, saying, If you cast us out, let us to go into that herd of swine.* [32] *He said unto them, Go. And when they were come out, they went into the herd of swine: and, behold, the whole herd went rushing down the bluff into the sea and drowned.*

Tombs, cemeteries, coffins and people that have been buried in tombs, all represent the past. The changes that have occurred in the past are dead, inert, non-mobile. Attachment to past memories and changes, restricts Self in the present. The past is no longer fruitful and productive. Release the past and move to the present. Demons represent a person caught up in negativity in the conscious mind. Trying to live in the past gives very little control in being productive in the present life. The person who has been abused as a child may, through the habit of old mental images in the mind, live in anger, abuse, and hatred throughout his/her life and may abuse his/her children. Little is produced in terms of productive learning in this way. Such a person can and may change in the present, leaving the past behind.

Jesus, the knower, symbolizes the knowing quality. This quality is required to cause all these negative, unproductive ways of being to be first recognized as habits and compulsions. This is symbolized by the movement of the demons into the herd of swine. Next, the habits and the compulsions must be changed in the conscious life experience through physical actions that are contrary to habit. *"The whole herd went rushing down the bluff into the sea and drowned"* symbolizes changing habits and compulsive limited negative attitudes by sending them into the experience of life (water). Water represents the conscious, day-to-day life experience. Maintain all the attention in the present so the mind does not have any time to dwell on reactions, pain, unproductivity, negativity, or hurts of the past. Live fully in the present.

> *33 They that kept them fled, and went their ways into the city, and told everything, and what was befallen to the possessed of the devils. 34 Behold, the whole city came out to meet Jesus: and when they saw him, they begged that he would leave out of their coasts.*

The people of the town begged Jesus to leave because they feared the rest of the swine in the town would run into the sea and be drowned. The villagers possessed (owned) the swine symbolizing emotional and physical attachment to limiting habits. When a habitual person becomes so engrossed in their brain pathways, they forget who they are and their true nature. True security does not reside in remaining the same or in maintaining the status quo within Self. True security and prosperity live in expanding consciousness through transforming change and growth in Self.

Self knowledge is always productive. Even when one discovers something that is a hindrance, the discovery of the hindrance enables one to move forward and progress. Discovering the cause behind any limitation is the first key to expanding beyond that limitation.

Symbols and Their Interpretation

Chapter Nine

1. Paralyzed - an aspect who has severely restricted motion
2. Sins - mistakes
3. Forgiven - to give for a purpose. For-give, for the purpose of giving.
4. Groom - subconscious mind
5. Wine - wisdom
6. Synagogue - Attention placed on knowing the mind
7. Woman - wo-man, conscious mind
8. Hemorrhages - aspect that is losing life force and refuses to hold on to Truth
9. Son of David - applying reasoning while initiating activity
10. Blind - refusal to use one's perceptive abilities
11. Mute - refusal to express one's thoughts and communicate with the inner Self
12. 12 - initiating a new cycle with the full understanding of the aggressive and receptive factors of creation
13. Harvest - to draw knowledge from the experience into the Self
14. Shepherd - one who directs aspects of Self in accordance with the plan held in superconscious mind
15. Heart - Self understanding
16. Demons - Aspects of conscious ego, especially related to unproductive and/or habitual thinking.

Chapter Nine

¹ He entered into a ship, and passed over, and came into his own town. ² Behold, they brought to him a paralyzed man, lying on a bed: and Jesus seeing their faith said unto the paralytic; Son, have courage; your sins are forgiven.

Paralysis in the <u>Bible</u> symbolizes immobility created by stagnant and restrictive thoughts. In addition to saying, *"Have courage,"* Jesus says, *"Your sins are forgiven."* Sins are the mistakes of the past that plague Self currently. Sins are mistakes. Mistakes are physical actions and thoughts that are limited, that are impermanent, that will not produce permanent learning. Permanent learning is stored in the subconscious mind for all time. A paralyzed man is a person who refuses to move forward and expand in the thinking. Fear and terror lead to avoidance which stops movement forward. In the context of the <u>Bible</u>, the paralyzed man represents an aspect of Self who needs to face and understand the unknown in order to produce motion. Towns and cities represent many aspects of Self. To identify specifically what aspects are involved, discern what the people are doing in that area. In other words discover their words, thoughts, and deeds. Jesus' own town was Nazareth.

³ Behold, certain of the scribes said within themselves, This man blasphemed. ⁴ Jesus knowing their thoughts said, Why do you hold evil in your hearts? ⁵ For which is easier, to say, Your sins are forgiven; or to say, Arise, and walk? ⁶ But so you may know that the Son of man has power on earth to forgive sins: I say to this paralytic: Arise, take up your bed, and go to your house. ⁷ The man arose, and departed to his house. ⁸ When the multitudes saw it, they marveled and glorified God, which had given such power unto men.

The scribes didn't think Jesus had the right to forgive people their sins for only God had that right. Well, the man stood up and walked, which is a type of motion. To walk is to cause motion. He rolled up his mat and walked home. Motion was created. The scribes were always writing down information. They recorded information. Recording information is a function of the brain. Anything recorded on paper can dry up, burn up, blow away, or be destroyed. Information is recorded in the brain, but it is a temporary recording, for the brain will disintegrate at the end of a lifetime. Those memories stored in the brain will dissolve as the brain rots. The permanent memory Jesus developed and was using, indicates and demonstrates the memory stored in the inner mind, the subconscious mind, called permanent understanding or permanent learning which once gained, earned, and achieved will be a part of the Real Self forever. Use the imager to imagine what you want to become in the future, not what you were in the past. Imagination is added to memory and attention to form reasoning. Imagination is above and beyond what animals are capable of utilizing. Reasoning is a step above logic. Reasoning traces cause to the thought of the thinker.

> [9] *As Jesus moved on, he saw a man named Matthew, at his post where taxes were collected: and he said unto him, Follow me. And Matthew arose, and followed him.*

Matthew wanted to learn from Jesus and be one of his followers. He wanted to learn through Jesus the inner secrets. So Jesus took him home for dinner. Jesus' disciples saw Matthew and complained because he was a tax collector. In those days, tax collectors were often dishonest people who overcharged other people on their taxes and then pocketed the extra money. This issue concerning tax collectors indicates why Jesus said, *"Give unto Caesar what is Caesar's"* for it meant recognize the value of your life and give to others in your physical environment. Give that value to the physical. Money received in taxes shows value. In this instance, this is a physical value not a mental or inner value. Jesus the knower recognizes a foundation has been constructed on which to build true inner value which is the construction of the edifice of Self understanding. Matthew becomes a disciple meaning he developed mental discipline. No physical object is bad or evil. It is how one either uses or refuses to use productively the physical existence that determines the usefulness of one's life.

> [10] *It came to pass, as Jesus sat eating at the table in the house, many tax collectors and sinners came and sat down with him and his disciples.* [11] *When the Pharisees saw this they said to his disciples, Why does your teacher eat with tax collectors and sinners?* [12] *Jesus heard them and said, They who are whole do not need a physician, those who are sick do.* [13] *Go you and learn what that means, I will have mercy, and not sacrifice: for I have not come to call the righteous, but sinners to repentance.*

Lamsa translates the words, while Jesus was at the table, as, *"And while they were guests in the house."* When an aspect of Self, as represented by Matthew, recognizes a greater source of value than previously experienced that awareness benefits other similar aspects of Self. One new learning leads to another and when one door is opened many new avenues of possibilities often present themselves. The tax collectors and sinners joining Jesus and his disciples at dinner present an image of those aspects of the Self who have previously been engrossed in the physical existence now come to recognize a source of greater knowledge as symbolized by the dinner meal. They recognize the usefulness of Self discipline represented by the disciples. Jesus, the one who is building the quality of knowing, is building permanent understanding in the conscious mind and drawing out from the inner mind to the conscious mind the understandings already stored there from previous lifetimes. Jesus in essence says that people who are in good health do not need a doctor, sick people do. It is mercy he desires, not sacrifice. When a person recognizes they are making a mistake in activities and thoughts that are limiting or restricting then realizes there is more to learn, they can improve themselves. The first step to change is identifying the restriction, constriction, reaction, and limitation. When a person thinks they know it all and are Self righteous, they have blocked the learning and they remain without forward motion and locked in their limitations. The message of this whole verse in the language of mind is to always look for the learning that is involved in any situation and to be ready to learn. Do not think that you know everything. There is always a place to learn no matter where you are, or how old you are, or how much fame has been gained. The desire is to learn wherever you are and move into greater areas of learning, Self development, and leadership.

> [14] *Then came to him the disciples of John, saying, Why do we and the Pharisees fast often, but your disciples do not*

Notes:

> fast? [15] *Jesus said to them, Can the*
> *wedding guests mourn as long as the*
> *groom is with them? The days will*
> *come, when the groom will be taken*
> *from them and then will they fast.*

This passage indicates John the Baptist's disciples have some similar actions or qualities as the Pharisees. John represents the action of believing and Jesus symbolizes the knowing quality. By developing the knowing through discipline, there is no reason to mourn or to practice only assimilation. Rather one can be fulfilled and joyful because one experiences learning and growth every day. It is the difference between practicing physical discipline or physical exercises every day versus practicing mental discipline through meditation and concentration. One builds the body, while the other builds the permanent Self. The body is temporary; I Am is eternal. Use information, knowledge, and experience fully and consistently then all knowledge is used completely.

> [16] *No man puts a piece of new cloth*
> *on an old garment; for that which is*
> *substituted takes from the garment,*
> *and the tear is made worse.* [17] *Nei-*
> *ther do men put new wine into old*
> *wineskins: else the bottles break and*
> *the wine is lost, and the bottles per-*
> *ish: rather they put new wine into*
> *new wineskins, and both are pre-*
> *served.*

The new cloth represents the new, more expansive outer expression that will not function with the old worn out outer expression. Wine represents wisdom. Grapes represent knowledge, knowledge for the inner Self. As the grapes of knowledge are matured and developed into another product called wine, they represent wisdom. The knowledge applied to produce a greater prized product that can be stored and improves with aging, is the permanent wisdom. The experience, knowledge, and wisdom of the present cannot be adequately stored or limited in the wineskins of the past.

Anyone who tries to live in the past by constantly bringing old memory thoughts of the past to their conscious awareness will find the new wisdom available in the present is lost and spilled out, where the usefulness of the experience in the present is missed.

> *18 While he said these things to them, behold, there came a synagogue ruler, worshipping him, saying, My daughter is even now dead: but come and lay your hand upon her, and she will live. 19 Jesus arose and followed him, and so did his disciples.*

Synagogue is a Jewish temple. As a temple serves a function similar to a church so it represents placing greater attention on the spiritual part of Self; that is, the whole mind and the whole Self. The synagogue symbolizes using the mind to give greater attention to the spiritual side of Self. The first thing the man said was, *"Come and lay your hand upon her."* The key word is hand which symbolizes purpose. Identify with your purpose in this lifetime and gain the meaning of life. Feel more alive. Produce more with life, and accomplish much more. Life is motion. One who creates purpose in the life has the motivation to produce much more and on a more expansive scale — mentally, emotionally and physically.

> *20 Behold, a woman, who had suffered from hemorrhages for twelve years, came behind him, and touched the hem of his garment: 21 For she said within herself, If I may but touch his garment, I will be whole. 22 But Jesus turned, and when he saw her, he said, Daughter, be comforted; your faith has made you whole. And the woman was made whole from that hour.*

Lamsa translates *"was made whole"* as *"having been healed"*. The woman had been living the life based on untruth; the limitations that waste the energy or life force of a lifetime. The woman's faith signals the willingness to move forward into a mental image greater than the past distractions, reactions, and attachment to limitations which waste energy and the life or life force one has prepared this lifetime to use. Hemorrhaging symbolizes waste of Truth through dishonesty. This is a waste of the life and inefficient use of the opportunities available. Cloak or clothing represents one's outer presentation; the way one expresses Self outwardly. A knower operates from permanent understandings, gives from the whole Self, and reaches toward Enlightenment. Everything a knower expresses outwardly is productive and useful for greater awareness. The aspects that come in contact with the productivity of an Enlightened aspect will be improved just as a person desirous of improving their life will associate with those of like mind and even those of greater Self awareness and consciousness so they may be taught and raised up to this higher level.

Why will faith restore one to health? Why will faith heal? To be healed is to become whole again. That is, to have all parts of one's Self; mentally, emotionally, and physically working in harmony once again. Faith heals because faith is the acceptance into one's Self of a new more expansive image of Self Enlightenment, purpose, and creation. This more expanded image-attitude is reflected in the body as wholeness. Hemorrhage is the escape of blood from a blood vessel; heavy bleeding. Blood in the language of mind represents Truth or life force. One who is hemorrhaging symbolizes an aspect of Self that refuses to use and therefore retain the understanding of universal Truth previously gained. There is also the refusal to utilize the energies of Self (life force) for the advancement of Self, thus the years and energy of one's life slips away without adding to one's total storehouse of understandings and soul awareness. To accept a new, productive, outer expression based on the knowing quality of learning and growth allows one to create a receptive space in Self and to receive new Truths into Self.

> [23] When Jesus came into the ruler's house, and saw the minstrels and the people making a noise, [24] He said to them, Leave all of you: for the girl is not dead, but only asleep. And they laughed at him scornfully. [25] But when the people were put outside, he went in and took her by the hand, and the maid arose. [26] The fame hereof went abroad into all that land.

Hand symbolizes purpose. Constantly align with the soul's purpose in order to produce forward motion. Move toward alignment and develop the whole Self. Death is a type of change and as such represents change within the Self. After death, an assimilation process of the previous life's learning occurs. In sleep each night an assimilation process also occurs, only in sleep the assimilation is of the previous day's experience only. To state as Jesus did *"the girl is not dead, but only asleep"*, is to understand the process of assimilation and to know how to initiate the learning process and reason for existence. When the purpose of a lifetime is understood, the life takes on greater meaning and fulfillment. The district or area presents an image that this ability to heal an immobile aspect of Self is beneficially affecting other surrounding aspects and aspects that are similar. For example, Self value. It requires respect and receptivity for they all entail listening and receiving from the environment.

> [27] *When Jesus departed there, two blind men followed him, crying, and saying, You Son of David, have mercy on us.* [28] *When he came into the house, the blind men came to him: and Jesus said unto them, Are you confident I can do this? They said unto him, Yea, Lord.* [29] *Then he touched their eyes, saying, According to your faith be it unto you.* [30] *Their eyes were opened; and Jesus commanded them, saying, See that no man know it.* [31] *But when they were departed, they spread abroad his fame in all that country.*

Eyes and eyesight indicate perception. They called Jesus — Son of David — which symbolizes the aggressive learning and use of reasoning. This is the first time Jesus is referred to as Son of David. David represents reasoning so the symbolic image created is reasoning and building on reasoning to produce perception and intuition as the development of the spiritual Self. Jesus said, *"Are you confident I can do this?"* In other words, have you pictured clearly the healing that is going to occur and there is no doubt in your mind; nothing to block the healing change. There must be nothing in the imagination to block the newer, greater thoughts from occurring. Perception improves when there is the accurate and clear imagination of what is desired added to the reasoning capabilities already in place. Perception is also gained when one honestly and with undivided attention observes the environment and the Self, without allowing preconceived biases and prejudices to interfere with the perception of what is presently transpiring in the life.

> [32] *As they went out, behold, they brought to him a mute who was possessed with a demon.* [33] *When the demon was expelled, the mute spoke: and the multitudes marvelled, saying, It was never so seen in Israel.*

Mute is one who is unable to speak therefore incapable of expressing the thoughts of Self. The difficulty presented here is in bringing the thoughts from the mind into the physical life. Therefore, communication is impeded. There was a totally negative attitude that this one had taken on that was in opposition to the soul's desires, as represented by the demon. Demon symbolizes unproductive attitudes that one has dwelled on so often that they have taken control of Self. The expanded mental image strengthened with will and discipline, will crowd out old limited memory. Use discipline to crowd out the old negative attitudes. The expulsion of the demon and gaining the ability to talk symbolizes the student's efforts and learning to communicate his or her experiences in order to use future experiences for greater learning for the inner Self and to communicate with the inner Self.

> [34] But the Pharisees said, He expels demons through the prince of the demons.

The Pharisees being hypocrites were jealous of Jesus' abilities, authority, and respect. Jealousy is a product of refusing to act on your desires. It is caused by passivity. When the passive person notices others with will power are accomplishing their goals and desires, he or she becomes jealous. One who is jealous will tend to attempt to put down one who is accomplishing something productive. Hatred will never crowd out hatred. Resentment will not crowd out resentment. Purpose replaces resentment. Understanding replaces hatred. Never allow jealousies to get in the way of producing greater creations. Observe someone else who is producing something greater, then use this as a stimulus to produce greater in your own life. Move forward, instead of avoiding and ignoring change.

> [35] Jesus journeyed to all the cities and villages, teaching in their synagogues and preaching the gospel of the kingdom, and healing every sickness and every disease among the people. [36] When he saw the multitudes, his heart was moved with compassion, because they fainted, and were scattered abroad, like sheep in need of a shepherd.

Unproductive thoughts or attitudes being changed to productive attitudes that produce learning, growth, and maturity as a mental creator for the whole

Self is the example here. Jesus cured every sickness and disease presenting a clear picture of one capable of changing any unproductive aspect into whole learning for the whole Self.

> *37 Then said he unto the twelve, The harvest truly is plenty, but the laborers are few; 38 Pray you therefore the Lord of the harvest, that he will send forth laborers into his harvest.*

For the individual to become Enlightened, there must be the constant vigil to improve the Self, overriding the past with present successes and expanding the consciousness so the old, outworn limitations are released. The only way a release can occur is by expanding the consciousness of the individual not by thinking the limitations will go away. The harvest is the knowledge capable of being produced by a disciplined, willful reasoner who uses the experiences with full attention to glean their essence which can then be added to permanent, subconscious, soul memory. As more thoughts are turned from attachment to physical limitation toward thoughts and mental images of the highest awareness and Enlightenment, one gradually becomes the Enlightened Self one images.

Symbols and Their Interpretation

Chapter Ten

1.   Apostles - disciplined part of Self that teaches others
2.   Simon Peter - disciplined effort to understand the will
3.   Andrew - disciplined effort to understand imagination
4.   James - disciplined effort to understand the knowing quality
5.   John - disciplined effort to understand believing
6.   Philip - disciplined effort to understand attention
7.   Bartholomew - disciplined effort to understand honesty
8.   Thomas - disciplined effort to understand productive thinking
9.   Matthew- disciplined effort to understand value
10. James, Son of Alphaeus - disciplined effort to understand memory
11. Thaddaeus - disciplined effort to understand commitment
12. Simon the Zealot party member - disciplined effort to understand determination
13. Judas Iscariot - disciplined effort to understand productive motivating action of the conscious ego
14. Hair on head - conscious thoughts
15. Sparrows - subconscious thoughts
16. Samaritan - productive aspects that do not know the inner Self
17. Gift - exchanged value
18. Gold - value of wisdom
19. Silver - value of knowledge
20. Brass - value of information
21. Blessing - knowing an imaged creation will work and function well
22. Gentile - any aspect that has no information about I AM, the one living God
23. Death - change
24. Cross - understanding of vertical (mental) and horizontal (physical) time
25. Holy - whole

Chapter Ten

[1] He called to him his twelve disciples, giving them power against unclean spirits, to expel them, and to heal all manner of sickness and all manner of disease. [2] Now the names of the twelve apostles are these; The first, Simon, who is called Peter, and Andrew his brother; James the son of Zebedee, and John his brother; [3] Philip, and Bartholomew; Thomas, and Matthew the tax collector; James the son of Alphaeus, and Lebbaeus, whose surname was Thaddaeus; [4] Simon the zealot party member, and Judas Iscariot, who also betrayed him.

The twelve disciples symbolize the twelve major aspects of Self. They offer an image of a disciplined conscious mind. When the disciplined mind (the twelve major aspects) are identified and then used, then Self begins to teach and offer to others what one has learned. The disciples become apostles when they begin to teach. When there is the recognition of the twelve major parts of the inner Self and when you have identified them outwardly in your physical existence, then Self has the freedom to change these as need be. Once the awareness and understanding of healing, curing sickness, and expelling unclean spirits has been achieved then one can begin to use this ability in all facets and all areas of one's life. The twelve qualities of Self are being understood. Simon the Zealot was also known as Simon of Canaan.

[5] These twelve Jesus sent forth, and commanded them, saying, Do not visit pagan territory and do not enter Samaritan towns, [6] Go instead after the lost sheep of the house of Israel.

Contrary to Jesus' command, Paul (Saul of Tarsus who never met Jesus in his physical life) went to pagan territory for his salesmanship of his version of Christianity that I term "Paulinity". Paul's doctrine is different than what Jesus teaches here. Jesus says *"Do not visit pagan territory and do not enter Samaritan towns. Go instead after the lost sheep of the house of Israel."* The first mission for the disciplined thinker is to gather the lost sheep of the house of Israel. The Israelites are the teacher aspects of Self, the keepers of the secrets. Discover the inner secrets. For any student of the mind, any student of Metaphysics, the first effort needs to be discovering the secrets of how to use the whole mind. Concentration, stilling the mind, meditation, and going within must be accomplished. Then daily application of the awareness of the inner Self, the God Self, in the day-to-day physical life can be practiced. Once the awareness has been developed in the Self, all the outer and all the inner aspects can be given direction bringing them into alignment within the whole Self. The aspects who were lost, symbolized by the lost sheep of the house of Israel, represent one who is unaware of many different aspects of Self. People need to wake up and be aware of who they are to recognize I AM.

> [7] *As you go, preach, saying, The kingdom of heaven is at hand.* [8] *Heal the sick, cleanse the lepers, raise the dead, expel devils: freely you have received these gifts, freely give them.* [9] *Provide neither gold, nor silver, nor brass in your purses,* [10] *Nor script for your journey, neither two coats, neither shoes, nor yet staffs: for the workman is worthy of his meat.* [11] *And into whatever city or town you will enter, inquire who in it is worthy; and there stay till you go there.*

The reign of God connotes the individual responsibility to the whole Self. Become aware and cultivate a desire to know the inner Self. One is taught how to start this process, then the responsibility of the whole Self is at hand. Hand represents purpose. It is one's duty to uncover one's purpose for being in the physical lifetime. It is right here within one's grasp. To look for a worthy person in every town is to gain perception of an aspect you possess that can be productive and is ready to hear the Truth. This worthy person, this aspect of Self, can be used to develop one's mind until all parts of Self, all parts of mind, are understood and united by full Self realization.

12 When you come into an house, salute it. 13 And if the house be worthy, give it your blessing: but if it be not worthy, let your peace return to you. 14 Whoever will not receive you nor hear your words, when you depart out of that house or city, shake the dust off of your feet. 15 Verily I say to you, It will be more tolerable for the land of Sodom and Gomorrah in the day of judgment, than for that city.

As you give freely so you will receive whether or not your gift has been utilized appropriately by another. This is a Truth physically when giving to another person. It is also true mentally within Self when one gives to aspects of Self freely for the growth and benefit of the whole Self. Those aspects who do not receive discipline and make it a part of the life will never know the inner or whole Self. Therefore learn to practice and teach those parts of Self who are most conducive and receptive to learning and growth instead of entrapment. Sodom and Gomorrah were known since the time of Lot, nephew of Abraham, as cities of sin and evil. They were so filled with sin that two angels of the Lord were sent to destroy them with sulfurous fire. The symbolic message in this passage is that to receive and fail to use the information about the value of disciplining the mind is worse than never even being aware of the value of discipline in the conscious mind.

16 Behold, I send you forth as sheep in the midst of wolves: be you therefore wise as serpents, and innocent as doves. 17 Beware of men: for they will deliver you up to the councils, and they will flog you in their synagogues; 18 You will be brought before governors and kings for my sake, for a testimony against them and the Gentiles. 19 When they try you, take no thought how or what you will speak: for it will be given you in that same hour what you will speak. 20 For it is not you who speaks, but the Spirit of your Father which speaks through you.

Serpents symbolize the conscious ego and the need to create as a creator made in the image and likeness of the Creator (God). The serpent first appears in the Bible in *Genesis 3:1*. The serpent tempted the woman to eat the fruit of the tree of knowledge of good and evil. To be wise as a serpent is to be consistently Self motivated to create, change, learn, grow and expand one's consciousness. The duty of the ego is to motivate the Self forward. Doves, being flying birds, represent subconscious thoughts. Following the flooding of the earth, Noah (*Genesis 8:8*) sent out a dove to see if water had lessened on the earth. The first time the dove came back. The second time the dove came back with an olive leaf. The third time the dove did not return indicating to Noah that the flood had receded and there was dry land again.

Subconscious thoughts appear to us in dreams and intuitive perceptions. The subconscious mind will never lie, but the conscious mind can be very dishonest to Self. Since one's subconscious mind is always honest and ready to receive more and greater learning, it is innocent. Just as a young child who is always eager to learn and who has not been taught dishonesty by adults is innocent or pure. To be pure and innocent is to be undiluted. To be pure is to have refused to allow the real desires from the inner Self for Enlightenment to be diluted with engrossing physical desires and sensory stimulation. Jesus always referred to the productive aspects who believed in his teaching of the inner secrets as the sheep. The wolves are the compulsive aspects of the physical. To be innocent as doves is to align your outer, conscious mind with your inner Self. Use the Kundalini for creativity. Keep Self in alignment with the Universal Laws. Don't go against the Universal Laws. When the attention is on building the whole Self, when it is time to speak the Truth, the Truth will flow from within.

> *21 Brother will deliver up brother to death, and the father the child: and the children will rise up against their parents, and cause them to be put to death. 22 You will be hated of all men for my names sake: but he who endures to the end will be saved. 23 When they persecute you in this city, flee you into another: for verily I say unto you, You will not have gone over the cities of Israel, till the Son of man comes.*

To escape death is to be free of the clutches of restriction of the physical engrossment or entrapment. The Son of Man is the one who is aggressive in the conscious mind in understanding the subconscious mind. Man is the thinker. To explore all levels of mind one needs to understand and employ the receptive and aggressive qualities of creation, then one can understand the subconscious mind. El is the name of God in the first chapter of *Genesis* whose plural form is Elohim.

Elohim is the <u>us</u> and <u>our</u> of *Genesis 1:26. Ra* is also the name for *God. Ra* is the name of God for the Egyptians. He is the Egyptian Sun God Amen-Ra. It is the shortened version of the name of another Egyptian God. Isis was an Egyptian God-dess from which the *Is* in *Israel* is taken.

> ²⁴ *No student is better than his teacher, nor is the servant above his lord.* ²⁵ *It is enough for the disciple that he be like his master, and the servant like his lord. If they have called the master of the house Beelzebub, how much more will they say about them of his household?*

Beelzebub was the name of a false God to the Israelites, the keepers of the secrets. He was a god of religions foreign to the Hebrew. Beelzebub represents worshipping the physical and its sense entanglements as one's god.

> ²⁶ *Do not fear them: for there is nothing covered that will not be revealed; nor hid that will not be known.* ²⁷ *What I tell you in darkness, that speak you in light: and what you hear in private, proclaim from the housetops.* ²⁸ *Fear not them who kill the body but are not able to kill the soul: but rather fear him who is able to destroy both soul and body in Gehenna fire.* ²⁹ *Are not two sparrows sold for almost nothing? not one of them falls on the ground without your Father knowing.* ³⁰ *The very hairs of your head are all numbered.* ³¹ *Have no fear, you are of more value than many sparrows.* ³² *Whoever therefore will acknowledge me before men, him will I acknowledge also before my Father which is in heaven.* ³³ *But whoever will deny me before men, him will I also deny before my Father which is in heaven.*

The soul cannot be destroyed, but the opportunity for the soul to grow, mature, gain, and progress this lifetime can be destroyed if one allows other people's gossip, lies, negativity, and resentment to dictate one's thoughts and actions. Do not allow the environment to dictate limitations. Rather move beyond limitations. Transcend limitations. Every hair on your head has been counted means that each conscious thought is valuable and has an affect on Self, others, and the environment. Thoughts are real and thoughts are things.

Yet individuality, "I Am", is worth more than any subconscious or conscious thought. To acknowledge is to give recognition and knowledge. Whoever gives knowledge (knowing) of Self to the conscious mind and physical aspects will gain in understanding and fulfillment of the plan held in superconscious mind.

Notes:

> ^{34} *Think not that I am come to send peace on earth: I came not to send peace but division.* ^{35} *I am come to set a man at variance against his father, and the daughter against her mother, and the daughter in law against her mother in law.* ^{36} *A man's foes will be those in his own household.*

Lamsa translates division as a sword. The reasoner must realize the division and difference between conscious mind and subconscious mind in order to use both effectively. Why would a knower want to be at odds with his or her Self? Identify any aspect which is not productive. Any part of Self that has separated from the whole, thinking everything is fine, is in for a rude awakening when the Self finds the need to interact with people. Interact with people and there is a reaction. Re-actions indicate the need to change in order to cause the true peace, the inner peace within the Real Self. Peace is not gained by running away from everything or avoidance. Self can exist in the physical world without being caught up in the entrapment of the world. Learn to be the real Self wherever and whenever. Growth is never accomplished by avoidance but rather by constantly embracing the opportunities for growth that are available; be they pleasant or unpleasant.

> ^{37} *He who loves father or mother more than me is not worthy of me: and he who loves son or daughter more than me is not worthy of me.* ^{38} *He who does not take his cross and follow after me, is not worthy of me.* ^{39} *He who seeks only himself brings himself to ruin, he who brings himself to nought for me discovers who he is.*

Jesus mentions the cross in verse 38. This is a prelude to the cross Jesus will bear later in Matthew's account. To take up one's cross is to realize one is not the physical body; one is entrapped in a physical body. Such a one realizes he or she is an immortal soul and therefore knows the purpose of existence in the physical body is to build permanent memory called understandings. The horizontal bar of the cross represents horizontal or physical time and the vertical board of the cross symbolizes mental or subconscious time. The nature of time must be understood by anyone desiring Enlightenment.

> *40 He who receives you receives me; and he who receives me receives him that sent me. 41 He who receives a prophet in the name of a prophet will receive a prophets reward; and he who receives a Holy man in the name of a righteous man will receive a Holy man's reward.*

Holy man is one who is reasoning, using the mind productively, and committed to learning to use the whole mind. To welcome discipline is to embrace and create the opportunity to build permanent knowing or knowledge. One who embraces a Holy man is a prophet for he is one who creates goals and moves to them.

> *42 Whoever will give to drink unto one of these little ones a cup of cold water only in the name of a disciple, verily I say unto you, he will in no way lose his reward.*

Water symbolizes conscious experience. Any aspect who is cooperating in using the experiences that are available and creating new experiences for the disciplined thinker, will receive the greatest reward of value which is permanent soul growth.

Symbols and Their Interpretation

Chapter Eleven

1. Teach - to give of the learning one has gained
2. Royal Palaces - accumulation of value and authority in the conscious mind
3. Elijah - goal setter. Creates the ideal of the believer and caused change
4. Children - quality of infancy, willing to receive new learning
5. Tyre and Sidon - understanding structure of mind
6. Sodom - engrossment in the sensory experiences
7. Yoke - yoga; union of conscious and subconscious minds

Chapter Eleven

* It came to pass, when Jesus had finished instructing his twelve disciples, he went to teach and to preach in their towns.*

The one who employs discipline to align the twelve major aspects in Self, can go to all parts of mind; instructing and teaching many parts of Self.

² When John heard in the prison the works of the Christ, he sent two of his disciples, ³ Instructing them to ask of him, Are you he that should come, or do we look for another?

Prison represents restriction and that shows the knowing of Self and creation is becoming more and more strengthened while believing, symbolized by John, is seen to be less and less powerful as knowing supplants it. Knowing is necessary, important, and very powerful for the reasoner. In order to create intuitive man within Self, build the knowing quality by creating permanent learning at an accelerated rate. The personal learning experience needs to be taught to others until the understanding of the Universal Laws governing the many aspects of the Self are completely understood. To develop the motivating factor of the quality of believing, one must exercise discipline.

⁴ Jesus answered and said unto them, Go and show John again those things which you do hear and see: ⁵ The blind receive their sight, and the lame walk, the lepers are cleansed, the deaf hear, the dead are raised up, and the poor have the gospel preached to them. ⁶ Blessed is he, whoever will find no stumbling block in me.

By a man's works will he be known. A creator will create. A builder will build and add to what was initiated. A knower is one who is able to consistently increase and improve perception; cause productive continual forward motion where there was none before. Such a one is able to conquer hate and destructive attitudes replacing them with love. He learns to cause inner listening to the subconscious and superconscious minds, and create learning opportunities where none previously existed. He produces mental, emotional, and physical prosperity while gaining understanding of the high Self in all parts of one's being.

> *⁷ As they departed, Jesus began to say unto the crowds concerning John, What did you go out into the wasteland to see? A reed swaying in the breeze? ⁸ But what did you go out to see? A man clothed in rich clothing? behold, those who dress luxuriously are to be found in royal palaces.*

John, is the epitome of the believing quality's power. Right believing has discipline, as John the Baptist had disciples. The believing quality is strong and decisive, not *a reed swaying in the breeze* which moves to whichever direction the environment or conscious thoughts influence it. The power of believing is not expressed fully outwardly in one's expression. Rather it is the motion towards a goal of awareness. A prophet (John) creates the goal of Enlightenment.

> *⁹ But what did you go forth to see? A prophet? yes, I say to you, and more than a prophet. ¹⁰ For this is he, of whom it is written, Behold, I send my messenger before your face, which will prepare your way before you.*

Reference is made to *Malachi 3*, *Mark 1* and *2*, and *Luke 1*. A messenger represents the quality of believing that comes before knowing in order to produce true and full understanding. A prophet represents a goal setter. One who has set the goals to be a whole functioning Self and is willing to move forward with the life. To be more than a prophet is to consistently create ideals, move forward, and to actually fulfill those ideals as well as the goals of the Self. Jesus represents achieving the ideal of Enlightenment.

¹¹ Verily I say unto you, History has not known a man born of woman greater than John the Baptist: not withstanding, the least born into the kingdom of heaven is greater than he. ¹² From the days of John the Baptist until now the kingdom of heaven suffers violence, and the violent take it by force.

Believing can only function as far as the conscious mind will move the Self. To know the inner Self one must move into knowing which is direct personal experience with the inner Self through practical application of the universal Truths in daily life. One can be a great salesman and motivate from believing and imagining goals. One works toward the goal with Self motivation but one will never be Enlightened that way. The ideal must be Enlightenment.

¹³ For all the prophets and the law prophesied until John. ¹⁴ If you will receive it, he is Elijah, the one who was certain to come. ¹⁵ He that has ears to hear, let him hear.

This is a reference to *Malachi 3:24, 2nd Kings 2, John 9:1, 3-17* and other references in the Bible. *John 14:12* quotes Jesus as saying, *"greater things than I do, you will also do."* We each may use the example, teachings, and opportunities available from Jesus the knower to cause our quickened evolution.

The prophets predicted and imaged the ideal of Enlightenment. With the advent of Jesus, this ideal is fulfilled. Therefore, there is no more need to prophesy the coming of the Messiah, the Saviour. Verse 14 has Jesus stating that John the Baptist is a reincarnation of Elijah. This is a direct reference to reincarnation if one is to read this physically.

The symbolic, mental interpretation is that there are steps to building the complete and full believer as there are steps to creating the fully Enlightened knower. In a similar fashion, one must move through infancy and adolescence to achieve adulthood and old age-wisdom.

¹⁶ But what comparison will I liken this generation? It is like children sitting in the markets, calling to their fellows, ¹⁷ Saying, We have piped unto you, and you have not danced; we have mourned unto you, and you have not lamented. ¹⁸ For John came neither eating nor drinking, and they say, He is mad. ¹⁹ The Son of man came eating and drinking, and they say, Behold a man gluttonous, and a drunkard, a friend of tax collectors and sinners. Yet time will prove where wisdom lies.

Notes:

Do not expect one who is leading a life to become Enlightened to live a life similar to those who are more material minded. Such a one will not be moved by petty reactions to changes in the physical environment. It is the mental attitude and intention behind those actions which creates karma. It appears that one who is engrossed and refuses to change, does not wish to understand an Enlightened One and therefore criticizes whatever they do.

> [20] *Then he began to upbraid the cities where most of his mighty works were done, because they did not reform.* [21] *It will go ill with you Chorazin, and worse for you Bethsaida! for if the mighty miracles which were done in you had been done in Tyre and Sidon, they would have reformed long ago in sackcloth and ashes.* [22] *I say unto you, It will be more tolerable for Tyre and Sidon at the day of judgment than for you.* [23] *You, Capernaum, which are exalted unto heaven, will be brought down to the realm of death: for if the mighty miracles which have been done in you had been done in Sodom, it would have remained until this day.* [24] *But I say unto you, That it will go easier for the land of Sodom in the day of judgment than for you.*

Reform means change. Re-form is to re-structure, to form a valuable, productive structure greater than the previous one. If it isn't valuable and constructive, it needs to be reformed into a structure that is valuable, important, and productive. One that will add permanently to the learning and growth of Self.

Tyre and Sidon are Phoenician cities and its peoples, who under the direction of King Hiram built King Solomon's temple. They symbolize an understanding of the structure of mind. Sodom has been referred to previously in its symbolic meaning. The concept here is once a person has been exposed to and given the Truth they are more responsible for using that Truth than one who has never been aware of the Truth. Also, one who is steeped in the information of Truth can go down farther with indebtedness to themselves by misusing that information.

> ²⁵ *At that time Jesus answered, saying, I thank you, O Father, Lord of heaven and earth, because you have hid these things from the learned and clever, and have revealed them unto the merest children.* ²⁶ *Father it is true; for that is how your divine pleasure could be manifested before you.* ²⁷ *All things are delivered unto me of my Father: and no man knows the Son, but the Father; neither knows any man the Father, save the Son, and he to whomever the Son will reveal him.*

To enter the kingdom of heaven, which is the inner levels of mind, one will learn as a child. Child symbolizes the stage of learning called infancy which has as its qualities to be always willing to absorb and add to the learning. A child does not know restrictions, preconceptions, biases, or prejudging -- prejudices. A child is able therefore to learn without restrictions. Learning, changing, and growing without restriction enables one to be able to make the expansion of consciousness that is necessary to know the inner thinker. A clever person or intellectual does not have this ability to enter the inner levels.

> ²⁸ *Come to me all you that labor and are heavy laden, and I will give you rest.* ²⁹ *Take my yoke upon you, and learn of me; for I am gentle and humble in heart: and you will find rest unto your souls.* ³⁰ *For my yoke is kindly, and my burden is light.*

It may seem difficult at first to begin on the spiritual path because it requires discipline. However, a mentally disciplined life is the easiest, most enjoyable, fun way to live, because this is living the Truth and the true life. One can answer the questions, "Why am I here? What is my purpose in life? Why do all these painful or pleasant things happen to me?" The disciplined one knows the answer to these questions and applies this knowledge to create a greater world.

Yoke symbolizes connecting or yoking together the conscious and subconscious minds. The word yoke is derived from the Sanskrit word *yoga* which means *union*.

Notes:

Symbols and Their Interpretation

Chapter Twelve

1. Grain - knowledge
2. Cure/Heal - to make whole, to change an attitude from being unproductive to productive
3. Beelzebub - satan; devil; conscious ego, the motivator
4. Jonah - learning commitment to fulfill one's assignment for a lifetime
5. Nineveh - engrossment in the physical senses
6. Queen of the south - receptive authority to create expansion
7. Seven - number of control

Chapter Twelve

¹ At that time Jesus went on the Sabbath day through the standing grain; and his disciples feeling hunger began to pluck the heads of grain, eating them. ² But when the Pharisees saw it, they said unto him, Behold, your disciples do what is not lawful to do upon the Sabbath day. ³ But he said unto them, Have you not read what David did when he was hungry, and those who were with him; ⁴ How he entered into the house of God and did eat the holy bread, which was not lawful for him to eat, neither for them which were with him, but only for the priests?

The knower has full command of the reasoning capabilities and its three factors of memory, attention, and imagination. The memory of the Holy Works is utilized here for Jesus is able to use the priests' own source of authority to expose their hypocrisy. Grain symbolizes direct use of knowledge. The Sabbath is the day of rest. The Sabbath symbolizes a regular period of assimilation. The meaning of the injunction against working (activity) on the Sabbath is there is a need to assimilate regularly the experience one has received. However, a Knower and reasoner is constantly assimilating the learning in each experience and therefore does not need a specific time set aside for this. There is no lag time in the learning for the knower.

⁵ Or have you not read in the law, how that on the Sabbath days the priests in the temple profane the Sabbath, and are blameless? ⁶ But I say unto you, That in this place is one greater than the temple.

The knower is greater than the mind. I AM is greater than mind for mind is a vehicle for I AM.

⁷ But if you knew what this means, I will have mercy and not sacrifice, you would not have condemned the guiltless.

A priest on temple duty is one whose attention, time, and effort engaged fully in serving creation and knowing mind. In this case, such a one or such an aspect is constantly assimilating into the inner Self the knowledge available from the experience.

To give mercy is to spare a life preserving the opportunities for learning and growth. This action of mercy is more important than giving your habits to God. The Israelites sacrificed animals (habitual brain pathways). The attention is more usefully applied by directing one's mind to learning and using experiences for knowledge, rather than placing the attention on habits and then trying to change and grow.

> *⁸ For the Son of man is superior to the Sabbath.*

The Pharisees, the priests of the corrupt temple of Jesus' time, were locked into limiting rules and regulations rather than living according to the spirit of the law which is to have a productive intention for every action of Self. This productive intention is called "right thinking" by Gautama the Buddha. This correct intention relieves karma creating in Self the opportunity to expand the learning in one's life.

The knowing aspect, Jesus, does not allow rules and regulations symbolized by the Pharisees (the hypocritical part of Self) to bind Self. Rules and regulations are provided to give a structure to be used in the life. But when rules and regulations are misused to bind or restrict Self this constitutes a misuse of the structure. The Son of Man, the thinker aggressively moving forwards, is not to be restricted. True reasoners are to use the structure that is available in order to keep the goal of complete Enlightenment of Self. The Sabbath symbolizes the goal. By holding this goal Holy, Self can move on to a higher level of awareness. The Self, however, is more important than any goal. The structure and rules in first grade and in kindergarten are not the structure and rules of high school. These are not the structure and rules of a job or college, nor are they the structure and rules of a city, or a state, or a country. As one grows, the field of perception, awareness, and responsibility expands and grows so the rules symbolizing structure become more expansive also.

The natural motion of physical life is change. Therefore to work hard to try to keep the life the same, to maintain balance, is to create difficulty in life because you are opposing the natural motion of physical life. In every motion there is a point of stability, or steadiness, or quiet.

> *⁹ When he left there, he went into their synagogue: ¹⁰ Behold, there was a man who had a withered hand. And they asked him, saying, Is it lawful to heal on the Sabbath day? so that they might accuse him. ¹¹ He said unto them, What man will there be among you, that will have one sheep, and if it fall into a pit on the Sabbath day, will he not lay hold on it, and lift it out? ¹² How then is a man better than a sheep? Therefore it is lawful to do well on the Sabbath day.*

One can use a compulsion to learn to discipline Self. One can make a habit of meditating every day. Even when it is a habit there is some benefit gained. The Sabbath is when the activity starts. The seventh day symbolizes assimilation of the previous day's experience and planning the activity of the next week or time period. A man with a shriveled or withered hand symbolizes one who has not created nor used purpose in their life for a long time. When purpose is created then assimilation of the knowledge of experiences can occur regularly and constantly.

> *¹³ Then said he to the man, Stretch forth your hand. He stretched it forth; and it was restored whole, like his other. ¹⁴ Then the Pharisees left and held council against him, plotting how they might destroy him. ¹⁵ Jesus knew their plans and withdrew from that place: great multitudes followed him and he healed them all; ¹⁶ He sternly ordered them not to make public what he had accomplished.*

Purpose has been regained as symbolized by the healing of the withered hand. The Sabbath represents the completion of the ideal and the beginning of activity. The three necessary ingredients for success in learning and growth are ideal, purpose, and activity. Ideal, purpose, and activity were present in the knower, Jesus, and he brought these aspects of Self into alignment. These parts of Self were not to make public what he had done because there were still too many negative, engrossed aspects of the knower and knower has not yet gained full Enlightenment. Nurture any new quality and learning through infancy and adolescence into adulthood where it will develop into a new understanding. Then from this understanding, Self can handle any limitation in the conditional world.

> *¹⁷ That it might be fulfilled which was spoken by Isaiah the prophet, saying ¹⁸ Behold my servant, whom I have chosen; my beloved, in whom I am well pleased: I will endow him with my spirit, and he will proclaim justice to the Gen-*

Notes:

> *tiles. [19] He will not strive, nor cry; nor will his voice be heard in the streets. [20] A bruised reed he will not break, and a smouldering wick he will not quench, till his judgement is victorious. [21] In his name the Gentiles will find hope.*

The quote is from *Isaiah 42:1-9.* Lamsa translates *"Gentiles"* as *"peoples".* Isaiah does not use the term gentiles instead he uses the word nations. Regardless, the mental picture is the same. Both represent aspects of the Self that have not yet identified as soul instead of just physical body, and have yet to fully realize the purpose for existence in the physical world. They are entrapped aspects that live their life for physical reasons.

Spirit is mind. To be endowed with the spirit of God is to know the mind of God. To know the mind of God is to know and fully use the plan of creation and operate according to Universal Law. The fire of expansion will never be extinguished, for the reasoner will complete and transcend all the lessons, rules, and limitations of the physical existence.

> *[22] Then one possessed with a devil, blind and dumb, was brought to him and he healed him, inasmuch that the blind and dumb both spoke and saw. [23] All the people were amazed, and said, Is not this the son of David? [24] But when the Pharisees heard it, they said, This fellow does not expel demons, but by Beelzebub the prince of the demons.*

The Pharisees are aspects of Self that rely on what has been; what the rules convey. This leads to an attitude of unhealthy skepticism because the faculty of imagination is not employed to understand the purpose of the rules or laws. Skepticism is related to rebelliousness and rejection of authority. Skepticism occurs when the mind is closed and, therefore, reasoning is lessened.

²⁵ Jesus knew their thoughts, and said unto them, Every king-
dom divided against itself is brought to desolation; and ev-
ery city or house divided against itself will not stand: ²⁶ If
Satan expels Satan, he is divided against himself; how then
will his kingdom stand? ²⁷ If I by Beelzebub expel demons,
by whom do your children expel out? therefore they will be
your judges. ²⁸ But if I expel demons by the Spirit of God,
then the kingdom of God is come to you. ²⁹ How can one
enter into a strong man's house and spoil his goods, except
he first bind the strong man and then he will spoil his house.
³⁰ He that is not with me is against me; and he that does not
gather with me scatters.

To be possessed is to have a demon or disincarned entity trying to
control one's body. The need in this case is for one to practice will power so
that one is making one's own decisions rather than passively allowing others
to do so. Blindness symbolizes the need to practice, improve, and build one's
mental perception. To be healed after being mute is to cause communication
where none previously existed. It is to voice one's thoughts, sharing them
with others, thereby creating a space within Self where one can once again
receive the learning available from the environmental activities.

All aspects of Self need to work together, in harmony for the common goal of Enlightenment, if the household of mind is to be developed and
employed to its utmost. Demons symbolize negative, habitual attitudes that
one mistakenly believes to be the Self. Habits can never cause the alignment
of mind nor the identification of aspects of Self. To gather with Jesus is to
bring into a common ideal, aspects of Self.

³¹ Wherefore I say unto you, All manner of sin and blas-
phemy will be forgiven unto men: but the blasphemy against
the Holy Spirit will not be forgiven unto men.

The Holy spirit is the whole mind. You must use, not misuse the
mind. For greater spiritual growth and awareness, view the Self as an ever-
changing, ever-learning, individual. When you recognize something inside
the Self that is new -- whether this is a new awareness, a new question or a
new way of looking at life -- then embrace this eagerly rather than being afraid
that this will destroy what you have built the life upon.

³² Whoever speaks a word against the Son of man, it will
be forgiven him: but whoever speaks against the Holy Spirit,
it will not be forgiven him, neither in this age or in the age
to come. ³³ Either make the tree good and his fruit good; or
else make the tree corrupt and his fruit corrupt: for the tree

Notes:

> *is known by his fruit.* [34] *O genera-*
> *tion of vipers, how can you, being*
> *evil, speak good things? The mouth*
> *speaks words describing whatever*
> *fills the mind.* [35] *A good man out of*
> *the good treasure of the heart brings*
> *forth good things: and an evil man*
> *out of the evil treasure brings forth*
> *evil things.* [36] *But I say unto you,*
> *That every idle word that men will*
> *speak, they will be held accountable*
> *for.* [37] *For by your words you will be*
> *acquitted, and by your words you will*
> *be condemned.*

Sins, which are mistakes, can be corrected so learning can once again occur. Thinking and verbalizing thoughts contrary to using the whole mind will never propel the Self forward. A person can tell from the knowledge one receives into Self whether one is producing subconscious understanding. A brood of vipers are aspects of the conscious ego that are unproductive. Thoughts are things. Your thoughts of today create your world of tomorrow. As a person thinks so they become. Your words describe where you are in soul progression. What you meant to say describes where you want to be. Your words describe your thoughts and your levels of consciousness. In fulfilling the goal of healing the blindness and lameness, and in expelling the demons, Jesus was accused of being a demon himself. That is ridiculous. Good or productive begets more of the same. Unproductive destroys.

> [38] *Then certain of the scribes and of*
> *the Pharisees answered, saying,*
> *Master, we want to see a sign from*
> *you.*

That is like saying, we want you to perform tricks so that we can believe. Belief doesn't work that way! Belief in something does not originate from someone or something outside of Self. This can only provide a stimulus for belief to be conceived in the mind of the thinker. Belief comes from one's own direct experience. No one can prove anything to another. The only real proof is Self proof. When the mind is open and reasoning is free to blossom and to be used fully, there is an increase and enhancement of awareness that benefits the Self and others immediately. Meditate every day, practice concentration every day, remember dreams writing them down and interpreting them every day. Practice daily directing and focusing the mind. Listen to the inner Self. Still the mind so the mind can be turned back on itself and know Self.

> *[39] He answered saying to them, An evil and adulterous gen-eration seeks after a sign; and there will no sign be given to it, but the sign of the prophet Jonah: [40] For as Jonah was three days and three nights in the whale's belly; so will the Son of man be three days and three nights in the belly of the earth.*

Lamsa translates belly as heart. Jesus' body, after being removed from the cross, was placed in Joseph of Arimethea's cave which served as a tomb for three days and three nights. Both show existence in a restrictive place where there is the identification of the restrictive thoughts, attitudes, and aspects of Self. Then one is ready to move forward once again to fulfill the assignment of Self, because such a one has identified the limitation that is creating pain and desires and is willing to move beyond that limitation. As a person transforms the prejudices one has held against vulnerability, open-ness, and Self examination there is the coming into awareness of one's true nature in a much deeper way. There will then be freedom and exaltation of Self as spirit.

> *[41] The men of Nineveh will rise in judgment with this gen-eration, and will condemn it: because their minds were changed at the preaching of Jonah; and, behold, a greater than Jonah is here.*

Jesus is greater than Jonah for the knower is greater than the goal setter.

> *[42] The queen of the south will rise up in the judgment with this generation, and will condemn it: for she came from the uttermost parts of the earth to hear the wisdom of Solomon; and, behold, a greater than Solomon is here.*

The queen of the south is the Queen of Sheba referred to in *I Kings 10:1-13.*

I Kings 10 [1] When the queen of Sheba heard of the fame of Solomon concerning the name of the Lord, she came to prove him with hard questions. [2] She came to Jerusalem with a very great train, with cam-

Notes:

els that bore spices, and very much gold and precious stones. When she came to Solomon, she communed with him all that was in her heart. [3] *And Solomon answered all her questions: no thing was hidden from the king.* [4] *When the queen of Sheba saw all Solomon's wisdom, and the house that he had built,* [5] *the meat of his table, the sitting of his servants, the attendance of his ministers and their apparel, his cupbearers, and his ascent by which he went up unto the house of the Lord; there was no more spirit in her.* [6] *She said to the king, It was a true report that I heard in my own land of your acts and of your wisdom.* [7] *However, I didn't believe the words until I came, and my eyes saw it: and the half was not told to me: your wisdom and prosperity exceeds the fame which I heard.* [8] *Happy are your men, happy are these your servants who stand continually before you and hear your wisdom.* [9] *Blessed be the Lord your God, which delights in you, to set you on the throne of Israel: because the Lord loved Israel forever, therefore he made you king to do judgment and justice.* [10] *She gave the king a hundred and twenty talents of gold, and of spices very great store and precious stones: there came no more such abundance of spices as these which the queen of Sheba gave to king Solomon.* [11] *And the navy also of Hiram, that brought gold from Ophir, brought in from Ophir great plenty of almug trees, and precious stones.* [12] *The king made of the almug trees pillars for the house of the Lord, and for the kings house, harps also and psalteries for singers: there came no such almug trees, nor were seen unto this day.* [13] *And king Solomon gave unto the queen of Sheba all her desire, whatsoever she asked, beside that which Solomon gave her of his royal bounty. So she turned and went to her own country, she and her servants.*

Jesus is greater than Solomon because wisdom is a product of knowledge gained from experience and applied in the life for Self and others, while knowing is permanent memory called understandings added to the inner and Real Self. Both cases show the overcoming of entrapment. You want a sign? Watch Jesus; for he is not entrapped like the Pharisees and Sadducees. That is the sign.

> *43 When the unclean spirit is gone out of a man, he walks through dry places, seeking rest, and finds none. 44 Then he said, I will return into my house from whence I came out; and when he is come, he finds it empty, swept, and garnished. 45 Then goes he, and takes with himself seven other spirits more wicked than himself, and they enter in and dwell there: and the last state of that man is worse than the first. Even so will it be also unto this wicked generation.*

The seven unclean spirits shows the more one thinks negatively, the more negativity grows. Engrossment and complete entrapment in negativity and limitation occurs. This is when mistakes, evil, unpleasant happenings occur in life; such as hate, resentment, anger, and jealousy. Exercise will power and Self discipline while redirecting the thinking.

> *46 While he yet talked to the people, behold, his mother and his brother stood without, desiring to speak with him. 47 Then one said unto him, Behold, your mother and your brother stand without, desiring to speak with you. 48 But he answered and said unto him that told him, Who is my mother? and who is my brother? 49 He stretched forth his hand toward his disciples, and said, Behold my mother and my brother 50 For whoever will do the will of my Father which is in heaven, the same is my brother, and sister, and mother.*

To build a new spirituality and awareness of Self, don't put Self in a negative, hateful, destructive environment. Enter an environment which is conducive to what is desired to be learned. These people (aspects) are spiritual kindred of the Real Self. You are only cooperative when you aid others to fulfill desires. Whatever you want, you need to find out or figure out that you are wealthy enough to give in order to receive your desire. Then you will learn you are abundant. If you want to be wealthy to receive something, you must first be wealthy enough to give. Through one's giving, one achieves a higher state of awareness so that one experiences and knows one's own influence and importance. When one gives, one experiences love and joy.

Notes:

Symbols and Their Interpretation

Chapter Thirteen

1.   Seeds - seed thoughts given from conscious mind to subconscious mind
2.   The evil one - devil; conscious ego
3.   Weeds - restricting, limited, and unproductive thoughts that crowd out productive and fruitful ideas
4.   Mustard seed - a powerful idea, seed thought
5.   Sky - superconscious mind
6.   Dragnet - tool for gaining spiritual awareness

Chapter Thirteen

Chapter thirteen is special because it begins the presentation of parables. Jesus is revealing inner secrets through teaching in parables. The essence of these parables is there is more than one level for speaking Truth. There is the inner spiritual level. Jesus gives the parable of the seed.

> [1] *The same day went Jesus out of his house, and sat by the sea side.* [2] *Such great multitudes were gathered drawn to him, that he got on a boat, and sat; while the whole multitude stood on the shore.* [3] *He spoke many things to them in parables, saying, Behold, a sower went forth to sow;* [4] *When he sowed, some seeds fell by the wayside, and the fowls came and devoured them up:* [5] *Some fell upon stony places, where they had not much earth: and forthwith they sprung up because they had no deepness of earth:* [6] *When the sun rose, they were scorched; and because they had no root they withered away.* [7] *Some fell among thorns; and the thorns sprung up, and choked them:* [8] *But others fell into good ground and brought forth fruit, some an hundredfold, some sixtyfold, some thirtyfold.* [9] *Let everyone listen to what he hears.*

The seed represents whole and complete ideas. Seeds that have been placed in the ground symbolize thoughts planted in subconscious mind substance. To fulfill desires first image the "seed" ideas and move the activity toward achieving the ideal imaged desire. It is important that Jesus, the knower, teaches others and learns how to fulfill desires because it is through the fulfilling of desires that we become desireless and achieve a state of desirelessness. Thorns represent doubts and indecisions which are obstructions to producing knowledge. The zeros in 100, 60, or 30 indicate power. By using this power we add to the whole Self. Standing on a boat while addressing the crowd on land symbolizes having one's awareness in the conscious physical life while addressing aspects in the subconscious. Only a knower can accomplish this.

Notes:

> [10] *The disciples came, and said to him, Why do you speak to them in parables?* [11] *He answered and said to them, Because it is given to you to know the mysteries of the kingdom of heaven, but to them it is not given.* [12] *For whoever has, to him will be given, and he will have more abundance: but whoever has not, from him will be taken away even that he has.*

The key to abundance is to give. The key to prosperity is to teach. Jesus speaks in parables because the public does not know the secrets of the inner levels of mind. A parable is a metaphor. To the thinker who has knowledge of the inner secrets, practicing and applying them, more will be given. He who does not use Universal Laws is not aware of the inner secrets. The Laws keep operating but the ignorance is not in harmony with the Laws and such a one will lose the little awareness they may have. When one thinks only physically then that which is of the inner levels of mind and of a higher consciousness can only be explained in parables and allegory. Parables are the elementary and beginning stages of learning to receive and communicate in the Universal Language of Mind. As one gains greater awareness of the inner Self, communication can occur in that inner language of mind. By communicating one's ideals, one can gain greater benefit from an association.

> [13] *Therefore I speak to them in parables: because they look but do not see; they hear but they do not listen, neither do they understand.*

One who believes all of existence to be comprised only of what can be experienced with the five senses will only think physical. There is a need to mentally understand the real Self and the higher consciousness which is not physical and therefore can be explained physically only as symbol.

14 In them is fulfilled the prophecy of Isaiah, which said, By hearing you will hear, and will not understand; and seeing you will see, and will not perceive: *15 For this people's heart is waxed gross, and their ears are dull of hearing, and their eyes they have closed; lest at any time they should see with their eyes, and hear with their ears, and should understand with their heart, and should be converted, and I should heal them.* *16 But blessed are your eyes, for they see: and your ears, for they hear.* *17 For verily I say unto you, That many prophets and righteous men have desired to see those things which you see, and have not seen them; and to hear those things which you hear, and have not heard them.* *18 Hear you therefore the parable of the sower.* *19 When any one hears the word of the kingdom, and understands it not, then comes the evil one, and steal away that which was sown in his mind. This is he which received seed by the way side.* *20 But he that received the seed into stony places, he that hears the message, and at first with joy receives it;* *21 Yet has he no roots, so he lasts for only a while: for when some setback or persecution arises because of the word, by and by he falters.* *22 He also that received seed among the thorns is he that hears the word; and the worries of this world, and the strategy of money making, choke the word, and he becomes unfruitful.* *23 But he that received seed into the good ground is he that hears the word, and understands it; which also bears fruit, and brings forth, some one hundredfold, some sixty, some thirty.*

When one turns the attention to the inner Self then one begins to understand the inner Truths. One will not experience in one's consciousness the higher Truths by hearing the words of Truth only. One must experience Truth. Then the wholeness of healing can occur.

The seed along the path represents the one who reads good books of Truth but never applies them. Such a one never practices meditation, concentration, directed imaging, or dream interpretation. The information stored in the brain as memory is lost or 'stolen' at the completion of a lifetime. Rocks symbolize will. The seed that falls on rocks is a person using willpower to initially apply information given and takes some initial steps in meditation and Self discipline. Yet after a few days, weeks, or months, he or she gives up and goes back to the old limited ways. The seed sown among thorns (Lamsa - thistles) is the one who hears the universal Truth and has the information of Self transformation. Yet, this aspect of Self allows doubts of one's ability to achieve Enlightenment to cloud the judgment therefore clutching fruitlessly to physical security, losing it all at the end of a lifetime. To receive seed into the good ground is to discipline the Self with mental exercises in order to understand the Truth through direct, repetitive experience to which reasoning is applied for producing knowledge of Self, consciousness, and creation. Fruit symbolizes knowledge.

> [24] *Another parable put he forth to them, saying, The kingdom of heaven is like a man who sowed good seed in his field:* [25] *But while the man slept, his enemy came and sowed tares among the wheat, and went his way.* [26] *But when the blade was sprung up, and brought forth fruit, then appeared the tares also.* [27] *So the servants of the householder came and said unto him Sir, did not you sow good seed in your field? Where are the weeds coming from?* [28] *He said unto them, An enemy has done this. The servants said unto him, Do you want us to go out and pull them up?* [29] *But he said, Nay; lest while you gather up the weeds, you root up also the wheat with them.* [30] *Let both grow together until the harvest: and in the time of harvest I will say to the reapers, Gather you together first the weeds, and bind them in bundles to burn them: but gather the wheat into my barn.*

Seed represents visualized or imaged thoughts that can be matured by the thinker (man) into knowledge (wheat). The enemy is any non-productive thought that any aspect of Self creates. It is usually associated with the conscious ego. Satan is referred to as the adversary. Hate destroys and this is the enemy's weed-seed. Doubt blocks new action and expansive motion and is therefore the enemy's weed seed. Fear pushes the thinker's direction contrary to growth and is thus the enemy's weed seed. Jealousy draws the thinker into a greater physical entrapment through the thirst for other people's fame, fortune, possessions and power, and is thus the enemy's weed seed.

All this negativity, constriction, and limitation becomes obvious as one pursues the desire for a more fulfilling life. As knowledge matures in the conscious mind, which is relying on and in harmony with the subconscious existence, the thinker clearly is aware of the experiences and ways of thinking that produce knowledge in the life. The limitations, restrictions, and destructive attitudes are also clearly recognized and separated from the valuable and productive thoughts and experiences, and are transformed through the expansive power (burn) of rapid energy transformation. Barn symbolizes one's storehouse of understanding which is subconscious mind.

> *31 Another metaphor put he forth unto them, saying, The kingdom of heaven is like a grain of mustard seed, which a man took, and sowed in his field: 32 Which indeed is the least of all seeds: but when it is grown, it is so big a shrub, so that the birds of the sky come and build their nests in the branches thereof. 33 Another parable spoke he unto them; The kingdom of heaven is like unto leaven, which a woman took, and hid in three measures of meal, till the whole was leavened. 34 All these things spoke Jesus unto the multitude in parables. He spoke to them in parables only. 35 That it might be fulfilled which was spoken by the prophet, saying, I will open my mouth in parables; I will utter things which have been hidden since the foundation of the world. 36 Then Jesus sent the multitude away, and went into the house: and his disciples came to him, saying, Declare unto us the parable of the weeds of the field. 37 He answered and said unto them, He that sows the good seed is the Son of man; 38 The field is the world; the good seed are the children of the kingdom; but the weeds are the followers of the evil one; 39 The enemy that sowed them is the devil; the harvest is the end of the world; and the harvesters are the angels. 40 As therefore the weeds are gathered and burned in the fire; so will it be in the end of this world. 41 The Son of man will send forth his angels, and they will gather out of his kingdom all who draws others to apostasy, and all evildoers; 42 And will cast them into a furnace of fire: there will be wailing and gnashing of teeth. 43 Then will the righteous shine forth as the sun in the kingdom of their Father. Who has ears to hear, let him listen.*

When a seed desire is planted in subconscious mind it can manifest in a powerful desire fulfillment as long as it is nurtured in the conscious mind. One's greatest desire manifestations being initiated from a seed idea, produce great opportunities for understandings to be added to one's subconscious storehouse of experience. This is in fulfillment of the plan of creation held in superconscious mind.

Woman (wo-man) symbolizes the conscious mind which is an extension of subconscious mind. The leaven is also one's seed ideas. Adding prepared knowledge (meal) to a seed idea produces an opportunity for the Self knowledge to grow and be developed into a more palatable use (bread).

Symbology is a method of explaining inner secrets to one who thinks physically yet desires to know the universal Truths — the real explanations of the inner secrets.

The Son of Man is the thinker who is initiating continual forward motion in the life so the opportunity for learning will present itself. The field is the world, and the world is mind. The children of the kingdom are those aspects who are openly producing permanent Self understanding. The weeds are the negative attitudes of Self that are caught up in egoic reactions which is the enemy. The end of the world is the completing of one's learning in the physical plane of existence. Angels are the productive thought forms of Self that allow the reception of knowledge.

Sooner or later every attitude, action, and thought which is counterproductive will have its energy released and the energy will be broken down to its constituent parts in order that it may be recycled. Those aspects willing to undergo this process will gain the divine radiance of alignment.

> [44] *Again, the kingdom of heaven is like unto treasure hid in a field; the which when a man has found, he hides, and for joy thereof goes and sells all that he has, and buys that field.* [45] *Again, the kingdom of heaven is like unto a merchant man, seeking goodly pearls:* [46] *Who, when he had found one pearl of great price, went and sold all that he had, and bought it.* [47] *Again, the kingdom of heaven is like unto a dragnet, that*

was cast into the sea, and gathered of every kind: [48] *Which, when it was full, they drew to shore, and sat down, and gathered the worthwhile into containers, but cast the useless away.* [49] *So will it be at the end of the world: the angels will come forth, and sever the wicked from among the just,* [50] *And will cast them into the furnace of fire: there will be wailing and gnashing of teeth.* [51] *Jesus said unto them, Have you understood all these things? They say unto him, Yea, Lord.* [52] *Then said he unto them, Therefore every scribe which is instructed unto the kingdom of heaven, is like unto a man that is an householder, which brings forth out of his treasure things new and old.* [53] *It came to pass, that when Jesus had finished these parables, he departed there.*

To recognize knowledge and learning in the life where none was previously seen and to recognize the value of the abundance of the universe, is to begin possessing knowledge of the Self called understanding. This is the pearl of great price. It signifies a recognition, on the part of a person who understands value, that offers the greatest worth to Self. That which is permanent has the greatest value and is called understanding. Understanding is stored in subconscious mind.

The vessels are the subconscious mind storehouse. Each of the many understandings are stored in their own vessel or space. When an area of learning in Self is completely understood then the vessel of understanding is stored in subconscious mind as permanent learning and memory. That which is bad or worthless is any object, habit, brain pathway or possession that is left behind at the end of a lifetime. Only the permanent has lasting value. Only the temporary becomes useless. Scribes represent brain pathways. House is mind. The storeroom is memory either subconscious or conscious. To combine these in new ways is imagination, which is the vehicle of quickened evolution of Self. This completes the learning of this part of mind, which part is entitled communication in the symbolic language of mind.

[54] *When he came into his own country, he taught them in their synagogue, inasmuch that they were astonished, and said, Whence has this man this wisdom, and these mighty works?* [55] *Is not this the carpenter's son? is not his mother called Mary? and his brother, James, and Joseph, and Simon, and Judas?* [56] *His sisters, are they not all with us? Where did this man gain all this?*

Jesus' native place is Nazareth symbolizing commitment to the creative urge (God). Mary symbolizes the nurturing quality of love in the conscious mind (woman). Joseph, symbolizing perception, is the name of Jesus' earthly father as well as his brother. This indicates the need for a knower who is moving towards Enlightenment to constantly use perception. The same is true for Simon symbolizing determination which is to be built into willpower as symbolized by Simon Peter, Jesus' disciple. The same is true of Judas (Lamsa = Judah) which symbolizes the forward evolutionary motivating factor of the ego. Judah, or in the Greek Judas, was a brother of Jesus. Judah (Judas) of Iscariot was a disciple of Jesus. The name James also is used by both a brother of Jesus and a disciple of Jesus. James, the disciple, is a brother of John. They also were fishermen.

In traveling throughout the world, Jesus was taught the inner secrets and passed the test of gaining the inner awareness of Self. He had the scripture memorized as did the Pharisees and the Sadducees, but he learned the real inner Truth during his travels and studies worldwide while the Sadducees and Pharisees had never practiced or applied themselves.

> *57 They were offended in him. But Jesus said unto them, A prophet is not without honor, save in his own country, and in his own house. 58 He did not work many miracles there because of their unbelief.*

No miracles were given there because of the lack of faith. The old compulsive parts of Self have old pictures or mental images called memories, doubts, limitations, and compulsions. The limitations and habits practiced the longest will be the hardest to change. They will be the parts that will be the last to change for these have been practiced the most and have therefore become the least productive. Faith must operate in the mind of one desiring to change and transcend. Faith is the ability to imagine something different from what is known or has been previously experienced. Faith put into action leads to an expansion of awareness and the utilization of knowing.

The activities of Jesus illustrate the willingness to aid others. His is a life of service. The benefit of learning to serve the whole Self of another is that this provides the opportunity for drawing out and identifying the understanding and wisdom that is present within the Self. This results in contentment, peace, and fulfillment.

Symbols and Their Interpretation

Chapter Fourteen

1. Herodias - receptive action of ego used to motivate Self in conscious mind by drawing Self toward object of desire
2. Herodias' daughter - aspect of conscious ego that aids to create change in identity
3. Five loaves - knowledge of reasoning
4. Two fish - spiritual awareness
5. 5000 - reasoning with the power of understanding
6. Shore - emotional level of mind
7. Ghost - inner level body
8. Walk on water - control of the conscious experience
9. Ship - physical body
10. Cloak - outer expression of one's inner thoughts and attitudes

Chapter Fourteen

The death of John the Baptist indicates knowing has taken full sway at this point so that one does not need to operate from the physical belief motivation anymore. Now Self operates from Self motivation to know the inner Self, creation, and Creator rather than external motivation for glory, fame, wealth, or religiosity. Herod had John arrested. The conscious ego, which Herod represents, shows the connection with believing and the motivation for physical goals with the ego. There is a recognition on the part of the individual that he is now operating from the standpoint of learning and growth. Every action is accomplished for learning and growth rather than for any physical goals; wealth, abundance, or fame. Everything is sacrificed toward the desire to know Self; the desire to know God and reach alignment. Willpower is exercised in determined steps to gain new awareness.

[1] At that time Herod Archelaus the tetrarch heard of the fame of Jesus, [2] And said unto his servants, This is John the Baptist; he is risen from the dead; and therefore mighty works do show forth themselves in him. [3] For Herod had laid hold on John, and bound him, and put him in prison for Herodias sake, his brother Philip's wife. [4] For John said unto him, It is not lawful for you to have her. [5] When he would have put him to death, he feared the multitude, because they counted him as a prophet. [6] But when Herod's birthday was kept, the daughter of Herodias danced before them, and pleased Herod. [7] Whereupon he promised with an oath to give her whatsoever she would ask. [8] And she, being before instructed of her mother, said, Give me here John the Baptizer's head on a platter. [9] The king was sorry: nevertheless for the oaths sake, and the guest sat with him, he commanded it to be given her. [10] He sent the order to have John beheaded in the prison. [11] His head was brought on a platter, and given to the girl: and she brought it to her mother. [12] His disciples came, and took up the body, and buried it, and went and told Jesus.

John the Baptizer represents the quality of believing that is further confined or diminished as the knowing of pure consciousness gains in power. The beheading of John symbolizes the change in identity of Self as this knowing quality becomes the full measure of one's thoughts and actions. The knower understands the secrets of creation and takes steps to ensure they are incorporated into Self. Herodias represents the receptive side of the conscious ego that draws Self to the object of desire. As Herodias was the sister-in-law of Herod, John complained about the two living together. The transgression of Herod represents the need for the conscious ego to constantly motivate Self to expand one's consciousness rather than inbreeding with what is familiar and comfortable which requires no stretching of the imagination. The daughter of Herodias represents the conscious ego's attempt to motivate through new ideas.

> [13] *When Jesus heard this, he left there by ship into a desert place: and when the people had heard thereof, they followed him on foot out of the cities.* [14] *Jesus went forth, and saw a great multitude, and was moved with compassion toward them, and he healed their sick.* [15] *When it was evening, his disciples came to him, saying, This is a deserted place, and it is already late; dismiss the crowds, that they may go to the villages, and buy themselves food.*

When a change of life occurs, the old way of life (believing) will no longer suffice. It has been changed, giving way to the need on the part of Self to go within and assimilate the transformation. Immediately, the knower processes the change in the core of his being and uses it to aid, improve, and make whole other aspects of Self. Evening symbolizes the end of a cycle.

> [16] *But Jesus said unto them, They need not depart; give them food to*

eat. [17] They said unto him, We have here only five loaves, and two fishes. [18] He said, Bring them to me. [19] He commanded the multitude to sit down on the grass. Taking the fives loaves and the two fishes; he looked up to heaven, blessed and broke them, giving the loaves to his disciples, who in turn gave them to the people. [20] They all ate, and were filled: The fragments remaining, when gathered up, filled twelve baskets full. [21] And they that had eaten were about five thousand, not counting women and children.

Five is the number of the reasoner. Its form is the shape of a triangle on top of a square formed by five dots which creates a shape of a house symbolizing the mind.

Loaves of bread symbolize knowledge. Fish symbolizes spiritual awareness. Grass is subconscious existence. Heaven symbolizes superconscious mind. The thinker and knower who directs their full perception to superconscious awareness will cause all knowledge to generate greater knowledge and a spiritual awareness which, in turn, generates greater spiritual awareness and expanded consciousness. There is plenty of knowledge for all twelve major aspects of Self and knowledge has been given fully to the reasoning quality; the five thousand fed.

There were twelve baskets remaining which is the same number as the twelve Apostles. The one who is disciplined with all twelve aspects will always have abundance. The number five shows the steps of reasoning. The two fish signifies the use of duality of spiritual awareness. This is understanding the aggressive and receptive factors of creation with reasoning, which will always produce abundance.

[22] Immediately Jesus constrained his disciples to get into a ship, and to go before him unto the other side, while he sent the multitudes away. [23] When he had sent the crowds away, he went up into a mountain by himself to pray: and when the evening was come, he was there alone. [24] But the ship was now in the midst of the sea, tossed with waves: for the wind was contrary. [25] At about three in the morning, Jesus went toward them, walking on the sea.

After giving of the expanded awareness of his greater identity as a knower (death of John) to thousands of aspects, Jesus the knower does go within and fully assimilate (symbolized by praying) all that has been gained.

Why is three in the morning important? Three is a creation number. Three is created by unifying the number one which symbolizes the aggressive factor and the number two which represents the receptive factor. This produces a third, just as a mother and father through their unity produce a child.

Notes:

> [26] *When the disciples saw him walking on the sea, they were troubled, saying, It is a ghost; and they cried out for fear.* [27] *But straightway Jesus spoke unto them, saying, Be of good cheer; it is I; be not afraid.* [28] *Peter answered him and said, Lord, if it be you, bid me come to you on the water.* [29] *He said, Come. And when Peter had come down out of the ship, he walked on the water, to go to Jesus.*

Will as symbolized by Peter is the most powerful factor to propel one to knowing. Yet, willpower alone will not master the conscious existence (water). To master the conscious existence one must have awareness of subconscious mind and apply it consistently. The knower's higher purpose is necessary in order for the will to be employed effectively and to rise above the physical, conscious experience.

Faith comes before believing which comes before knowing. Without faith, or believing, will is ineffectual for there is no imagination to direct the will. Lamsa translates fear as doubt. Doubt always blocks success. The boat represents the physical body.

> [30] *But when he perceived how strong the wind was, he was afraid; and began to sink, he cried, saying, Lord, save me.* [31] *Immediately Jesus stretched forth his hand, and caught him, and said unto him, O you of little faith, what did you hesitate for?* [32] *When they came into the ship, the wind ceased.* [33] *Then they that were in the ship came and worshipped him, saying, Of a Truth you are the Son of God.*

The wind connotes thought in motion. One who controls and directs their thoughts productively, using productive thought to direct the body in a productive growth-filled manner, is able to control the experiences of Self in the physical. Such a one's experiences are designed for the greatest growth in consciousness.

> ³⁴ *When they went over the waters, they came into the land of Gennesaret.* ³⁵ *When the men of that place had knowledge of him, they sent word throughout all that country, and brought to him all that were diseased;* ³⁶ *Seeking him that they might only touch the tassel of his cloak: and as many as touched were made perfectly whole.*

Lamsa translates *"tassel of his cloak"* as hem of his robe. To accept a new more productive, expression as one's own, using every word spoken and every action taken as a means of greater Self knowledge is to become a whole and completely understood aspect.

This indicates the ability to control the physical life experience and the conscious experience; awakening from the slumber of engrossed physical experience. This comes after the death of John the Baptizer showing that knowing has supplanted believing in the life of this individual. Control physical experience when attention is on spiritual awareness, and the full awareness of the inner Self is gained. This is the time when the disciples declared beyond a doubt, you are the Son of God. They did call Jesus, Son of Man. Yet, here they called him Son of God. Son of God is one whose full attention is on giving to knowing the real inner Self. From this time forward, the purpose of one's existence and everything that one accomplishes is dedicated to knowing the whole Self.

Notes:

Symbols and Their Interpretation

Chapter Fifteen

1. Mouth - communicating imaged thoughts or receiving knowledge
2. Canaanite - belief in the conscious mind that the physical environment controls your life
3. House of Israel - the mind of one who practices the inner secrets and who recognizes the one Living God, I AM
4. Table - tool for receiving knowledge
5. Deformed - refusal to construct productive structured mental images
6. Seven loaves - control of knowledge
7. Seven hampers - control of receptivity
8. 4000 - power of stability

Chapter Fifteen

¹ Then Jesus came to the scribes and Pharisees of Jerusalem, saying, ² Why do your disciples transgress the tradition of the elders for they do not wash their hands when they eat bread. ³ He answered them saying, Why do you also transgress the commandment of God by your tradition? ⁴ For God commanded, saying, Honor your father and mother: and, He who curses father or mother, let him die the death. ⁵ But you say, Whoever will say to his father or his mother, It is a gift, by whatsoever you might be profited by me; ⁶ And honor not his father nor his mother, he will be free. Thus have you made the commandment of God of no effect by your tradition.

Scribes symbolize information stored in the brain. Pharisees symbolize speaking words that are contrary to one's thoughts and actions. To be a Pharisee is to say one thing and to do something else. The Pharisees are not asking Jesus questions because they wish to know the Truth. They are asking questions only in the hopes of making the knower look like he is not teaching Truth. In verse seven, chapter fifteen, Jesus calls the Pharisees hypocrites. This is an apt description of the symbolic attitude being revealed because the Pharisees say one thing while they practice another.

⁷ You hypocrites, well did Isaiah prophesy of you, saying, ⁸ This people draws nigh unto me with their mouth, and honors me with their lips; but their heart is far from me. ⁹ But in vain they do worship me, teaching for doctrines the commandments of men.

Every time the Pharisees would quote a scripture to Jesus to emphasize his lack of obedience, Jesus would cite another revealing how the Pharisees were giving only lip service and failing to apply the Truth of that scripture. This testing is a part of life one must constantly face in order to build the full Truth in Self. The Pharisees are not one's enemies, they are the parts of Self who are not practicing full use of the mind and full discipline. Application of universal Truth in the day-to-day life is a must to develop the Enlightened One.

> [10] *He called the multitude, and said to them, Hear, and understand:* [11] *It is not that which goes into the mouth that defiles a man; but that which comes out of the mouth, this defiles a man.*

What comes out of your mouth is the direct reflection of what is in the mind; the thoughts and attitudes. When the attitudes are unproductive then there is restriction of one's own movement forward as a spiritualized being. It is one's unproductive repeated thoughts, called attitudes, which defile or makes a thinker impure. One's words are a reflection and a summation of one's thoughts and attitudes. Food does not cause a person to be unproductive in the life. Spiritual people all over the world, in all time periods, have eaten different diets and still achieved sainthood and Enlightenment.

> [12] *Then came his disciples, and said unto him, Know that the Pharisees were offended, after they heard this saying?* [13] *But he answered and said, Every plant, which my heavenly Father has not planted, will be rooted up.* [14] *Let them alone: they are the blind leaders of the blind. And if the blind lead the blind, both will fall into the pit.* [15] *Then answered Peter and said unto him, Tell us about this parable.* [16] *Jesus said, Are you also yet without understanding?* [17] *Do not you yet understand, that whatsoever enters in at the mouth goes into the belly, and is discharged into the latrine?* [18] *But those things which proceed out of the mouth come forth from the mind; and they defile the man.* [19] *For out of the mind proceed evil thoughts, murders, adulteries, forni-*

cations, thefts, false witness, blasphemies: ²⁰ *These are the*
things which defile a man: but to eat with unwashed hands
defiles no man.

The Truth the knower, Jesus, keeps making over and over again is
that <u>thought is cause</u>. Cause does not originate from the food (knowledge)
one ingests. Neither food or knowledge, force a person to think one way or
another. A person <u>chooses</u> what they will think; they <u>choose</u> to form and
retain attitudes and habitual ways of thinking. Thoughts are things and are
the source point of reality. Thoughts are the vehicle for the reality each individual constructs around him/her Self.

> ²¹ *Then Jesus went there, and departed into the coasts of*
> *Tyre and Sidon.* ²² *Behold, a Canaanite woman came out of*
> *the same coasts, and cried unto him, saying, Have mercy on*
> *me, O Lord, you Son of David; my daughter is grievously*
> *troubled with a demon.* ²³ *But he gave no word of response.*
> *And his disciples came and began to entreat him, saying,*
> *Send her away; for she cries after us.* ²⁴ *But he answered*
> *and said, I am not sent only to the lost sheep of the house of*
> *Israel.* ²⁵ *Then came she and worshipped him, saying, Lord,*
> *help me.* ²⁶ *But he answered and said, It is not right to take*
> *the children's bread, and to cast it to dogs.* ²⁷ *She said,*
> *Truth, Lord: yet the dogs eat of the crumbs which fall from*
> *their masters table.* ²⁸ *Then Jesus answered and said unto*
> *her, O woman, great is your faith: be it unto you even as you*
> *will it. And her daughter was made whole from that very*
> *hour.*

Any aspect, any part of the Self whether it is engrossed in the physical life or whether it believes in God, needs to mature and improve the Self
thus gaining greater awareness of the inner Self. The possibility exists for
this to occur. This part of the Self may be healed by expanding awareness,
improving, and building new and greater Self understanding. Tyre and Sidon
were ancient Phoenician cities. The Phoenicians invented the alphabet. King
Hiram of Tyre had his craftsmen build King Solomon's temple. It seems
there is always the awareness in Tyre and Sidon of the value of God's message. Thus the Canaanite woman represents an aspect who is not aware of the
inner secrets and Truths of mind, nor is this one a teacher of those Truths. Yet,
still this aspect has great faith which is the ability to image what one wants to
occur even if the clear image is stimulated from an outside factor.

> ²⁹ *Jesus departed from there, and went down by the sea of*
> *Galilee; and went up into a mountain, and sat down there.*

Notes:

> [30] *Great multitudes came unto him, having with them those that were lame, blind, mute, deformed, and many others, and laid them down at Jesus feet; and he healed them:* [31] *Inasmuch that the multitude wondered, when they saw the mute to speak, the deformed to be whole, the lame to walk, and the blind to see: and they glorified the God of Israel.*

Israel is the combination of three words; Is, Ra, and El. El is the name of God used in the first chapter of *Genesis*. The English term for deity is called God, but originally the name of God in *Genesis* was EL in Aramaic. The Plural of El is Elohim. Ra is a God of Egypt. Ra is the Sun God. The Israelites lived in Egypt for a time. They followed Joseph into Egypt and were led out of Egyptian bondage by Moses. Ra is the Sun God of Egypt. The Israelites spent time in Egypt and learned of that God, the God of the Sun. The Sun God, Ra, represents awareness. The letters Is come from Isis. Isis also is a God of Egypt. She is a deity with female or receptive attributes. Is-Ra-El is the many Gods or Aspects of awareness and light brought together into a whole being. As each person is made in the image of the Creator, with like attributes, then each person is potentially a creator and can become a whole person, a son of God.

> [32] *Then Jesus called his disciples unto him, and said, I have compassion on the multitude, because they continue with me now three days, and have nothing to eat: and I will not send them away hungry or they may collapse on the way.* [33] *His disciples say unto him, How could we ever get enough bread in this deserted spot, to fill so great a crowd?* [34] *Jesus said unto them, How many loaves have you? And they said, Seven, and a few little fishes.* [35] *He commanded the crowd to sit down on the ground.*

36 He took the seven loaves and the fishes, and gave thanks, and broke them, and gave to his disciples, and the disciples to the crowd. 37 They all ate, and were filled: and they gathered up of the fragments that were left over seven hampers were full. 38 They fed four thousand men, beside women and children. 39 And he sent away the multitude, and took a ship, and came into the coasts of Magdala.

The image presented here is similar to the image of the previous example of feeding the multitudes, but the numbers are different. Instead of feeding 5000, Jesus the knower, feeds 4000. Instead of having 12 hampers of food left over, he has seven. Seven is the number indicating control — control having to do with the seven levels of mind as well as controlling the conscious mind and the seven major energy transformers or chakras. The seven hampers show that seven levels of mind are being filled with divine understanding and spiritual awareness. This indicates also that the seven chakras are being used to recycle used energy back into the inner levels of mind so that more of the physical experience can be used productively. 4000 shows stability is being gained in learning to use the physical for growth in awareness. Four is the number of the physical and the quality of physical existence is stability. In the previous example of feeding the multitudes the knower was applying the reasoning quality which had been completely understood (symbolized by the number 5000) to give knowledge to all aspects. As one gives of themselves freely, there is always much knowledge and spiritual awareness produced and retained as symbolized by the seven hampers of left over fragments of food. This time 4000 people are fed which is a multiple of 4 and also 40. Jesus spent 40 days in the wilderness assimilating his life experiences to that point. Feeding 4000 denotes that stability has been achieved in nourishing and giving knowledge and spiritual awareness to many aspects of Self. This capability produces the power of understanding within Self as symbolized by the three zeros following the number 4 in 4000.

Notes:

Symbols and Their Interpretation

Chapter Sixteen

1. Yeast - Imagination as an initiator of growth and preparer of knowledge
2. Yeast of the Pharisees - memory, no imagination
3. Messiah - awareness of plan held in superconscious mind
4. Christ - superconscious awareness
5. Living God - I AM
6. Conduct - one's actions and the attitude-intention behind them

Chapter Sixteen

¹ The Pharisees also with the Sadducees came, and as a test asked him to show them a sign in the sky. ² He answered and said to them, When it is evening, you say, Red sky at night, the day will be bright, but in the morning, sky red and gloomy, the day will be stormy. O you hypocrites, you can discern the face of the sky; but can you not discern the signs of the times? ⁴ A wicked and adulterous generation seeks after a sign; and there will no sign be given unto it, but the sign of the prophet Jonah. And he left them, and departed.

The sign of Jonah is to stop running from commitment to Self and to fulfill one's assignment for a lifetime as symbolized by Jonah going to Nineveh to tell the people to reform and repent. No sign will be given except the sign of the prophet Jonah. Jonah spent three and one-half days in the belly of the whale which symbolizes one who is engrossed in the physical life and therefore imprisoned by their own lack of inner commitment. The sign to move out of entrapment is to live for the real, inner Self. Jonah, with reluctance, shared his prophetic message. John fulfilled his prophetic message in full. The Pharisees and Sadducees do not want to change. They have built their house on the shifting sands of false security of physical position and power. When the knower speaks with the wisdom and power of the permanent and everlasting Enlightenment it poses a threat to those physically bound aspects for they would need to change. They basically ask the knower, Jesus, to predict what will happen in the future as the example of red sky in morning predicts the rest of the day will be stormy. The knower's prediction is, therefore, that sooner or later everyone and everything will change, even the Pharisees and Sadducees. Sooner or later everyone will fulfill the commitment to Self.

⁵ When his disciples arrived at the other side, they had forgotten to take bread. ⁶ Then Jesus said unto them, Take heed and beware of the yeast of the Pharisees and of the Sadducees. ⁷ They reasoned among themselves, saying, It is because we have taken no bread. ⁸ Which when Jesus

Notes:

> *perceived, he said unto them, O you of little faith, why reason you among yourselves, because you have brought no bread?* [9] *Do you yet not understand, neither remember the five loaves of the five thousand, and how many baskets you took up?* [10] *Neither the seven loaves of the four thousand, and how many baskets you took up?* [11] *How is it that you do not understand that I spoke it not to you concerning bread, that you should beware of the yeast of the Pharisees and of the Sadducees?* [12] *Then they understood that he was not issuing a warning against the yeast of bread, but of the teaching of the Pharisees and of the Sadducees.*

Yeast is used to cause bread dough to rise and to expand. The yeast of the Pharisees is the thoughts and attitudes of the Pharisees (hypocrites) which produce no expansion in consciousness and no expansion in knowledge of Self. The yeast of the Pharisees is temporary expansion of negativity, because anything of the conscious mind only is temporary. Just memorizing scriptures and pointing them out to other people, saying you should practice this or that without using the information and applying it within Self, adds nothing to the permanent Self. The yeast or teaching of the Pharisees will add nothing to the permanent Self and will cause no permanent expansion of mind. Pretty or forceful words voiced in the physical may seem good for a little while but eventually will cave back in on themselves and their perpetrator.

> [13] *When Jesus came into the coasts of Caesarea Philippi, he asked his disciples, saying, Whom do men say that the Son of man is?* [14] *They said, Some say that you are John the Baptist; some, Elijah; and others Jeremiah, or one of the prophets.* [15] *He said unto them, But whom say you*

> *that I am?* ¹⁶ *Simon Peter answered and said, You are the*
> *Messiah, the Christ, the Son of the living God.* ¹⁷ *Jesus*
> *answered and said unto him, Blessed are you, Simon son of*
> *Jonah Barjona: for no mere man has revealed it to you, but*
> *my Father which is in heaven.* ¹⁸ *I say also unto you, that*
> *you are Rock, and upon this rock I will build my church;*
> *and the jaws of death will not prevail against it.* ¹⁹ *I will*
> *give unto you the keys of the kingdom of heaven: and what-*
> *soever you will bind on earth will be bound in heaven; and*
> *whatsoever you will loose on earth will be loosed in heaven.*
> ²⁰ *Then he charged his disciples that they should tell no*
> *man that he was the Messiah.*

Here Simon-Peter called Jesus the Son of God, not Son of Man. Examining this section in a physical manner, shows the people accepted reincarnation as a fact and believed Jesus to be a reincarnation of Elijah or Jeremiah. Jesus could not be a reincarnation of John for they both existed in the physical environment at the same time. But when examining the interactions between Elisha and Elijah as reported in the *Old Testament*, it becomes clear that Jesus aligns with Elisha and John with Elijah.

The one who has moved the Self forward with will power is capable of discerning the nature of the knower. Will is the factor and foundation needed for a reasoner to build his or her understanding of mind. Jesus refers to Simon Peter as son of Jonah. Jonah was spoken of by the knower Jesus in verse four of this chapter. To be a descendant or son of Jonah is to aggressively pursue the full use of commitment to one's assignment for the lifetime through the highest use of the factor of believing. The keys of the kingdom of heaven are the universal principles in which the Universal Laws and Truths are constructed.

> ²¹ *From that time forth Jesus began to indicate to his dis-*
> *ciples, how he must go unto Jerusalem, and suffer many*
> *things of the elders and chief priests and scribes, and be*
> *killed, and be raised again the third day.* ²² *Then Peter took*
> *him, and began to rebuke him, saying, may you be spared,*
> *Lord: this will not happen to you.* ²³ *But he turned, and*
> *said unto Peter, Get you behind me, Satan: you are an of-*
> *fense unto me: You are not judging by God's standards but*
> *my man's.*

Peter was trying to keep the knower Jesus from fulfilling his desires, his needs, his mission, and his assignment. This was due to Peter's attachment to Jesus. The knower is to fulfill his assignment to prove that no physical limitations can restrict the Enlightened One. Therefore, no attachments must impede this assignment not even the attachment to exercising will power to manifest physical desires. This is why Jesus at this point refers to Peter as Satan. The motivating ego (Satan) backed up by will (Peter) to move the Self forward is not to be used strictly to hold onto and clutch the physical in an effort to keep the environment from changing. Instead, the thinker is to move the attention and perception, symbolized by the phrase *"get you behind me,"* to God's standards which are the laws of creation called the Universal Laws. Direct the imagination with will power rather than escaping into fantasy. Escaping into fantasy is withdrawing the attention from what is occurring at the present period of time and refusing to imagine how to cause change and solutions. Fantasy is simply removing the attention to a place within the imagination that is not related to the current period of time and in which there is no intention of causing what is being imagined to come about.

> [24] *Then said Jesus unto his disciples, If any man will come after me, let him deny himself, and take up his cross, and follow me.* [25] *For whoever will save his life will lose it: and whoever will lose his life for my sake will find it.* [26] *For what is a man profited, if he will gain the whole world, and lose his own soul? or what will a man give in exchange for his soul?* [27] *For the Son of man will come in the glory of his Father with his angels; and then he will reward every man according to his conduct.* [28] *Verily I say unto you, There be some standing here, which will not experience death, till they see the Son of man coming in his kingdom.*

To deny one's Self is to recognize Self does not exist in the physical life solely for the sense gratification. Therefore, the instruction from the knower is to first refuse to allow physical information and brain pathways in the conscious mind to control Self. Second, to take up his cross is to live the life fully with the effort to understand mental time (vertical part of the cross) and horizontal physical time (horizontal bar of the cross) and to live the life fully for vertical time. The third requirement is to move in the same direction and with the same activities as the knower. All physical possessions and accomplishments are released at the end of a lifetime. What remains is understanding, consciousness, and I AM. Some aspects are not entrapped and therefore need not be restricted or transformed.

Symbols and Their Interpretation

Chapter Seventeen

1. Transfigured - change and transformation to a higher form of existence
2. Sun - superconscious awareness, the highest part or division of mind
3. Radiant - expressing inner awareness
4. Moses - imagination
5. Demented - refusal to reason
6. Temple tax - value of structure
7. Coin - value

Chapter Seventeen

¹ After six days Jesus took Peter, James, and John James' brother, and brought them up to a high mountain by themselves, ² He was transfigured before their eyes: and his face did shine as the sun, and his clothes were radiant as the light. ³ Behold, there appeared unto them Moses and Elijah talking with him. ⁴ Then Peter said to Jesus, Lord, it is good for us to be here: with your permission, let us make here three altars; one for you, and one for Moses, and one for Elijah. ⁵ While he yet spoke, behold, a bright cloud overshadowed them: and behold a voice out of the cloud, which said, This is my beloved Son, in whom I am well pleased; listen to him. ⁶ When the disciples heard it, they fell on their face, and were overcome with fear. ⁷ Jesus came and touched them, and said, Arise, and be not afraid. ⁸ When they had lifted up their eyes, they did not see anyone but Jesus.

This section indicates full awareness of superconscious mind and alignment with all levels of mind. Illumination and awareness from the inner Self can move into one's conscious awareness. Moses represents the power of imagination to move beyond entrapment and to use the physical productively with reasoning. Elijah represents the power of believing that later becomes John the Baptist. Elijah expressed many of the qualities that Jesus had developed. Elijah healed the sick, raised the dead, and parted the waters. The first two letters of the name Elijah are EL. EL is the name of God in the first chapter of *Genesis*, before it was translated from Hebrew to Greek to Roman to German to English. Believing has certain Godlike qualities for inherent in believing is the ability to image and direct the productive use of the imagination.

⁹ As they came down from the mountain, Jesus charged them, saying, Tell the vision to no man, until the Son of Man has

Notes:

> come back from the dead. [10] *His dis-*
> *ciples asked him, saying, Why then*
> *say the scribes that Elijah must first*
> *come?* [11] *Jesus answered and said*
> *unto them, Elijah truly will first come,*
> *and restore all things.* [12] *But I say*
> *unto you, That Elijah is come already,*
> *and they knew him not, but have done*
> *unto him whatsoever they pleased.*
> *Likewise will also the Son of Man suf-*
> *fer at their hands in the same way.*
> [13] *Then the disciples understood that*
> *he spoke unto them of John the Bap-*
> *tist.*

Believing must come before knowing. The reference here is to the reincarnation of Elijah. Elijah had reincarned and was known as John the Baptizer. Elijah the prophet, who set the goal to achieve full know-ledge within Self and whose quality of believing, is at last fulfilled in John the Baptist. The prophecies of the *Old Testament* are fulfilled in Jesus, who in a previous lifetime as Elisha asked for and received a double portion of Elijah's spirit.

> *2nd Kings 2* [9] *It came to pass, when*
> *they had crossed over, Elijah said*
> *unto Elisha, Ask for whatever I may*
> *do for you, before I be taken away*
> *from you. And Elisha said, May I re-*
> *ceive a double portion of your spirit.*

By the time of Jesus and John the Baptist, Jesus had received the double portion of Elijah's awareness, healing abilities, and consciousness. Therefore, Elisha-Jesus moved ahead of Elijah-John in awareness toward Enlightenment. Jesus went on to accomplish the full Enlightenment of Self.

> [14] *When they came to the multitude,*
> *there came to him a certain man,*
> *kneeling down to him, and saying,* [15]
> *Lord, have mercy on my son; for he*
> *is demented, and in serious condi-*

tion: for many times he falls into the fire, and often into the water. ¹⁶ *I brought him to your disciples, and they could not cure him.*

Discipline of itself is not enough to cause expansion of consciousness. The effective utilization of the imagination must be employed to give direction to the mind and to conceive an expanded image that Self can move into. The expansion of consciousness proceeds from the application of the imaginative faculty to move Self from Reasoning Man to Spiritual Man. This expansion of consciousness must be mastered by the thinker who desires to become Enlightened.

¹⁷ *Then Jesus answered and said, O faithless and perverse generation, how long will I be with you? How long will I suffer you? Bring him here to me.* ¹⁸ *Jesus rebuked the demon; and he departed out of him: and the child was cured from that very hour.* ¹⁹ *Then came the disciples to Jesus privately, and said, Why could not we cast him out?* ²⁰ *Jesus said unto them, Because you have so little faith: for verily I say unto you, If you have faith as a grain of mustard seed, you will say unto this mountain, Remove hence to yonder place; and it will remove: and nothing will be impossible unto you.* ²¹ *This kind does not leave but by prayer and fasting.*

Nothing is impossible. Mountains represent obstacles or challenges. There is no obstacle or challenge that cannot be overcome when Self will imagine. Faith indicates imagining something more than is already accomplished based on someone else's expectations. To imagine something greater is the first step to accomplish anything. To trust one's Self is to practice success many times until there is no doubt of success and one is secure in success. Discipline by itself will not produce wholeness (healing and whole knowing) in the Self. The disciplined will must be combined with imaginative believing.

²² *While they met again in Galilee, Jesus said to them, The Son of man will be betrayed into the hands of men:* ²³ *They will kill him, and the third day he will be raised again. And they were exceedingly saddened.*

The Son of Man is the initiatory activity of the thinker towards knowing the Self. Men represent the physically engrossed aspects of Self. Full admittance of being engrossed in the physical body is necessary so there can be the full demonstration of overcoming of the physical engrossment and moving out of that entrapment. To be raised from the dead is to gain continual consciousness. The fully conscious one does not go to sleep and lose consciousness at night. To be raised up is to gain permanent motion and permanent consciousness.

> [24] *When they came to Capernaum, the collectors of the temple tax came to Peter, and said, Does not your master pay tribute?* [25] *He said, That is right. And when he had come into the house, Jesus asked without giving him time to speak. What think you, Simon? Of whom do the kings of the earth take custom or tribute? Of their own children, or of strangers?* [26] *Peter said unto him, Of strangers. Jesus said unto him, Then are the children free.* [27] *Notwithstanding, so we don't offend them, go to the sea, and cast a hook, and take up the fish that first comes up; and when you have opened his mouth, you will find a coin worth twice the temple tax: that take, and give to them for me and you.*

Pay all that is owed to the physical because physical existence provides a place and a structure to learn. To improve one's financial situation, realize that physical finances are a reflection of the degree to which value is given and value is utilized. When a person understands a deeper concept of service and commits Self to giving completely and wholly in service there will be the recognition of the value of what is offered. Therefore, the recognition of this value will be recognized by others.

The kings of the world represent physical authority. They represent any accepted authority outside of Self. The temple tribute or tax is value one gives to the physical life. Most people place their value on objects, people, places, and events (as represented by the strangers) rather than within the Self. The solution is to go into the day-to-day life, the conscious experiences of Self, in order to gain spiritual knowledge (fish) from the learning available in the experiences. There one will find the abundant value needed to use the physical life successfully.

Any creation requires the development of three principles called ideal, purpose, and activity. The purpose presented in this passage is the enhancement and increase of Self value and worth. The activity is shown in the action of catching the fish (spiritual awareness) from the waters (conscious life experiences). The ideal is to exist in the world but not be of the world; to know Self as a spiritual being while incarned in physical form. This means to use the lifetime and its physicality fully, without becoming engrossed in sensory experiences.

Symbols and Their Interpretation

Chapter Eighteen

1.   Millstone - will
2.   Neck - will
3.   Foot - spiritual foundation
4.   Maimed - refusal to respect and create structure
5.   Heavenly Father's face - High Self identity
6.   99 - completion of a cycle
7.   Brother - environment related attitudes that affect aspects of Self
8.   Father's plan - blueprint for creation and for Self to gain Christ awareness
9.   King - ruler; authority; ability to cause imaged thoughts to manifest with control
10. Prison - Self restriction

Chapter Eighteen

The quality of infancy is the key to all new learning, new ideas, new awareness, and new cycles of growth. The abilities of infancy are first, absorbing information and experience; second, an openness and a desire to receive; third, learning without restriction of doubt and fear; fourth, constant action and love fueling the desire to learn. These are the exact attitudes the student needs to have when approaching the spiritual teacher. Whatever the Self will direct the mind to image and therefore conceive, it is capable of achieving. Image new learning which leads to the growth in Self and expansion of consciousness. Feeling is not bad, and the child does not avoid what he or she experiences emotionally. By dulling the emotions, one is separating the Self from the Self. This keeps the conscious Self ignorant of one's inner and subconscious Self. It is productive and beneficial to be purposeful in the use of the emotions.

> [1] *At the same time Jesus' students came to him, saying, Who is the greatest in the kingdom of the skies?* [2] *Jesus called a little child to him, and set him in the midst of them,* [3] *And said, I assure you that, Except you change, and become like little children, you will not enter into the kingdom of the skies.* [4] *Whoever therefore will humble himself as a child, the same is greatest in the kingdom of God.*

A child symbolizes the quality of infancy. The child is able to absorb experience freely without prior concepts or restrictions. The child's brain may be likened to a sponge which absorbs every liquid with which it comes into contact. In similar fashion, a child's brain receives impressions through the five senses, absorbing experiences and information freely without restriction. It is only later, as the child physically matures and creates brain pathways, habits, and limitations that the opening to the complete learning which incorporates the inner Self is closed.

Infancy is the time and stage of most rapid learning. In order to enter the kingdom of God, which is superconscious mind, one must set aside

Notes:

the egoic reactions and habitual brain pathways so that new more expansive learning may occur. When infancy is denied respect, one can become cynical; skepticism occurs when the mind is closed obstructing the natural receptivity of infancy. One who is operating from habit rather than perception will continually miss opportunities — mentally, emotionally, and physically. The habitually constricted person will also misinterpret present situations and interactions with others by stubbornly trying to make the new situation and expansive learning fit into the much smaller and more limited old thought pattern. Be willing to learn from each and every experience as does a child. Absorb the learning, like a sponge absorbs water. Grow, receive, and absorb; learning freely. Change, by constantly adding to the learning instead of refusing it.

> [5] *Whoever welcomes one such little child in my name welcomes me.* [6] *But whoever will offend one of these little ones who believe in me, it were better for him that a millstone were tied around his neck and that he were drowned in the depth of the sea.* [7] *Woe unto the world because of scandal for it is inevitable that scandal should occur. but woe to that man by whom the scandal comes!* [8] *Therefore if your hand or your foot offend you, cut them off, and cast them from you: it is better for you to enter into life crippled or maimed, rather than being thrown with two hands or two feet into everlasting fire.* [9] *If your eye offend you, pluck it out, and cast it from you: it is better for you to enter into life with one eye, rather than having two eyes to be cast into fiery Gehenna.*

Use the childlike attitudes of being open to learning throughout your life. One who is unwilling to cause renewed learning needs to examine their own will, or lack of it. One who is unwilling to move forward in the life will find the environment changing around them. They will find others more than willing to apply will power to produce change. Therefore, the lack of use of will power will lead one to the depths of engrossment with the weight of indecisiveness *tied around the neck.*

If one's purpose (hand) is unproductive then completely formulate a new, more expansive purpose. If the spiritual foundation (foot) is inadequate then create a new foundation based on more effective means of mental discipline such as concentration, meditation, and imaging.

The everlasting fire symbolizes what occurs when a person refuses to change and expand his or her consciousness. Such people find the world expands and changes around them. They experience the endless pain and suffering caused by lack of control in one's environment. Control can only be gained by change, growth, and expansion of consciousness. Use the correct perception available. Constantly cause expanded perception. If perception is cloudy, if perception is unproductive, then it is better to change and cause thought to expand. Cause a fresh start. Discontinue the unproductive.

> *[10] See that you never despise the little ones; for I say unto you, that in heaven their angels always behold my Heavenly Father's face. [11] For the Son of man has come to save that which was lost. [12] What do you think about this? If a man has one hundred sheep, and one of them be gone astray, does he not leave the ninety-nine, and go into the mountains, and seek that which is gone astray? [13] And if he finds it, verily I say unto you, he rejoices more of that sheep, than of the ninety-nine which went not astray. [14] Even so, it is no part of your heavenly Father's plan that one of these little ones should perish.*

This section is the key indication of the plan held in the superconscious mind. The plan is for Self to be a Christ, to gain the Christ consciousness and to be a whole functioning Self. Even so it is not the will of your Father which is in heaven that one of these little ones should perish indicates one is willing to cause infancy to learn from every experience. Learn and grow. Cause learning where no learning existed before. Then you will never perish! It is only when the learning is blocked that the potential growth in awareness is lost.

Ninety-nine symbolizes the completion of preparation for gaining power by understanding creation. The number one hundred symbolizes the power of understanding creation. Every aspect willing to be devoted to Christ consciousness will gain superconscious awareness.

> *[15] Moreover if your brother will trespass against you, go and tell him his fault between you and him alone: if he will*

hear you, you have gained your brother. [16] *But if he will not hear you, then take with you one or two more, that in the mouth of two or three witnesses every word may be established.* [17] *If he will neglect to hear them, tell it unto the church: but if he neglect to hear the church then treat him as a Gentile or a tax collector.* [18] *Verily I say unto you, Whatsoever you will bind on earth will be bound in heaven; and whatsoever you will loose on earth will be loosed in heaven.*

Lamsa translates verse eighteen as, *"Truly I say to you, Whatever you bind on earth will be bound in heaven, and whatever you release on earth will be released in heaven."* The restriction, constriction, limitation and refusal to learn that a person employs will slow his or her soul progression and the fulfillment of the plan held in superconscious mind (heaven). Whatever is loosed or released on earth is the freedom created by the effective use of free will and individual responsibility. The freedom to create enables one to practice creation and to move toward compatibility with the Creator. Give instruction to the various aspects of Self. Point out and admit the faults and weaknesses of Self, then change them. Use every method available to eliminate the walls of protective limitation that bind Self. In short, use every method available to change, grow, transform, and enlighten Self so the consciousness may expand.

[19] *Again I say unto you, That if two of you will agree on earth by joining your voices to pray for anything, whatever, it will be done for them by my Father which is in heaven.* [20] *For where two or three are gathered together in my name, there I am in their presence.*

When many people get together to pray it does have power; the power of thought. Two or more aspects of Self aligned with a common ideal and purpose, will cause more of the whole mind -- the whole attention, the whole desire, the whole activity -- to move toward knowing who Self is and one's relationship to one's Creator. The aspects of Self must come together. To know is to understand the answers and the questions. Discover the answers. When more than one division of mind functions in harmony and alignment with the others then does the Christ awareness appear. When conscious and subconscious are each fulfilling their duty to the other then knowing is built within Self. There the Knower, Jesus, resides.

> [21] *Then came Peter to him, and said, Lord, how often will my brother sin against me, and I forgive him? Seven times?*
> [22] *Jesus said unto him, No, not seven times: but, I'm telling you up to seventy times seven.*

The aspect of Self that is making a mistake needs attention and giving to that part or aspect. Teach and give until one produces change within Self. When you give, you open the previously closed doorways to your inner Self. Then and only then does the new learning have an opening to enter the real you. Give to the Real Self. Seven indicates control and seventy times seven equals 490. Power, symbolized by zero, is in 490. Four plus nine equals thirteen which shows full mastery is gained. The number 490 symbolizes the understanding of creating a stable foundation of learning so you have the ability to complete any permanent understanding. *Genesis 4* shows Cain to be avenged seven fold if anyone kills him. The number seven indicates the seven chakras. Seven times seventy represents the seven major chakras and the major-minor chakras.

> [23] *Therefore is the kingdom of heaven likened unto a certain king, which decided to settle the accounts of his servants.* [24] *When he had begun to reckon, one was brought unto him, which owed him ten thousand talents.* [25] *But inasmuch as he had not the money to pay, his lord commanded him to be sold, and his wife, and children, and all that he had, and payment to be made.* [26] *The servant therefore fell down, and worshipped him, saying, Lord, have patience with me, and I will pay you all.* [27] *Then the lord of that servant was moved with compassion, and let him go, and forgave him the debt.* [28] *But the same servant went out, and found one of his fellow servants, which owed him an hundred pence: and he laid hands on him, and took him by the throat, saying, Pay me that you owe.* [29] *His fellowservant fell down at his feet, and besought him, saying, Have patience with*

Notes:

> me, and I will pay you all. [30] He
> would not: but went and cast him into
> prison, till he should pay the debt.
> [31] So when his fellowservants saw
> what was done, they were very sorry,
> and came and told unto their lord all
> that was done. [32] Then his lord, af-
> ter that he had called him, said unto
> him, O you wicked servant, I forgave
> you all that debt, because you desired
> me: [33] Should you not have also had
> compassion on your fellowservant,
> even as I had pity on you? [34] His
> lord was angry, and delivered him to
> the torturers, till he should pay all
> that was due to him. [35] So likewise
> will my heavenly Father do also to
> you, unless each of you forgives ev-
> eryone of his brothers from his heart.

One limits Self and places limits on Self by making a prison of his or her own mind. To obtain mercy is to forgive the limiting and habitual mental images of the past so one's attention can fully move to the present and imagine the future. As you think, so you become. A person will continue to torture Self as long as the conscious mind is restricted. The conscious mind will never be able to give to the whole Self when it is undisciplined, dishonest, and compulsive. The whole Self must mature. The symbolic message is always to give to the whole Self by giving to others.

Standards are a code of ethics, particularly what is permanent and lasting and will benefit other people.

In order to gain authority and autonomy, practice extending one's thinking to visualize the ideal outcome desired in any action. In this way, you will begin to unfold the purpose for why certain actions are more beneficial or more productive, and therefore correct to pursue.

Prison represents one's own walls of limitation placed around Self. You move beyond your prison of limitation by giving to others in a more expanded way and imaging yourself being different, more productive and more capable.

You do not have to be in a specific person's presence to build an understanding. However, when two people are brought together; by recognizing the other's needs and aiding them to fulfill their needs, one is able to build and deepen one's own understanding.

Symbols and Their Interpretation

Chapter Nineteen

1.   Divorce - Breaking the commitment to the permanent; the inner Self
2.   Sex - harmony between conscious and subconscious mind
3.   Love - non-separateness; non-avoidance, receiving others and creation as yourself
4.   Needle - connector of outer expression to the inner Self
5.   Throne - point of control

Chapter Nineteen

¹ It came to pass, that when Jesus had finished these sayings, he departed from Galilee, and went into the regions of Judea across the Jordan; ² Great multitudes followed him; and he healed them there.

When the knower develops to the level of awareness presented here then Self causes a continual process of creating wholeness within aspects of Self. All aspects follow the intelligent and soul fulfilling direction of the thinker.

³ The Pharisees also came unto him, tempting him, and saying unto him, is it lawful for a man to divorce his wife for any reason whatever? ⁴ He answered and said to them, Have you not read, that the Creator made them from the beginning male and female. ⁵ And He said, Because of this a man will leave father and mother, and will cleave to his wife: and they two will be one living thing? ⁶ Wherefore they are no more two, but one flesh. What therefore God has joined together, let no man divide.

Jesus is quoting from *Genesis 2:18-25.*

Genesis 2 ¹⁸ The Lord God said: "It is not good for the man to be alone. I will make a suitable partner for him." ¹⁹ So the Lord God formed out of the ground various wild animals and various birds of the air, and he brought them to the man to see what he would call them; whatever the man called each of them would be its name. ²⁰ The man gave names to all the wild animals; but none proved to be the suitable partner for the man. ²¹ So the Lord God cast a deep sleep on the man, and while he was asleep, he took out one of his ribs and closed up its place in his flesh. ²⁰ The Lord God then built up into a woman the rib that he had taken from the man. When he had brought her to the man,

Notes:

> [20] The man said: "This one, at last, is bone of my bones and flesh of my flesh; This one will be called 'woman,' for out of 'her man' this one has been taken." [24] That is why a man leaves his father and mother and clings to his wife, and the two of them become one body. [25] The man and his wife were both naked, yet they felt no shame.

Man represents subconscious mind and woman represents conscious mind. Marriage symbolizes the commitment made between conscious and subconscious minds. Therefore, one will not break the commitment to the inner Self. Man (subconscious-soul-Self) has left the Superconscious mind (mother-father) to gain experience in the conscious mind (woman). Through the use of commitment and the resulting harmony between these parts of mind, there is a cooperative working together to produce wholeness, a union.

> [7] They said to him, Then why did Moses command divorce and command giving of a divorce decree? [8] He said unto them, Moses because of the hardness of your hearts let you divorce your wives: but from the beginning it was not so. [9] I say to you, Whoever will divorce his wife, except it be for fornication, and will marry another, commits adultery: and whoever marries a divorced woman commits adultery.

Any conscious mind that refuses to identify its own thoughts and harmonize them with subconscious mind, and any subconscious mind that attempts to move into another body, breaks the commitment from inner to outer mind and outer to inner mind. The subconscious mind makes a commitment to a physical body and conscious mind at the time of incarnation and will remain committed to that conscious mind for the duration of the lifetime. The aware conscious mind will remain committed to its duty of adding understandings to subconscious mind throughout the lifetime. Subconscious mind serves its duty by aiding the conscious mind to fulfill its desires throughout the lifetime.

> [10] *His disciples said to him, If the case of the man be so with his wife, it is not good to marry.* [11] *But he said unto them, All men cannot receive this teaching, save they to whom it is given.* [12] *For some men are incapable of sexual activity from birth; some have been deliberately made so and some there are who have freely renounced sex for the sake of God's reign. Let him accept this teaching who can.*

In essence Jesus says he who divorces his wife and marries another commits adultery and the man who marries a divorced woman commits adultery. Marriage indicates a commitment to the inner Self. The outer Self existing in the conscious mind must realize the need for and create this commitment. Divorce indicates breaking the commitment which has been made. The degree or level of commitment created and made to one's learning and growth, is to be continually enriched. As progress is made, add to that commitment, never going back and being less committed to Self than a day, a week, a month, or a year before. The aggressive response to the creative urge is to be used to create the Christ consciousness within the Self and gain the divine radiance of full compatibility with creation.

> [13] *Then were there brought unto him little children, that he should put his hands on them, and pray: and the disciples rebuked them.* [14] *But Jesus said, Let the little children come to me, and do not forbid them to come to me; for of such is the kingdom of heaven.* [15] *He laid his hands on them, and departed there.*

The disciples scolded him for spending valuable time with children. They wanted him to give his full time and attention to adults, especially them. Yet, great importance lies in giving attention to and identifying all the infantile, adolescent, and immature aspects of Self, as symbolized by Jesus placing his hands on the children in prayer. The Knower needs to create a great purpose for these aspects so, as they mature, they will be in alignment with the plan to become Enlightened.

> [16] *Behold, one came and said unto him, Master Teacher, what good thing will I do, that I may have everlasting life?* [17] *He said unto him, Why call you me good? there is none good but one, that is, God: but if you will enter into life, keep the commandments.* [18] *He said unto him, Which*

commandment? Jesus said, You will not murder, you will not commit adultery, you will not steal, you will not bear false witness, [19] *Honor your father and your mother: and, you will love your neighbor as yourself.* [20] *The young man said unto him, All these things have I kept from my youth up: what do I still need?*

The new commandment, that Jesus offers beyond the ten commandments which God gave to Moses and which Moses then offered to the Israelites, is *"Love your neighbor as yourself"*. Jesus adds love to the human equation.

Creating a purpose for everything you do is of utmost importance in fulfilling all of the commandments originally given in *Exodus*. There are three aspects of developing and having purpose in your life. 1] Helping other people. 2] Expressing your talents. 3] Following your inner urge, following your dreams, following the great ideal of Self awareness.

Exodus 20 [1] *And God spoke all these words, saying,* [2] *I am the Lord your God, which have brought you out of the land of Egypt, out of the house of bondage.* [3] *You will have no other gods before me.* [4] *You will not make unto you any graven image, or any likeness of any thing that is in heaven above, or that is in the earth beneath, or that is in the water under the earth.* [5] *You shall not bow down yourself to them, nor serve them: for I the Lord your God am a jealous God, visiting the iniquity of the fathers upon the children unto the third and fourth generation of them that hate me;* [6] *And showing mercy unto thousands of them that love me, and keep my commandments.* [7] *You shall not take the name of the Lord your God in vain: for the Lord will not hold him* *guiltless that takes his name in vain. ⁸ Remember the Sabbath day, to keep it holy. ⁹ Six days shall you labor, and do all your work: ¹⁰ But the seventh day is the Sabbath of the Lord your God: in it you shall not do any work, you, nor your son, nor your daughter, your manservant, nor your maidservant, nor your cattle, nor your stranger that is within your gates: ¹¹ For in six days the Lord made heaven and earth, the sea, and all that in them is, and rested the seventh day: wherefore the Lord blessed the Sabbath day, and hallowed it. ¹² Honor your father and your mother: that your days may be long upon the land which the Lord your God gives you. ¹³ You shall not kill. ¹⁴ You shall not commit adultery. ¹⁵ You shall not steal. ¹⁶ You shall not bear false witness against your neighbor. ¹⁷ You shall not covet your neighbors house, you shall not covet your neighbors wife, nor his manservant, nor his maidservant, nor his ox, nor his ass, nor any thing that is your neighbor's.*

Jesus was born to Mary, the embodiment of the nurturing quality of love in the conscious mind. Caring for others while at the same time learning to care for Self is the "golden cord" that binds all the ten commandments together.

²¹ Jesus said unto him, If you will be perfect, go and sell all that you have, and give it to the poor, and you will have treasure in heaven: and come and follow me. ²² But when the young man heard that saying, he went away sorrowful: for he had great possessions.

Here is presented the attitude necessary to ensure the physical does not entrap Self. One must use the physical existence and its objects, but Self must not be possessed and engrossed in the sensory entrapment of the changing physical life.

²³ Then Jesus said to his disciples, I assure you, only with difficulty will a rich man enter into the kingdom of heaven. ²⁴ Again I say to you, It is easier for a camel to go through the eye of a needle, than for a rich man to enter into the kingdom of God. ²⁵ When his disciples heard this they were exceedingly amazed, saying, Who then can be saved? ²⁶ But Jesus said to them, for men this is impossible; but with God all things are possible.

What is translated in the King James version as *camel* is more accurately interpreted as *rope*. Lamsa translates verses 24 as, *"Again I say to you, it is easier for a rope to go through the eye of a needle, than for a rich man to enter the kingdom of God."* Rope was mistranslated as camel because the Aramaic word used here — *gamia* — is a word meaning both *rope* and *camel*. In the Universal Language of Mind this passage speaks to the Truth that physical possessions are physical and therefore cannot enter subconscious or superconscious mind which is not physical. One who is owned by his or her possessions can never "suture" or bind the conscious and subconscious minds together with the "needle" or implement of yoga, for yoga means union. *Sutra* means *to suture*, as in suturing a wound together or suturing the minds together. This process is impossible for one who possesses no thread but only rope. The thread symbolizes one's ability to use the physical for learning and growth by combining the minds. The rope symbolizes one's collection of objects as a means to find false security.

> [27] *Then Peter answered and said to him, Behold, we have put everything aside and followed you; what can we expect from it?* [28] *Jesus said unto them, Verily I say unto you, That you who have followed me, in the regeneration when the Son of man will sit in the throne of his glory, you also will sit upon twelve thrones, judging the twelve tribes of Israel.* [29] *Every one who has forsaken houses, or brother, or sisters, or father, or mother, or wife, or children, or lands, for my name's sake, will receive an hundredfold, and will inherit everlasting life.* [30] *Many who are first will be last; and the last will be first.*

In order for any type of creation to occur, structure is necessary. The twelve thrones and twelve tribes define part of the structure of creation. The twelve thrones are the twelve tribes of Israel. The twelve tribes of Israel are the 12 major inner subconscious aspects of Self. The twelve disciples or apostles indicate the twelve major outer conscious aspects of Self. When the twelve major inner aspects and twelve major outer aspects are aligned, then *"the first will come last and the last will come first"*. The parts or aspects of Self that are already completely understood and free from entrapment will aid the aspects which have not yet gained Enlightenment. The conscious awareness will go marching into mind with full awareness ready to claim the kingdom of God. Everlasting life is permanent consciousness with full awareness of creation and without cessation.

Notes:

Symbols and Their Interpretation

Chapter Twenty

1.   Right - righteous; productive
2.   Jericho - most ancient use of mind

Chapter Twenty

¹ For the kingdom of heaven is like the man that was a house-holder, who went out early in the morning to hire laborers into his vineyard. ² When he had agreed with the laborers for the usual daily wage, he sent them into his vineyard. ³ He went out about midmorning, and saw other men standing idle in the market place, ⁴ And said to them; You go also into the vineyard, and whatsoever is fair I will pay you. And they went their way. ⁵ Again he went out about noon and midafternoon and did likewise. ⁶ About late afternoon he went out, and found others standing idle, and said to them, Why do you stand here all the day idle? ⁷ They said to him, Because no man has hired us. He said to them, You go also into the vineyard; and whatsoever is fair, that will you be paid. ⁸ So when evening came, the lord of the vineyard said unto his foreman, Call the laborers, and give them their hire, beginning from the last to the first. ⁹ When they came that were hired late in the afternoon, they received a full days pay. ¹⁰ But when the first came, they supposed that they should have received more; yet they received the same daily wages. ¹¹ When they had received it, they complained about the owner. ¹² Saying, These last have worked but one hour, and you have made them equal to us, who have borne the burden and heat of the day. ¹³ But he answered one of them, and said, Friend, I do you no wrong: did you not agree to work for the usual wages? ¹⁴ Take your pay, and go home: I intend to give this man who was hired last the same pay as you. ¹⁵ Is it not lawful for me to do what I will with my own money? Or are you jealous because I am gener-ous? ¹⁶ So the last will be first, and the first last: for many are called, but few chosen.

The laborers in the vineyard is a story about the workers who are all paid the same wage — even the ones who work the hardest or longest in the field. The vineyard represents the knowledge that can be gained from the physical life for the inner Self. Self chooses how much abundance is enough. How low one goes or how high one will move in life and learning is a choice. Those who perceive much value in what they do and are willing to recognize that value will gain increased Self worth from the experience.

Chapter Nineteen ends with a verse very similar to verse sixteen. *"Many who are first will be last, and the last will be first."* Whenever a statement is repeated by the knower, Jesus, be certain that this message is of utmost importance to the thinker. The last or most recent understanding the thinker has developed will be employed in the conscious mind to the highest degree during that lifetime. Everyone, until they achieve Enlightenment, has many understandings stored in subconscious mind that are not being used. The understandings the individual has constructed and developed this lifetime, are the understandings most frequently used. The other older permanent understandings stored from previous lifetimes must be drawn into the conscious awareness of Self through meditation, concentration, dream interpretation, teaching many people what one has learned, and the willingness to move beyond any previously accepted limitations. This expansion beyond limitations creates a space within Self where one may receive in greater proportion the learning and knowledge that is available.

> *[17] Jesus traveling to Jerusalem took the twelve disciples aside and said to them, [18] Behold, we go up to Jerusalem; and the Son of man will be handed over to the chief priests and scribes, and they will condemn him to death, [19] and will deliver him to the Gentiles to mock, and to scourge, and to crucify him: but on the third day he will be raised up.*

The word Jerusalem is a combination of the words Jeru and Salem. Salem was the place where Melchizedek a priest of the God Most High resided. Melchizedek was a priest of the God Most High and he never died. He represents an aspect that has gained

Enlightenment. Melchizedek lived in Salem. Jeru-salem indicates the place, in the physical, where the mind can be directed in order to gain awareness of the inner Self and align with the superconscious mind.

> *Genesis 14* ¹⁷ *When Abram returned from his victory over Chedorlaomer and the kings who were allied with him, the king of Sodom went out to greet him in the Valley of Shaveh (that is, the King's Valley).* ¹⁸ *Melchizedek, king of Salem, brought out bread and wine, and being a priest of God Most High, he blessed Abram with these words:* ¹⁹ *"Blessed be Abram By God Most High, the creator of heaven and earth;* ²⁰ *And blessed be God Most High, who delivered your foes into your hand."* *Then Abram gave him a tenth of everything.*

The limitations of the scribes (which represent brain pathways) are very restrictive when compared to the free flow of will power and reasoning. Habits are a part of the animal body which the thinker inhabits. Habits and compulsion are created through the faculty of memory, which was developed in animals as a precursor of and in preparation for the reasoner. Memory can be and needs to be used effectively by the reasoner. Memory alone will not propel the reasoner forward to the next stage of evolution. Memory must be combined with attention (on the present experience) and imagination (to image the future or the next advancement in one's growth) in order for the reasoner to function. Imagination is the great tool of the reasoner that is to be employed to move forward to greater stages of Enlightenment.

> ²⁰ *Then the mother of Zebedee's children with her sons, came to him, worshipping him and desiring a certain thing of him.* ²¹ *He said to her, What is it you want? She said to him, Grant that my two sons may sit, the one on your right hand, and the other on the left, in your kingdom.* ²² *But Jesus answered and said, You know not what you ask. Are you able to drink of the cup that I will drink of, and to be baptized with the baptism that I am baptized with? They say unto him, We are able.* ²³ *He said unto them, You will drink indeed of my cup, and be baptized with the baptism that I am baptized with: but to sit on my right hand, and on my left, is not mine to give, but it will be given to them for whom it is prepared of my Father.* ²⁴ *When the ten heard it, they were outraged at the two brothers.* ²⁵ *But Jesus called them to him, and said, You know how those who exercise authority among the Gentiles lord it over them, and their great ones make their importance felt.* ²⁶ *But it will not be so*

among you: but whoever will be great among you, let him serve the rest. [27] *Whoever wants to rank first among you, let him serve the needs of all:* [28] *Even as the Son of man came not to be served by others but to serve, and to give his own life as a ransom for many.*

The two sons of Zebedee are James and John. James and John were the third and fourth disciples called by Jesus the knower. Simon, known as Peter, and his brother Andrew were the first two disciples called by the knower. All four were fishermen when Jesus called them.

Matthew 4 [18] *Jesus, walking by the sea of Galilee, saw two brothers, Simon called Peter, and Andrew his brother, casting a net into the sea: for they were fishermen.* [19] *He said to them, Follow me, and I will make you fishers of men.* [20] *They immediately left their nets, and followed him.* [21] *Going on from there, he saw two other brothers, James the son of Zebedee, and John his brother, in a ship with Zebedee their father, mending their nets; and he called them.* [22] *They immediately left the ship and their father, and followed him.*

The question of sitting on the left and right hand of Jesus indicates a desire to identify with and be in constant communion with Enlightenment. The other ten disciples became indignant which is to be jealously insecure. The instruction which the knower then offers to his disciples is to be the greatest (and therefore sit at the right or left hand of Jesus) one must be the greatest server. All the greatest spiritually Enlightened individuals have been world teachers and world servers. The egoic reactions, the dishonest ego and conscious mind, are made honest and in alignment with the inner Self through service to others. When one is serving and aiding others to growth, learning, and abundance there is no place for the conscious ego, the small Self, to act in any fashion other than for what it is intended which is as a motivator. Anyone who wants to become Enlightened must understand service to the whole world, to the whole planet, and give that service completely to all. As one serves others that person also learns to serve all aspects of Self.

> *29 As they left Jericho, a great multitude followed him. 30 Behold, two blind men were sitting by the side of the road. When they heard Jesus passing they cried out, Have mercy on us, O Lord, you son of David. 31 The multitude rebuked them, because they should be quiet, but Jesus stood still, and called them, and said, What do you want me to do for you? 33 They said unto him, Lord, our eyes. 34 Jesus had compassion on them, and touched their eyes: and immediately their eyes received sight, and they followed him.*

Jericho is the oldest city in the world that is known to be continuously inhabited to the present time and as such represents a part of mind that has been with the individual for a long time preserved as understanding. Two blind men represent the quality of perception that is lacking and needs to be addressed. The Lord, Son of David, shows that perception must build on reasoning. David indicates reasoning. The request to open our eyes means these aspects have a visualized image that is complete and there is no doubt that perception is possible. When this occurs there is perception. When one is willing to change the Self and move through initiations so that experience and knowledge can be received into Self where none previously existed, then perception is functioning effectively. As long as one is judging, thinking, or reacting, one is constantly forming pictures that are not being received from the environment. Therefore, they may have little or no relation to what is actually occurring around the Self.

Notes:

Symbols and Their Interpretation

Chapter Twenty-One

1.   Mount of Olives - Challenge to knowledge overcome
2.   Ass - control of will
3.   Zion - High place in mind; highest achievement of mind
4.   Hosanna - attention on intuitive thinker
5.   Money sellers - stealing value from Self
6.   Vineyard - subconscious experience that provides knowledge
7.   Keystone - foundation for using the whole mind
8.   Structure - mind and Universal Laws
9.   Fig tree - knowledge produced from subconscious experience

Chapter Twenty-One

Jesus taught in the surrounding countryside and cities as described in the previous chapters of the *Book of Matthew*. Chapter Twenty-one begins with the triumphal entry into Jerusalem. This symbolizes that the thinker has fully understood and disciplined the conscious mind so control can be gained from the conscious level in all other parts of the mind. Jeru indicates the physical life and environment and Salem indicates the spiritual life or the superconscious mind. The word *Salem* means *peace*. The triumphal entry shows the mind has been disciplined. The twelve disciples connote discipline of Self. Self is first taught the inner secrets and the Universal Laws and then becomes a teacher of what has been understood. Self will teach the multitudes. One must multiply the learning and the knowledge as indicated by the story of the loaves and the fishes. Overcoming every obstacle and every unproductive habit is symbolized by the healing of the sick and the lame. Life is a process of becoming and to become one must know the starting point of Self; where the Self is. The knower is aware of his or her level of understanding and awareness.

> *¹ When they drew near Jerusalem, entering Bethphage, the mount of Olives, Jesus sent two disciples, ² Saying unto them, Go into the village straight ahead of you and you will find an ass tied, and a colt with her: loose them, and bring them unto me. ³ And if any man say anything to you, you will say, The Lord has need of them; and immediately he will send them. ⁴ All this was done, that it might be fulfilled which was spoken by the prophet, saying ⁵ Tell you the daughter of Zion, Behold, your King comes unto you, without display, and sitting upon an ass, the foal of a beast of burden.*

Verse five is a quote from *Zechariah 9:9* and Isaiah *62:10-12*:

> *Zechariah 9 ⁹ Rejoice greatly, O Daughter of Zion! Shout, Daughter of Jerusalem! See, your king comes to you righ-*

teous and having salvation, gentle and riding on a donkey, on a colt, the foal of a donkey.

Isaiah 62   [10] Pass through, pass through the gates! Prepare the way for the people. Build up, build up the highway! Remove the stones. Raise the banner for the nations. [11] The Lord has made proclamation to the ends of the earth: Say to the Daughter of Zion, See, your Savior comes! See, his reward is with him, and his recompense accompanies him. [12] They will be called the Holy People, The Redeemed of the Lord; and you will be called Sought After, The City No Longer Deserted.

Time after time, Jesus the knower fulfilled the predictions of the goal-setters; the ideal-creating prophets.

[6] The disciples went, and did as Jesus commanded them, [7] And brought the ass, and the colt, and put on their cloaks and he mounted. [8] A very great multitude spread their garments on the road; others cut down branches from the trees, and strewed them on the path. [9] The multitudes that went before, and that followed, cried, saying, Hosanna to the son of David: Blessed is he that comes in the name of the Lord; Hosanna in the highest. [10] When he came into Jerusalem, all the city was moved, saying, Who is this? [11] The multitude said, This is Jesus the prophet of Nazareth of Galilee.

Mount shows that the challenges have been met and overcome. Learning has occurred because the olive trees on the Mount of Olives represent the subconscious experience which is the result of the use of discipline, knowledge, and wisdom added to the inner Self. Jesus rides a donkey or an ass into the town showing the full control of the will. This is the fulfillment of the prophecy that the knower would have the full power to control the Self and the will. As Jesus is coming into Jerusalem the people say *"Hosanna to the son of David"*. Jesus is the son of David because this is the full development of the reasoning capability that produces a knower who is one capable of causing greater awareness and knowledge in Self. This prophet, Jesus of Nazareth, continually is referred to as a Nazarene. A Nazarene in the *Old Testament* is one who is committed to God, symbolizing commitment to knowing the whole Self as a spiritual being and understanding creation. Samson and Samuel were Nazarenes.

> *12 Jesus went into the temple of God, and cast out all them that sold and bought in the temple, and overthrew the tables of the moneysellers, and the seats of those who sold doves, 13 He said to them, It is written, My house will be called the house of prayer; but you have made it a den of thieves. 14 The blind and the lame came to him in the temple; and he healed them. 15 When the chief priests and scribes saw the wonderful things that he did, and the children crying in the temple, saying, Hosanna to the son of David; they were bitterly displeased, 16 And said unto him, Hear you what these say? And Jesus said unto them, Yes, have you never read: Out of the mouth of babes and sucklings you have framed a hymn of praise? 17 He left them, and went out of the city into Bethany; and he stayed there.*

The cleansing of the temple shows that anything remaining within the mind that is unproductive, that is disrespectful to the Self, that is not producing value, that is distracting from the real purpose of the mind which is to know God, Self, and the whole mind will be eliminated from the mind. The chief priests and elders are jealous and feeling threatened because Jesus is teaching the people with authority which lessens an intellectual's pseudo-informational authority and subsequently the intellectual's feeling of importance. Egoic, jealous aspects attempt to destroy the knowing quality. Place faith in learning. Place attention on how to build authority and add to the learning so as to have and build the value seen in others. The reason the knower runs the money changers out of the temple is they were using the temple for their own personal profit. They cheated the pilgrims out of money by overcharging them for money exchange and for animals used in sacrifice, basically through having a monopoly on such goods. Responsibility and discipline enhance creativity by giving structure to mind, thought, and life. The aspects known as the money changers were being irresponsible.

Notes:

¹⁸ *At dawn, as he returned into the city, he was hungry.* ¹⁹ *When he saw a fig tree in the way, he came to it. Finding nothing but leaves on it, he said to it, Let no fruit grow on you from now on. At once, the fig tree withered away.* ²⁰ *When the disciples saw it, they marveled, saying, How soon is the fig tree withered away.* ²¹ *Jesus answered and said to them, Verily I say unto you, If you have faith, and doubt not, you will not only do this which is done to the fig tree, but also if you will say to this mountain, Be lifted up, and be thrown into the sea; it will be done.* ²² *You will receive all that you pray for, provided you have faith.*

Dawn follows night. Night is a time of sleep. Sleep is the time when the process of assimilation occurs. During daytime one creates many experiences for Self, each yielding the opportunity for knowledge to be gained from these experiences. The knowledge produced in the conscious mind through one's daily experiences must then be assimilated into the inner subconscious mind, the soul of Self. After this assimilation process has occurred Self is prepared to begin a new day with an expanded awareness through use of the information presented in dream imagery. When all food has been assimilated, the body once again grows hungry. In a similar fashion, once knowledge from the previous day's experience has been assimilated into the subconscious mind a person develops a yearning and hunger for further knowledge. Figs symbolize knowledge. The fig tree that bears no fruit symbolizes an avenue of experiencing that produces no knowledge necessary for further advancement. An example of this is psychic impressions one may receive yet not find useful for producing any changes within Self. Another example is the refusal to reason, living in one's thoughts where there is no new learning.

The important instruction that Jesus offers to his disciples from the withered fig tree is that the one who has built trust in Self (*"faith with no doubt"* in the Lamsa translation) will be able to surmount and overcome all obstacles. Such a one will control any creation of Self so that creation challenges the Self enabling forward movement in awareness to occur rapidly and easily. A person who trusts no one else rarely, if ever, trusts him/her Self.

Every conscious thought and desire given to subconscious mind will be received in time by the conscious mind from subconscious mind. Prayer is the action of giving one's desire, thought, questions, or petition to the subconscious mind. Meditation is the action of receiving the answers to one's prayers.

Lamsa also translates verse twenty-two as, *"And everything that you will ask in prayer believing, you will receive."* The knower Jesus does not say you *may* receive, or perhaps you'll receive. The knower declares that you *will* receive that for which you pray. The subconscious mind's duty is to fulfill all of the conscious mind's desires if allowed to do so by the conscious mind. This means in order for the subconscious mind to aid the conscious mind to fulfill desires, you the individual must initiate regular, consistent, daily activity towards your goals. Those images created in the conscious mind and projected into subconscious mind will manifest in the physical life. This is a use of the image making faculty given by Elohim, the plural God, of *Genesis 1:26.*

To believe, to have faith, and to trust, is to create a mental image of what is desired to occur and to allow no doubt which would cloud or destroy the mental image desired. The subconscious mind then receives the desired image as it was intended and is free to act on the desired image and move it from thought to condensed thought substance into the matter manifestation of one's physical life.

> [23] *When he came into the temple, the chief priests and the elders of the people came to him as he was teaching, and said, By what authority are you doing these things? and who gave you this power?* [24] *Jesus answered and said unto them, I also will ask you one thing, which if you tell me, I likewise will tell you by what authority I do these things.* [25] *What was the origin of John's baptism? Was it divine or merely human? And they reasoned with themselves, saying, If we will say, From heaven; he will say unto us, Why then didn't you believe him?* [26] *But if we will say, Merely human, we will have a reason to fear the people; for all regard John as a prophet.* [27] *They answered Jesus, and said, We do not know. And he said to them, Then neither will I tell you by what authority I do these things.*

The temple is the mind that gives full attention to higher spiritual development and Enlightenment. The high priests represent those aspects of

Notes:

Self who are firmly entrenched in old limited concepts of God, immortality, and creation. The elders are the mature aspects of Self. Some of these have gained a degree of wisdom, others have not. All of them have become more set in their ways as the inertia of physical existence has had time to affect these aspects. These aspects which are restrictive have the intention of trying to discredit the knower. This is the purpose of their question. The knower, Jesus, responds in like kind by asking them a question that clearly presents the limitations of physical, temporary experience especially in comparison to permanent learning that the knower has developed.

John's baptism with water symbolizes commitment to use the physical to produce success, learning, and to fully understand the power of imagery through belief. John's baptism was both divine and human for John represents using and building the step on the evolutionary path called believing. It is thus divine in that this belief adds to the whole Self. John's baptism is human because it involves reasoning in the conscious mind.

The chief priests and elders feared the repercussions of their answers because they lived in limitation. The aspects of Self who live in limitation, fear being drawn out where all aspects of Self can see the falsity and restriction of this part of Self. Therefore, these engrossed aspects have not earned the right to question the knower's authority.

> [28] *What do you think of this situation? A certain man had two sons; and he came to the first, and said, Son, go work today in my vineyard.* [29] *He answered and said, I will not; but afterward he repented, and went.* [30] *And he came to the second, and said likewise. And he answered and said, I go, sir; and went not.* [31] *Which of the two did the will of his father? They say unto him, The first. Jesus said unto them, Verily I say unto you, That the tax collectors and the harlots go into the kingdom of*

God before you. [32] For John came unto you in the way of
righteousness, and you believed him not; but the tax collec-
tors and the harlots believed him: and you, even when you
had seen him, did not convert to believing him afterwards.

The tax collectors and prostitutes are likened to the son who said he
would not go to work in the vineyard yet regretted it and went and worked
anyway. The one who commits to activity to produce knowledge and wisdom
(grapes and wine) will gain awareness of superconscious mind (heaven) long
before anyone who professes to have information and knowledge yet never
practices it.

Prostitutes symbolize conscious aspects who misuse the creative
energy. Tax collectors are aspects of Self who have no value or steal value
from Self and do not respect the value of others.

[33] Listen to another comparison: There was a certain house-
holder, which planted a vineyard, and hedged it round about,
and dug a winepress in it, and built a tower, and let it out to
husbandmen, and went into a far country: [34] When the time
of the fruit drew near, he sent his servants to the husband-
men, that they might receive the fruits of it. [35] The husband-
men took his servants, and beat one, and killed another, and
stoned another. [36] Again, he sent other servants more than
the first: and they did unto them likewise. [37] But last of all
he sent to them his son, saying, They will respect my son. [38]
But when the husbandmen saw the son, they said among
themselves, This is the heir; come, let us kill him, and let us
seize his inheritance. [39] They caught him, and threw him
out of the vineyard, and killed him. [40] When the lord of the
vineyard comes, what will he do unto those husbandmen?
[41] They say unto him, He will destroy those wicked men,
and will let out his vineyard to other husbandmen, who will
deliver him the fruits in their seasons.

Vineyards are often referenced in the Bible. The fruit of the vine is
grapes, which are food. Food symbolizes knowledge. Transforming grapes
into wine shows the mutation of the knowledge into wisdom. Wine was held
in high esteem in this part of the world during the historical time of Jesus.
Wine shows the transformation of knowledge into wisdom. The lesson to be
learned from this parable is: when producing knowledge one doesn't just
walk away and leave it but gives it attention from time to time; continually
adding to one's knowledge, continually building and creating.

Notes:

> [42] *Jesus said to them, Have you never read in the scriptures, The stone which the builders rejected has become the keystone of the structure: this is the Lord's doing, and it is amazing in our eyes?* [43] *Therefore say I to you, The kingdom of God will be taken from you, and given to a nation bringing forth the fruits thereof.* [44] *Whoever will fall on this stone will be broken: but on whomever it will fall, it will scatter them to pieces.* [45] *When the chief priests and Pharisees had heard his parables, they perceived that he spoke of them.*

That which does not at first look so powerful in the physical will, in the long run, build and be the most important of all. When the attention is on the inner Self and the ability to cause creation because it is permanent not temporary, then great learning will occur. Evil and sin represent that which is temporary. Good and Godlike is permanent. Creation is permanent. God is permanent. Total understandings are permanent. So in the long run the true owners of the vineyard — the ones who own the land and produce the knowledge, setting up the structure for learning to occur as symbolized by the vineyard, the winepress, and tower— are the ones who gain Enlightenment called the kingdom of heaven.

> [46] *When they sought to lay hands on him, they feared the crowds who regarded him as a prophet.*

The last verse of Chapter Twenty-one presents a new insight. As Jesus is presenting the story of the tenant farmer (who killed the slaves or servants who came to get their payments and the son of the owner being killed), he is educating the high priests and Pharisees who try to destroy the knowing quality called Jesus. The knower is building for the whole Self rather than feeding the ego and conscious mind. This is the first instance where they try to arrest Jesus which shows the willingness of the knower to submit to the restriction in the physical environment and the physical body. If a person is arrested and thrown in prison, that one is a prisoner and has lost some freedom. The point that is going to be shown throughout the resurrection is that for one who has gained Enlightenment the physical no longer can control or limit Self. The physical existence can no longer restrict Self when movement and motion of Self is used to create as a creator and to fulfill one's purpose for this lifetime.

The aspects that are not so heavily invested in physical security protect and embrace the higher teachings. The Israelites hoped and prayed for a prophet who would deliver them from their oppressors. The Knower does deliver entrapped aspects of Self from their engrossment by leading them to Self understanding and higher consciousness.

Symbols and Their Interpretation

Chapter Twenty-Two

1. Wedding - manifestation of commitment in the physical
2. Caesar - physical authority from experience and memory
3. Resurrection - continued awareness
4. Commandments - Universal principles
5. Lord - I AM
6. Spirit - mind
7. Enemies - unproductive, negative attitudes
8. Egypt - Physical engrossment

Chapter Twenty-Two

Jesus the knower enters Jerusalem as presented in Chapter 21. From this point forward, *Matthew* builds to the climax in Jerusalem and its environs: the knower's crucifixion and resurrection. The area where Jesus did most of his ministry and gathered his disciples was in Galilee; the area north of Jerusalem. Galilee, Nazareth, Capernaum, Bethsaida, Gadara, and Chorazin are all towns or villages around the Sea of Galilee. This is the area where Jesus the knower accomplished most of his ministry up to the time of his entry into Jerusalem portrayed in Chapter 21. The main Jewish temple was located in Jerusalem and as such served as the main seat of Jewish learning and religious life. This was the headquarters of the Pharisees and Sadducees, whom Jesus instructed and battled. They became jealous of the knower because he knew the essence and authority of the Holy Scriptures which they did not. The knower had not gone through the steps of training of the Pharisees and Sadducees, yet he possessed knowledge they did not have. Because of this, they were jealous, perceiving Jesus as a threat to their so-called physical security. Rather than changing and starting anew in infancy, they chose to try to destroy the new learning and awareness so they themselves would not have to experience the discomfort of change. No growth ever comes from being comfortable. A child never learned to walk by being comfortable. An adult never learned to speak a new language by being comfortable. Rather they extend and stretch themselves, being out of balance, so they can move forward. When walking there is a moment of imbalance as one foot moves ahead of the other and the weight shifts forward. Sitting in a chair is comfortable, but it doesn't get you anywhere.

> [1] *Jesus answered in a parable saying,* [2] *The kingdom of heaven is like a certain king, who gave a wedding banquet for his son,* [3] *He sent his servants to call them who were invited to the wedding: but they would not come.* [4] *Again, he sent other servants, saying, Tell them who are invited, Behold, I have prepared my dinner: my steers and my fat calves are killed, and all things are ready: come to the wedding.* [5] *But they made light of it, and went their ways, one to his farm, another to his shop:* [6] *The rest took his servants,*

Notes:

and insulted them spitefully, and
killed them. [7] But when the king
heard of this, he was furious: and he
sent forth his armies, and destroyed
those murderers, and burned up their
city. [8] Then said he to his servants,
The wedding is ready, but they who
were invited were not worthy. [9] Go
therefore into the highways, and as
many as you will find, invite to the
wedding. [10] So those servants went
out into the highways, and gathered
together as many as they found, both
bad and good: and the wedding was
furnished with guests. [11] When the
king came in to see the guests, he saw
there a man who was not properly
attired for a wedding: [12] He said unto
him, Friend, how is it that you came
here not properly attired? And he had
nothing to say. [13] Then said the king
to the servants, Bind him hand and
foot, and take him away, and cast him
into outer darkness; there will be
weeping and grinding of teeth. [14]
Because many are called, but few are
chosen.

Lamsa translates verse fourteen as, *"For many
are called and few are chosen."* King James translates
verse fourteen as, *"For many are called, but few are
chosen."* Jesus is in Jerusalem which symbolizes the
knower has recognized and understood the productive
use of the conscious mind. The knower is using every
experience to create and build permanent understandings which will be stored in subconscious mind. Jesus
gives a parable about the wedding banquet. The wedding symbolizes the commitment made between the
inner and outer Self or more specifically the subconscious and conscious minds. The woman represents
the conscious mind. The man represents the subconscious mind. The parable is a mental picture story which
Jesus used to explain the concept or universal Truth of
commitment. King symbolizes inner authority. One's

inner authority is a product of fulfilling the plan held in the superconscious mind. Completing this evolutionary blueprint of creation adds to the conscious and subconscious mind's knowledge. The marriage is therefore the union of two divisions of mind, the conscious and subconscious, under the direction of the father of the son (superconscious aspect) who has the authority of a King. A banquet symbolizes many aspects of Self coming together for the purpose of receiving knowledge and to give full attention and acknowledgment to the union of the inner subconscious mind and outer conscious mind. The guests who refuse to come to the wedding symbolize those aspects of Self who refuse to acknowledge the need to make a commitment to the subconscious mind. The guests who refuse to come to the wedding are missing out on the reason for physical existence which is to add to the inner Self. Those guests who laid hold of and killed the servants of the King are those aspects which destroy learning opportunities for Self. When one is jealous of another's accomplishments that jealousy tends to lead a person to attempt to destroy outwardly what one has not been willing to produce inwardly. The cause of jealousy is a person refusing to practice and apply the will power, effort, and discipline to accomplish what is desired and yet being aware that another person has been willing to do just that. You see the results of their accomplishments but you are unwilling to change so you attempt to destroy the productive changes of another and in so doing destroy or constrict many aspects of learning and growth in Self. The aspects of Self who are destructive must be changed and transformed into a higher purpose by the thinker. This is the meaning of verse seven. The King (inner authority) destroyed the murderers (changed and transformed those aspects who do not want to align with their superconscious mind and refuse to use the experience as commitment to growth and Self understanding and in fact destroy the learning of others).

The phrase, *the wedding is ready but they who were invited were not worthy*, represents the knowledge of Self and mind that is constantly available when the conscious mind and its aspects are prepared through mental discipline. One must recognize all aspects and parts of Self and draw them into commitment to the subconscious mind or soul and then to the superconscious awareness or Spirit. The man not properly dressed (translated by Lamsa as *"not wearing wedding garments"*) symbolizes any aspect of Self who refuses to use the outer expression to communicate with others appropriately as a tool for learning and further Self understanding. The one who refuses to express the inner Self adequately in their physical life will find the learning and growth to be very limited and constricted. In fact, they will find their purpose (hand) and spiritual foundation (foot) very limited and restricted. They will, in effect, lose their freedom.

15 Then the Pharisees went off and began to plot how they might trap him in his words. 16 They sent their disciples with the Herodian sympathizers to him, saying, Teacher, we know that you are truthful, and teach the way of God in Truth, you court no one's favor and do not act out of human respect. [17] Tell us therefore, What think you? Is it lawful to pay tribute to Caesar, or not? [18] But Jesus perceived their intentions, and said, Why do you test me, you fakes? [19] Show me the coin paid in taxes. And they brought to him a small Roman coin. [20] He said to them, Whose image and inscription is this? [21] They said to him, Caesar's. Then said he to them, Render therefore unto Caesar the things which are Caesar's; and unto God the things that are God's. [22] When they had heard these words, they marvelled, and left him, going on their way.

Herodian sympathizers represent those aspects of Self which use the conscious ego as a motivator to try to physically control events and people around them. Lamsa translates the sentence out of verse sixteen that says, *"You court no one's favor and do not act out of human respect"* as, *"You do not favor any man, for you do not discriminate between men."* This is a statement in effect saying Jesus, the Knower, recognizes the value of all aspects of Self. The question in this section starts with the Pharisees trying to trap Jesus by saying, "Should you pay tax to the Emperor or not?" Because they knew that he would be thrown into prison if he would try to say you shouldn't pay taxes. The Pharisees based their power on intellectualism which is all memory. Memory is of the conscious mind and of the past. The past does not exist. Only the present exists and we are creating our future. So intellectualism is very limited.

Jesus' answer to the Pharisees concerning the coin is the famous *"Give unto Caesar what is Caesar's and give to God what is God's."* The inner meaning is to give to the physical the value and due that it deserves and merits. Respect the physical body. Feed, clothe, and shelter the body because it serves you. The body serves the mind, the inner Self or soul, and I Am while one is in the physical existence. Remember the primary duty of Self is to learn. At the same time one must take care of the physical body so the physical body can serve the thinker. Meditate every day and place attention on the inner Self. Learn to still the mind, focus the attention, and listen to the inner Self, day by day. In this manner one learns to align the conscious, subconscious, and superconscious minds. One then develops full awareness of who one is and his or her relationship to creation.

> [23] *The same day the Sadducees came to him, who say that there is no resurrection, and asked him,* [24] *Saying, Teacher, Moses said, If a man dies, having no children, his brother will marry his wife, and produce offspring for his brother.* [25] *Once there was with us seven brothers: and the first, when he had married a wife, died, and, having no issue, left his wife to his brother:* [26] *Likewise the second also, and the third, and so on to the seventh.* [27] *Finally, the woman died also.* [28] *Therefore in the resurrection, whose wife will she be of the seven for they all had her.* [29] *Jesus answered and said unto them, You are wandering in circles, not knowing the scriptures, nor the power of God.* [30] *In the resurrection they neither marry nor are given in marriage, but are as the angels of God in heaven.* [31] *Regarding the fact that the dead are raised, have you not read that which was spoken to you by God, saying,* [32] *I am the God of Abraham, and the God of Isaac, and the God of Jacob? God is not the God of the dead, but of the living.* [33] *And when the multitude heard this, they were astonished at his teaching.*

Marriage is a physical custom that is used to symbolize the inner marriage, the marriage between the conscious and subconscious minds. At the time of death the soul withdraws from the physical body, leaving behind and releasing the conscious mind which has been used for learning throughout the duration of the lifetime. After physical death one will not have a conscious mind. The ultimate effort needs to be toward aligning Self with the superconscious mind and becoming compatible with one's Creator. In this way one creates his or her own home in superconscious mind and lives in the heavenly Father's mansion. As the Bible says, *"In my Father's house there are many mansions"* which is to live in compatibility with one's Creator.

The Sadducees believed there is no resurrection. The idea of the resurrection as physical bodies getting up out of their graves and walking around is a very physically engrossed manner of approaching this section. The true resurrection is the resurrection of consciousness from its dormancy,

Notes:

stagnancy, and no-change to the continuous motion and awareness of true life. True life is awareness of one's real Self as the driver and motivating force for the physical body. When one's consciousness is resurrected out of engrossment in the five senses then the mind is free to contemplate and understand God and creation. The number seven is the number of control. The basic issue of this passage is an evaluation; to determine which aspect of the subconscious will have control and which subconscious aspect will be committed to the conscious mind. When and as the Self gains awareness of the true purpose of life, all aspects of subconscious mind are united within conscious awareness and Self is prepared for Enlightenment. At the final stage of moving beyond the limitations of the conscious mind there is no marriage of man and woman because the consciousness has been resurrected and now resides with full superconscious fulfillment and I Am awareness. Therefore, all divisions of mind and all minds exist in eternal, continuous union and creation. The Self has in effect gone beyond the subconscious mind (man) and conscious mind (woman) to have superconscious awareness of creation (God in heaven). Creation occurs from forward motion (living) not from stagnancy or attachment to the past (dead). Memory consists of mental images of the past. Memories of the past will not propel one to enlightenment. The One Living God is I Am. The motion of one's true identity must move forward through a combination of imagination and will.

> [34] *When the Pharisees heard he had silenced the Sadducees, they gathered together.* [35] *Then one of them, who was a lawyer, asked him a question, testing him, saying,* [36] *Teacher, which commandment is the greatest law?* [37] *Jesus said to him, You will love the Lord your God with all your heart, and with all your soul, and with all your mind.* [38] *This is the first and greatest commandment.* [39] *And the second is like it, You will love your neighbor as yourself.* [40] *From these*

two commandments come all the law and the prophets.

Jesus added his own commandment because he said, *"I came to fulfill what was already given."* His commandment was *"You will love your neighbor as your Self."* Jesus adds the quality of complete love to all his teachings, indicating that he was as great as Moses, and even greater, because Jesus connected all ten commandments with the Golden Rule, a cord of love so that others might benefit. This shows a maturation of the quality of love given to Jesus by his mother Mary. To increase the ability to love Self and therefore others, practice discipline, still the mind, and consider Self and the soul important rather than only focusing on the physical body, physical Self, and physical production. Jesus (the Knower) added his own commandment which fulfilled and completed the learning of the practical application of the image-making faculty. The next complete step in evolution is to be fully Enlightened. To achieve this, one must be a world server which is to serve the world. All great spiritual leaders who have found Enlightenment have also been great teachers and have taught the Universal Truths and inner secrets of the mind to those willing to learn. They taught as many people as were willing to learn. Teaching is part of the process of becoming Enlightened.

Exodus 19: [25] *So Moses went down to the people and told them this.* [20:1] *Then God delivered all these commandments* [2] *I, the Lord, am your God, who brought you out of the land of Egypt, that place of slavery.* [3] *You shall not have other gods besides me.* [4] *You shall not carve idols for yourselves in the shape of anything in the sky above or on the earth below or in the waters beneath the earth;* [5] *you shall not bow down before them or worship them. For I, the Lord, your God, am a jealous God, inflicting punishment for their father's wickedness on the children of those who hate me, down to the third and fourth generation;* [6] *but bestowing mercy down to the thousandth generation, on the children of those who love me and keep my commandments.* [7] *You shall not take the name of the Lord, your God, in vain. For the Lord will not leave him unpunished who takes his name in vain.* [8] *Remember to keep the Sabbath day Holy.* [9] *Six days you may labor and do all your work,* [10] *but the seventh day is the Sabbath of the Lord, your God. No work may be done then either by you, or your son or daughter, or your male or female slave, or your beast, or by the alien who lives with you.* [11] *In six days the Lord made the heavens and the earth, the sea and all that is in them, but on the seventh day he rested. That is why the Lord has blessed the Sabbath day and made it Holy.* [12] *Honor your father and your mother, that you may have a long life in the land which the Lord, your God, is giving you. [13] You shall not kill. [14] You shall not commit adultery. [15] You shall not steal. [16] You shall not bear false witness against your neighbor. [17] You shall not covet your neighbor's house. You shall not covet your neighbor's wife, nor his male or female slave, nor his ox or ass, nor anything else that belongs to him.*

Yahweh (Hebrew) translated as Lord (English) in the Bible is I Am who is learning to be a creator. Lord symbolizes I AM. Egypt, that place of slavery, indicates one's engrossment in the five physical senses. It is of utmost importance that each individual, each person, come to learn to image I AM. This means to use the imaging faculty, otherwise known as visualization or imagination, to create a mental picture of Self as Enlightened; with Christ awareness or consciousness made in the image and likeness of one's creator. The full attention is to remain on imaging Enlightenment to whatever degree one is capable. This may be in the form of concentration on an artist's conception of Jesus, Gautama the Buddha, or whoever one considers to be the epitome of Enlightenment.

The word God (English) is a translation of the word EL (Hebrew, plural Elohim) beginning with *Genesis* Chapter One. God is the English version of the German word for God; Gott. One is not to give their image-making faculty to spending time creating images of physical desires and sensory gratification. The majority of the imagination is to be used for creating the Godhood within. To name anything is to identify it. To take the name of the Lord, your God, in vain is to discredit and to mutilate the image that one holds of Self becoming Enlightened. Therefore, identify and understand Enlightenment and move into one's imaged form of knowing I AM.

In *Genesis* Chapter One we find that the Lord (Yahweh) did not make the heavens and the earth. Rather it was God (Elohim) who made the heavens and earth in six days and on the seventh day He (God-Elohim) rested. Six is the number of service showing that creation is and was an act of service by Elohim (God) to I Am (mankind). The number seven symbolizes control. The seventh day being a day of rest symbolizes there is a need for a time of assimilation for each learning. Reasoning is used with the experiences, combined with teaching the learning to others (six = service) and then assimilating the full use of that experience.

The fourth commandment is an admonition to assimilate all learning from all experiences of creation. Father and mother of the fifth commandment symbolize the aggressive and receptive factors of the superconscious mind. This commandment is an admonition to fulfill the plan held in superconscious mind for one's evolvement as a creator.

The meaning of the commandment you shall not kill is to be productive in all you do. Never destroy or restrict learning opportunities.

You shall not commit adultery is a command to maintain the commitment between the conscious and subconscious minds so the soul can evolve.

You shall not steal is the directive to always add value to the permanent Self. This means to always create permanent Self understanding from every experience.

You shall not bear false witness against your neighbor means to cause one's thoughts, words, and actions to match and align. It is the directive to make all one's actions and thoughts produce greater Truth within Self.

The tenth commandment is a directive to eliminate jealousy from the life. It is the directive to match willpower with desire in order to produce direction of growth and motion so that permanent learning can occur. Imaging the Self evolving to be a creator combined with love of all creation sums up the ten commandments. The Lord your God is I AM. Love is the complete fulfillment of giving and receiving finding its fulfillment in cooperation, and enhancing all of creation. Symbolically, whole heart is the action of using every understanding by the thinker to build further Self understanding. Whole soul is the use of the full force and energy of one's subconscious mind and past understandings permanently stored there. The phrase "all your mind" is indicative of the necessity of utilizing conscious, subconscious, and superconscious minds, which are the three divisions of mind. Mind is the vehicle of consciousness. Mind is the vehicle I Am employs to gain experience for further evolutionary momentum.

Your neighbor, as given by Jesus in his second commandment, is every aspect of Self as well as all of creation. The knower has thus directly and succinctly indicated the proper place for one's attention as well as the exact perspective needed by the thinker for Self evolution and expansion of consciousness. In order to cause the greatest and most rapid spiritual progress and evolutionary growth, each individual by necessity must direct all of one's learning and permanent understanding, one's soul that inhabits the physical body, and one's superconscious, subconscious, and conscious minds in alignment to know the whole Self, I Am. Thereby one can gain the Christ or Cosmic consciousness. Each individual will also learn to care for and give to all the rest of creation. The whole of Universal Law and the Universal Truths form the structure of mind. The Universal Laws and Truths are formed from the Universal Principles.

> *[41] While the Pharisees were gathered together, Jesus asked them, [42] Saying, What is your opinion of the Messiah? whose son is he? They said to him, The son of David. [43] Then he said to them, How then does David in spirit call him Lord, saying, [44] A Lord said to my Lord, sit at my right hand, while I pin your enemies underneath your feet? [45] If David then calls him Lord, how is he his son? [46] No man was able to answer him a word, therefore no one dared from that day forward to ask him any more questions.*

The last part of this chapter called *The Son of David*, deals with the issue of Jesus putting the question to the Pharisees, "Whose son is the Messiah?" They answer David because the Messiah, who is the savior, Jesus the Knower, is supposed to be descended from David. David was a great king of the physical existence and Jesus is to be a great king of the spiritual existence. Jesus is of the lineage of David. He is of the line of Judah, also David was of the lineage of Judah. David was an ancestor of Jesus through his physical or earthly father, Joseph, so Jesus quotes, *"A Lord said to my Lord sit at my right hand while I pin your enemies underneath your feet."* The Lord is, I Am, with a righteous purpose in alignment with the Creator. Tell your enemies (unproductive aspects of Self) that your restrictions are conquered. Get your own conscious ego, the little lord, the little I am, the conscious ego, in alignment with the true I AM. The word *ego* in Greek means *I AM*. Cause the two egos to be in alignment. All restrictions, limitations, and habits that are one's enemies need to be under foot so they are under the control of a firm, spiritual foundation.

Jesus is quoting in verse forty-four from the *Book of Psalms* in the *Old Testament* of the Bible. More specifically Jesus is quoting from *Psalms 110:1*. From *Psalms* Chapter 110:1, *"the Lord said to my Lord"* is literally and exactly translated as *"The oracle of the Lord (Yahweh) for my Lord."* "My Lord" is a Hebrew phrase used when a subject addresses his superior such as when a knight would address a duke by referring to him as "my Lord". In medieval Europe one of a lower station in life would address someone of a higher station as "my Lord." At the time of Jesus, King David was universally recognized as the author of this Psalm. This Psalm was also accepted as referring to the Messiah, the anointed one, the savior who was to come and save the people of Israel.

> *Psalms 110: [1]The Lord said unto my Lord, Sit at my right hand, until I make your enemies your footstool. [2] The Lord shall send the rod of your strength out of Zion: and you shall rule in the midst of your enemies. [3] Yours is princely power in the day of your birth, in holy splendor; before the daystar, like the dew, I have begotten you. [4] The Lord has sworn, and will not repent, You are a priest forever after the order of Melchizedek. [5] The Lord at your right hand shall strike through kings in the day of his wrath. [6] He shall judge among the heathen, he shall fill the places with the dead bodies; he shall wound the heads over many countries. [7] He shall drink of the brook in the wayside: therefore shall he lift up his head.*

David, the writer of this Psalm addresses the Messiah (Jesus) as his superior by saying, *"The Lord said to my Lord."* In other words David calls the Messiah *"my Lord"* showing that King David accepts and understands the knower's authority and superiority over David, the reasoning faculty. Jesus' point is that the Messiah, the knower, must be David's (reasoning) superior, instead of being his son or lesser.

Evolution is a forward moving process. This is why Homo sapiens are superior in reasoning abilities to Homo erectus. This is why hybrid corn produces more bushels per acre of corn than Indian or native corn. This is why the primates have evolved hands with opposing thumbs and larger brains than their forebears. A descendant does not have to be less than its ancestors. In fact, we would expect for one or more of the lineages proceeding from an ancestor to exceed that of its predecessors! And this is the answer to the question that Jesus called forth that the Pharisees were unable to answer!

As stated earlier Yahweh is interpreted in the English language as Lord. The oracle of Yahweh-Lord is communication from I AM to the productive conscious mind. An oracle communicates a message that is universal and is Truth. What is superior to reasoning? Reasoning can be used only to conquer the physical existence symbolized by Rajas gunas of the *Bhagavad Gita*. A true reasoner will transcend the conditional, conscious mind limited Self and will use reasoning to build permanent memory called understandings. David symbolizes reasoning. I AM indicates and communicates to the knower the need to remain righteous or productive (right hand). Each person has as the purpose for being in a physical body to produce Self understanding and move toward full Enlightenment. In time and with this effort, you will gain control of unproductive attitudes and aspects transforming them into full use of mind, aspects of Self, and a strong spiritual foundation.

Zion symbolizes superconscious mind. True power comes from fulfillment of the blueprint of creation held in superconscious mind. Lamsa translates daystar as *"I have begotten thee as a child of the ages!"* One begotten of God is I AM. A child of the ages is one willing to cause new learning continuously. Jesus the Knower is to be a priest forever, after the order of Melchizedek. Melchizedek never died. He was so highly exalted above Abraham that he could bless Abraham. Abraham even gave Melchizedek, King of Salem, one-tenth of his treasures as a tithe to the Lord. The order of Melchizedek is the commitment to Superconscious mind. The order of Jeru-Salem is a commitment to the conscious mind. The wayside in verse seven is the physical existence in which humanity is entrapped. To lift up the head of the knower is to know Self as creator and to identify one's full and complete identity.

In answer to the question of verse forty-five, *Matthew* Chapter Twenty-two, one needs to be continually initiating continuous, forward, motion of learning in the physical existence. Then one will always be greater today than yesterday, and will carry reasoning to its ultimate fulfillment which is to recognize thought as cause. As you think so you become, as you image so will you become. A Pharisee can never answer the question posed by the knower because a Pharisee refuses to cause permanent learning and therefore does not understand caused evolvement nor intentional fulfillment of the plan held in the superconscious mind. Therefore, a Pharisee remains bound to physical life and its attachments and entrapments.

Notes:

Symbols and Their Interpretation

Chapter Twenty-Three

1.   Rabbi - the inner Self
2.   Humble - productive ego
3.   Gnat - distracting habit
4.   Camel - habit
5.   Cup - receptivity
6.   Tombs - stagnancy in Self.
7.   Blood - Truth and life force
8.   Viper - dishonest ego
9.   Abel - reasoning from subconscious mind
10.   Zechariah - goal setter

Chapter Twenty-Three

*¹ Then spoke Jesus to the crowds, and to his disciples, ²
Saying, The scribes and the Pharisees sit in Moses' seat: ³
Therefore do whatever they tell you to observe, and do; but
do not follow their example: for they say things and then do
not do them. ⁴ For they bind us with heavy taxes that are
hard to pay, laying them on others shoulders, while they
themselves let no taxes within arm's length of them. ⁵ All
their works they do in order to be recognized by men: they
widen their phylacteries and enlarge the borders of their
garments, ⁶ They love the uppermost rooms at feasts and
the chief seats in the synagogues, ⁷ And greetings in the
markets, and to be called by men, Rabbi, Rabbi. ⁸ You should
avoid that title Rabbi: for one among you is the teacher and
the rest are learners. ⁹ And call no man upon the earth your
father: for only one is your Father, the one in heaven.*

Moses symbolizes the effective use of the imagination. The scribes
represent the memory experience of Truth stored in the brain. The thinker
employs the image-making faculty to move toward and into the thought form.
As this occurs, the brain records this forward progression as memory. Brain
memories of and by themselves produce no new growth. The Pharisees represent those aspects of Self who say what should be done but do not practice
it themselves. This is why the knower tells the crowds (representing many
aspects of Self) not to follow the example of the scribes and Pharisees. Memory
thoughts and words of Truth will do no permanent, lasting good until they are
applied and practiced to make the Truths a part of Self that can be stored as
subconscious, permanent understanding. Observation, attention, and perception are valuable and important when supported by will, desire, effort, and
discipline to change; then they produce forward motion and an expansive
consciousness in the life. Without change and growth, experiences have limited and temporary meaning.

Garments and robes represent one's outer expression, in other words
the way we present ourselves to others. To widen and lengthen one's garments is to place one's attention more and more on trying to impress others

outwardly without causing true transformation and growth within. The word Rabbi means teacher, but only Jesus who symbolizes the knower can be the teacher of Self. All other aspects need to be willing to learn of Self and grow in Self awareness. Father in heaven is the spirit of Self existing in superconscious mind. The Pharisees refuse to practice what they preach and say. They have good productive words stored in their brain but refuse to avail themselves of the wisdom and Truth of the *Old Testament*. The Pharisees and Sadducees represent temporary information, stored in the brain rather than practiced and applied for the betterment of the whole Self. By its temporary nature, there is nothing of permanent value. Jesus uses the Pharisees and Sadducees to illustrate the need for activity and practice for building that which is permanent. One must practice and apply Truth in one's life to make Truth real and alive in one's Self and life.

> [10] *Avoid being called teachers. Only one is your teacher, the Messiah.*

The one among you who is your teacher is I AM whose plan is held in superconscious mind. *The one* of verse 9 symbolizes I AM. *Father in heaven* is the authority aspect of Self that exists in superconscious mind. Through following the plan held in superconscious mind while listening to the direction of the soul residing in subconscious mind and causing the conscious mind to be productive in the physical life, one can follow the example of the superconscious mind in order for it to fulfill the master plan for Enlightenment. The inner teacher is the superconscious Self.

> [11] *For he that is greatest among you will be your servant.* [12] *And whoever will exalt himself will be abased; and he that will humble himself will be exalted.*

Whoever humbles himself will be exalted because he is the one who serves all. To be a world server is to dedicate the Self toward becoming Enlightened.

Service and Enlightenment go hand in hand. Teaching Self understanding and mind go hand in hand with Enlightenment. The humble person is willing to listen thereby receiving new knowledge. The egoic person thinks they already know all therefore they refuse to listen and receive new knowledge and new experience. Why is service so important to the expansion of consciousness? Service is the activity of moving beyond one's constrictions and limitations. Service is the means by which one can expand beyond the confines of his or her own limited thinking. By giving to something greater than one's Self, one expands one's consciousness beyond oneself. The one who serves others by teaching them to go beyond and transcend the limited, egoic-bound conscious mind is the one who grows in consciousness. The teacher is the one who gives their time, effort, and attention so that others might grow and expand their consciousness. In the process, the teacher clarifies in the conscious mind the understandings stored in the subconscious mind. The two minds of such a teacher become aligned and the reciprocating action of the functions of the two minds come into alignment.

The one who foolishly attempts to build the Self up on dishonest pride will find the world comes crashing down on them. The one who is consistently honest with Self will find the steps of soul development will be sure and the spiritual foundation will be secure. As learning occurs within Self in the conscious mind, the intelligent thinker will cause there to be an overlap of learning in one aspect of Self to another. Learning to be successful in one area of life can be used in another area of life and another aspect of Self by transferring the use of Universal Law and Truth from one area of Self to another. In this way, the whole conscious mind is inundated with the new learning. This new awareness is a full part of the conscious mind personality and will be utilized daily and consistently.

> *13 But woe to you, scribes and Pharisees, you frauds. You shut up the kingdom of God against men: for you neither go in yourselves, nor admitting those who are trying to enter. 14 Shame on you, scribes and Pharisees, you frauds. You devour widows houses, and for a pretense make long prayer: therefore you will receive the greater damnation. 15 Disgrace to you, scribes and Pharisees, hypocrites for you travel over sea and land to make a single convert; and when he is converted, you make a devil of him twice as wicked as yourselves. 16 Woe unto you, you blind guides, who say, Whoever will swear by the temple, it is nothing; but whoever will swear by the gold of the temple, that is what counts. 17 You blind fools: for which is greater, the gold or the temple that sanctifies the gold? 18 Whoever will swear by the altar, it is nothing; but whoever swears by the gift that is upon it, he is guilty. 19 You fools and blind: for which is greater, the*

Notes:

> gift, or the altar that makes the gift
> sacred? [20] Whoever therefore will
> swear by the altar, swears by it, and
> by all things thereon. [21] Whoever will
> swear by the temple, swears by it and
> by him that dwells therein. [22] He who
> will swear by heaven, swears by the
> throne of God and by Him who sits
> thereon. [23] Woe unto you, scribes and
> Pharisees, hypocrites for singling out
> the mint and herbs and seeds, and
> omitting the weightier matters of the
> law like judgment, mercy, and faith:
> these are the parts you should have
> done, and then the others shouldn't
> be omitted.

The conscious mind cannot go into the inner levels of mind. Consciousness uses the conscious mind and sub-conscious mind with awareness to move into the subconscious mind with permanent understanding. Thus the individual causes *awareness* of the whole Self. Thus, the conscious mind must be honest in order to be productive. One who believes the physical existence to be where security or fulfillment resides will not enter into the kingdom of God (superconscious awareness). A Pharisee or hypocrite — an aspect of Self that says one thing and practices another; who presents itself in one way but inwardly thinks differently — will remain physically bound and entrapped in the physical. A Pharisaical aspect of Self that is not made to be productive cannot possibly hope to aid or improve other aspects. Only through honesty with Self and all aspects of Self, can the individual move forward in steps of evolutionary growth. The dishonest conscious ego, called the devil or Satan in the <u>Bible</u>, will continue to take the physically engrossed person further and deeper down into the engrossment of the senses unless, through discipline and the help of a teacher, it is caused to be honest.

Gold represents value, while the temple of God symbolizes the attention of Self being on using the mind to know creation. To swear by the altar of the temple is to verbally — and mentally with one's full attention — commit to knowing mind and creation. To be sacred is to be Holy or consecrated to God, symbolizing the whole mind. The attention directed on using the whole mind to understand creation and consciousness is the greatest value one can gain. Tithes on mint, herbs, and seeds represent giving to others or to God while expecting to gain physical returns as subconscious mind does its duty of aiding the conscious mind to fulfill its desires without any thought of change or expansion of consciousness. Mint, herbs, and seeds symbolize subconscious existence and show up as psychic experiences. What really matters however is not so much psychic experiences as understanding Universal Law (law), karma (justice), change (mercy), and imagination (faith). These need to be practiced without neglecting one's basic physical needs.

> [24] *You blind guides, which strain at a gnat, yet swallow a camel.* [25] *Woe unto you, scribes and Pharisees, hypocrites for you make clean the outside of the cup and the platter, but within they are full of extortion and lustful appetites.* [26] *You blind Pharisee, cleanse first that which is within the cup and platter, that the outside of them may be clean also.*

Both gnat and camel symbolize habits. Gnats symbolize small, bothersome idiosyncrasies that distract one from the true ideals. Camels symbolize large and strong compulsions, representing the refusal to reason and use free will to make new and different decisions. Cup symbolizes one's receptivity or ability to receive. Extortion and lust are those experiences and possessions gathered for their own sake or so one can look good to others in the environment. To cleanse the inside of the cup is to rid the Self of all prejudices, biases, and negative attitudes so that one can learn to receive in a manner that is productive and without negative judgements. When the thoughts and attitudes are productive, the experiences of Self will be productive.

> [27] *Woe unto you, scribes and Pharisees, hypocrites for you are like whitewashed tombs, which indeed appear beautiful on the outside, but within are full of dead mens bones and of all kinds of filth.* [28] *Even so you also outwardly appear righteous unto men, but within you are full of hypocrisy and iniquity.* [29] *Woe unto you, scribes and Pharisees, hypocrites because you build the tombs of the prophets, and decorate the monuments of the saints,* [30] *And say, If we had lived in the days of our fathers, we would not have been partakers with them in the blood of the prophets.* [31] *You are witnesses unto yourselves, that you are the children of those who killed the prophets.* [32] *Take then the measure of your fathers.* [33] *You serpents, you generation of vipers, how can you escape*

Notes:

the condemnation of Gehenna fire?
[34] Behold, I send to you prophets and
wise men and scribes: some of them
you will kill and crucify; some of
them will you scourge in your synagogues and persecute them from city
to city: [35] Until retribution overtakes
you for all the righteous blood shed
upon the earth, from the blood of
righteous Abel to the blood of
Zechariah's son of Barachias, whom
you killed between the temple and the
altar. [36] Verily I say unto you, All
these things will come back upon this
generation. [37] O Jerusalem, Jerusalem, you that kill the prophets, and
stone them which are sent unto you,
how often I wanted to gather your
children together, even as a hen gath-
ers her chickens under her wings, but
you refused me. [38] Behold, you will
find your temple deserted. [39] For I
say unto you, You will not see me from
this time forward, till you will say,
Blessed is he who comes in the name
of the Lord.

In the Universal Language of Mind, tombs,
dead men, bodies, and corpses indicate mental stagnancy and attachment to old, worn out ways of thinking. Changes have been made in the past but there still
exists attachment to the old while trying to pretend to
be growing and moving forward in the present. This
misuse of old memories stored in the brain are symbolized by the scribes and the Pharisees. No productive growth is made by trying to live in old memory
pictures of the past. The only place to grow, learn, and
live is in the present. By living fully in the present,
one can build and practice the qualities needed to become a whole functioning Self. It is through this process that one learns, grows, and gains the Christ within.
What is referred to as hell in the King James version
and Gehenna in the Catholic version is the place where
all the refuse and trash was burned outside of Jerusa-

lem. Fire, which is used to burn trash, represents expansion in dream symbols. When the conscious mind refuses to learn and grow for too long a time then the desires will put Self in situations which are unpleasant, reducing the options and choices available. This restricts one's Self so much that it is eventually viewed as an unpleasant, limited, and unwanted position. Desiring to move out of the painful situation, Self <u>will</u> change. Sooner or later everyone will change. The quicker that change is caused to happen, the more pleasant is growth. The longer change is avoided, the less pleasant and seemingly more difficult growth will be. The Christ awareness will not be perceived until one is willing to identify with the inner Self and to utilize the inner Self for Enlightenment and awareness — fully and consistently — every waking minute of every day.

Symbols and Their Interpretation

Chapter Twenty-Four

1. World - the whole mind
2. Wars - conflict within Self
3. Nation - groups of aspects with similar qualities
4. Famine - refusal to learn from one's experiences
5. Birth - creation and manifestation of new idea
6. Daniel - goal setter, understanding of Language of Mind
7. Winter - infancy
8. Human - capable of physical reasoning
9. Lightning - sudden new awareness
10. Vultures - subconscious thoughts that practice recycling
11. Moon - subconscious awareness, the abode of the soul
12. Stars - conscious awareness
13. Door - opening to inner levels of mind
14. Clouds of heaven - superconscious awareness
15. Hosts of heaven - superconscious aspects
16. Trumpet - chakra; energy transformer
17. Four winds - four levels of subconscious mind
18. Noah - I AM
19. Ark - universal principles, laws and Truths
20. Drunk - passive, weak will

Chapter Twenty-Four

¹ Jesus went out, and departed from the temple: and his disciples came up to show him the buildings of the temple area. ² Jesus said unto them, Do you see all these things? verily I say to you, There will not be left one stone upon another here, it will all be torn down.

Everything that has been accepted as a limitation previously in the conscious mind is now to be given up and left behind for it no longer serves as a useful structure. Complete overcoming of the structure of physical entrapment is the next major step for the knower. Everything associated with limitation in the physical existence and the conscious mind is overturned as consciousness is expanded beyond any confines. During Jesus' time, the temple was controlled by the Pharisees (hypocrites), scribes (memory and brain pathways), and Sadducees (belief that the physical life is all there is to one's existence). In addition, these people were controlled by the Romans under the direction of Herod. Therefore the temple no longer served as a house (mind) of God (creation) rather it was a politically, power-based, controlling factor ruling the Jewish people -- the Pharisees and Sadducees who refuse to believe one can gain Christ consciousness this lifetime. The will (stone) together with the image-making faculty will completely transform the process by which mind (temple) is used. The mind is to be used as a vehicle for physically entrapped I AM to free itself and rise to heights of Divine Radiance.

³ As he sat upon the mount of Olives, the disciples came unto him privately, saying, Tell us, when will these things occur? What will be the sign of your coming; the culmination of time in the world? ⁴ Jesus answered and said unto them, Take heed that no man deceive you. ⁵ For many will come in my name, saying, I am the Messiah; and will deceive many. ⁶ You will hear of wars and rumors of wars: see that you are not troubled: for all these things must come to pass, that is how it is at the end. ⁷ For nation will rise

Notes:

against nation, and kingdom against kingdom: and there will be famines, and pestilences, and earthquakes, in many places. [8] All these are the beginning of the birth pangs. [9] Then will they deliver you over to be tortured, kill you: and you will be hated of all nations for my names sake. [10] Then will many falter and betray one another, and will hate one another. [11] Many false prophets will rise, and will deceive many. [12] Because of the increase of lawlessness, the love of many will grow cold. [13] But he that will endure to the end, the same will know salvation. [14] This gospel of the kingdom will be preached in all the world for a witness to all nations; only after this will the end of the world come.

The Mount of Olives represents an elevated state of consciousness achieved by the knower. This high place in mind is utilized effectively to produce greater knowledge and wisdom for Self. The consciousness of Self exists with awareness of subconscious existence. Most everyone would like to have some indication of what is to occur today, tomorrow, a year from now or ten years from now. It is not pleasant to unknowingly await unexpected events and effects in one's life; for then one re-acts to these actions finding little control or pleasure in trying to use events after they have already occurred. Many people and many negative aspects of Self will try to convince the conscious mind that terrible and painful events are about to occur portending disaster and fear. Yet fear, terror, doubt, and indecision are not the true ways of mind and Self. The real Self identifies with courage and love. The subconscious mind knows only forward motion and adding to its storehouse of understood experiences called permanent memory. There is nothing destructive or painful in this knowing process.

Groups of aspects (nations) will have conflict with other groups of aspects. The insecurity and limitation of the conscious mind and the physical body will react to loss of control over temporary attachments and slavery to the five senses. The subconscious mind, the soul, will fight to align the conscious mind with the duty and purpose of the subconscious mind Self. Changes will occur and Self will evolve as the expansion of consciousness proceeds. These are the early signs of the birthing of a new idea of Enlightenment as the purpose of life dawns within the Self.

The birth of the new awareness may seem like torture as the conscious mind of Self attempts to free itself of the shackles of limitation. Those aspects of the knowing Self, who commit to only those experiences that will expand one's knowledge of Self and consciousness, may find various reactions of anger, hate, passivity, and fear arising as one's habits tend to try to assert themselves. It will be easy to misuse one's developing image-making faculty (imagination) by employing visualization to accumulate physical possessions solely for the reason of sensory gratification and a false sense of security. However, the one who constantly holds in mind the image of the Enlightened One who desires to become compatible to his Creator will gain salvation; which is freedom from entrapment and Enlightenment as a spiritual being. When this occurs, all aspects of Self will be trans-formed and trans-figured as en-light-en-ment and inner awareness is accepted throughout one's being. Then the culmination of time will have come, meaning there will no longer be any need for reincarning in the physical schoolroom. The end of one's existence as Reasoning Man arrives as Self moves into the next stage of evolution called Intuitive Man (man meaning thinker, not male or female bodies).

Only after this awareness is achieved will freedom from entrapment occur. The end of the earthly cycle of reincarnation, the end of your entrapment in the physical, will only come when the good news which is discipline, use of the Universal Laws, application of them in your daily life, and using your experience to build permanent understandings, is accomplished. Until the total Self is Enlightened the soul will continue to reincarn and continue to be entrapped, existing within the realm of physical time instead of mental time.

> [15] *When you therefore will see the abominable and destructive desolation, spoken of by Daniel the prophet, stand in the holy place; whoever reads this, let him understand:* [16] *Those in Judea must flee to the mountains:* [17] *Let him who is on the roof of the house not come down to take any thing out of his house:* [18] *Neither let him who is in the field return back to take his cloak.* [19] *Woe unto those that are with child, and to those that are nursing mothers in those days.* [20] *But pray that you will not have to flee in the winter, neither on the Sabbath day:* [21] *For then will be great tribulation, such*

Notes:

> as was not since the beginning of the world to this time, or in all ages to come. [22] *If the period had not been shortened, not a human being would be saved: but for the chosen's sake those days will be shortened.* [23] *Then if any man will say unto you, Lo, here is Christ, or there; believe it not.* [24] *For there will arise false prophets, and false Messiahs, and will show great signs and wonders; so great that, if it were possible, they would deceive the chosen.* [25] *Behold, I have told you before.* [26] *So wherefore if they say to you, Behold, he is in the desert; go not forth: behold, he is in the secret chambers; do not believe it.* [27] *For as the lightning comes out of the east, and shines even unto the west; so will also the coming of the Son of man be.* [28] *For wherever the carcass is, there will the vultures be gathered together.*

Verse fifteen is a reference to the *Book of Daniel 11:30-31* of the *Old Testament.*

> *Daniel 11* [30] *For the ships of Kittim will come against him:* (the King of the north which is the physical and its entrapped existence) *therefore he will lose heart and retreat. Then he will direct his rage against the holy covenant: so will he do; he will even return, and single out those who forsake the holy covenant.* [31] *And armed forces will move at his command, and they will defile the sanctuary stronghold, and abolish the daily sacrifice, and they will set up the abomination that makes desolation.*

The knower is using a reference from the *Old* or inner mind *Testament* to give authority and fulfillment to his own mission as the Messiah; the one who is to save his people from their sins. The Holy place is one's attention focused on knowing the whole mind. Uncleanness and desolation is the refusal of the physically entrapped individual, who has free will, to use the mind and imagination productively to move forward in the evolutionary growth of the Self. To pollute the sanctuary is to refuse to use the opportunities available in one's experiences to promote soul growth. Defiling the sanctuary symbolizes the contraction of the mind caused by negative and unproductive thoughts. Destructive, limited, and unproductive thoughts pollute the mind of one engrossed in sensory experiences. Accumulation of unused physical possessions, without using these items and experiences for the benefit of the whole Self, creates pollution of the mind. For pollution is unused substance. Life is meant to be utilized completely, for the whole Self, so it can be broken down or reduced to its simplest parts while being employed for the quickened evolution of the thinker. Mind substance is reduced to its simplest components through the action of the image-making faculty. Directed imagery draws the Self forward through evolutionary learning. This frees the simplified mind substance to be recycled into subconscious mind where the inner mind begins the process once again of aiding in the manifestation of desires.

Daniel was a prophet of the tribe of Judah. He lived in Babylon at the time the Israelites existed in Babylonian captivity. This time of abominable and destructive desolation arrives for each individual when they realize that living life solely for physical ends does not bring the satisfaction and fulfillment required for a meaningful life. This is the time when each person individually must make a choice of living the life of sensory gratification and solely for physical comfort, or living the life for the greater awareness of Self. The greater accumulation of permanent understanding provides the greatest security, pleasure, joy, and happiness possible. Those in Judea (Judah) symbolize any aspect with enough understanding and awareness of I AM to know one is not a physical body but a soul. Judah knows the need to move away from or to flee the sensory entrapment. Such a one must place Self in a new learning environment conducive to his or her further movement toward Divine awareness. Whatever the level of Self awareness, when the desire to know the meaning and purpose to life occurs, the individual must immediately respond by pursuing the higher knowledge in order to keep from slipping backward into the morass of entrapped humanity.

The mountains referred to in verse sixteen symbolize the need to direct the attention and imagination constantly on something or someone greater than Self. It provides an ideal that one can move toward in order to expand and increase the Self as a son or daughter of the Creator. This is the process that eventually will produce a son of God; for as you think and that which you meditate upon, so you become. Verse seventeen is similar to verse sixteen and symbolizes the need to move forward in one's growth never looking back and never drifting backward. The mountains and roof of the house symbolize one's efforts to gain superconscious awareness, the *"high place in mind."* Field symbolizes subconscious existence. The person who has gained awareness and some understanding of one's existence in subconscious mind as soul, must not try to go backwards to the old way of expressing Self as symbolized by the cloak. One must constantly develop new associations, friendships, and ways of expressing the new awareness in order that Self may be fully established with the new understanding in the conscious mind. Those parts of Self or aspects that are developing new ideas will find there is a need to examine the ideas in the light of discerning if they will add to the total Self. If the ideas and aspects being nurtured will add to one's further growth in awareness as I AM, they must be understood.

The Sabbath represents the completion of a cycle or the completion of a stage of learning. It is the time when one assimilates the learning from the previous experiences and accomplishments. Winter represents a period of assimilation of the experiences and a beginning new growth in Self. The admonition given here is to constantly cause the learning required for soul growth and consistently create the opportunities in one's environment for Self knowledge to occur. When one first realizes the need for more fulfillment than the physical life alone can provide, that person has arrived at the most pivotal time in one's whole soul evolution. It is the time in one's life when he or she has the actual opportunity to quicken spiritual evolution. Thus, one can shorten their time of entrapment from many lifetimes to one or two. When the acceptance of the commitment to quicken one's evolutionary growth is fulfilled then the amount of physical time needed for the movement of the thinker forward from reasoning to spiritual or intuitive man is greatly shortened. The physical time needed for any learning to occur is shortened. Much less time is required because the keys to soul learning are understood and utilized through commitment to Self understanding and Enlightenment. The chosen (or chosen people) symbolize anyone committed, with the highest priority given, to knowing the assignment for this lifetime, fulfilling that assignment, and through this fulfilling the divine plan of creation.

A Messiah is a savior, but nothing will save one from the pains of constriction brought on by a habitual conscious mind refusing to change, except commitment to whole Self Enlightenment. The desert represents the unused parts of one's mind. There is no savior in unused mind. Saving from sins (mistakes) occurs when learning is derived from experience so one no longer creates the error filled ways. East symbolizes the innermost levels of the subconscious mind. The east is very important for it is from the depths of the subconscious mind that one's desires begin to manifest from thought, eventually becoming a part of one's outward physical life. Lightning flashing from east to west symbolizes the dawning of a new awareness moving from the innermost levels of subconscious mind that will eventually develop as full understanding in the conscious mind of one devoted to Self understanding. The Son of Man is such a one. Carcass symbolizes stagnancy caused by having one's attention on the past due to emotional and memory attachments. The vultures symbolize subconscious thoughts assimilating the experiences of the past so that subconscious mind can gain knowledge from those experiences and Self can move forward while releasing the past.

> ^{29} *Immediately after the troubles of those days the sun will be darkened, and the moon will not give her light, and the stars will fall from the skies, and the hosts of heaven will be shaken loose:* ^{30} *Then will appear the sign of the Son of man in heaven: and then will all the clans of earth strike their breasts, and they will see the Son of man coming on the clouds of heaven with power and great glory.*

The *"Son of man"* symbolizes the thinker (man) who is initiating sustained activity of forward motion towards the goal of knowing the ideal Self. Stress occurs when there is a conflict or dichotomy of opposing goals within the Self. The choice, as presented in the symbolical language of the Bible, is between the temporary false security of physical life as identified with one's five senses, and the permanent — therefore true and real — security of gaining and earning Self understanding. The sun, moon, and stars represent superconscious, subconscious, and conscious awareness respectively. The sun, moon, and stars darkening symbolize one's previous conceptions and limitations are being replaced by a more expansive vantage point. When one enters a new life with the more enlightening experience it brings, there is always a time of adjustment needed to be able to focus on the greater light of awareness. When a person steps from a lighted house to outdoors on a bright day the eyes need time to adjust to the greater light. When the physically engrossed Self realizes a life built only on the idea of physical sensory gratification and possession accumulation can never satisfy, there is a period of darkness as one searches and seeks for the meaning of life.

At each major step of growth there is a test one must pass. This test is the choice between the physical assumptions one has built the life upon and the soul urge impressing itself on the conscious mind. The sign of the Son of Man is the awareness one gains from placing as first priority one's learning, growth and Self understanding. Such a person develops an outshining awareness and a certain authority, such as Jesus portrayed in his teaching. The hosts of heaven represent the thought forms held in superconscious mind that explain and define the plan of creation. The conscious mind is now capable and prepared to understand the secrets of creation of the further Enlightenment of Self. All the clans of earth symbolize all the aspects of Self. The breast or area of the heart on the body symbolizes understanding. The Son of Man coming on the clouds of heaven is the thinker who is constantly initiating new, greater, and therefore different action and motion to understand, direct, and use the Universal Principles of which the plan of creation is constructed. This process grants to the thinker power to control and utilize Self and creation. This is the ultimate glory. This section harkens to *Revelation 22:5 "The night will be no more. They will need no light from lamps or the sun, for the Lord God shall give them light, and they shall reign forever."* It says there will be no need for light of the sun because the light will come from the inner light of the Self. In the last chapter of the *Book of Revelation*, when the awareness is so great within the Self that it shines forth to aid others, the full light of awareness of I Am is even greater than the light of awareness of subconscious or superconscious minds. All divisions of mind are vehicles to be used by I Am. I Am is always greater than conscious, subconscious, or superconscious, or all three together.

> [31] He will send his angels with a great sound of a trumpet, and they will gather together his chosen ones from the four winds, from one end of heaven to the other. [32] Now learn a parable of the fig tree; When his branch is yet tender, and sprouting leaves, you know that summer is

nigh: ³³ *So likewise, when you will see all these things happening, know that he is near, standing at your door.* ³⁴ *Verily I say unto you, This generation will not pass away, till all these things be fulfilled.* ³⁵ *Heaven and earth shall pass away, but my words shall not pass away.*

The four winds symbolize the four levels of the subconscious mind. The angels symbolize thought forms from I AM. A great sound of a trumpet represents the effective awareness, understanding, and evolution of Self to be able to direct the Kundalini through the crown chakra at will. The knower who gains Self understanding will control all of mind — conscious, subconscious, and superconscious. The fig tree represents knowledge and the alignment of subconscious experience. One who is constantly giving understanding to subconscious mind will find the availability of knowledge greatly increases, for the conscious mind of such a one is vastly improved in its capability to receive from the soul or inner Self. The branch which is sprouting leaves symbolizes growth in one's subconscious existence. This can only occur when the conscious mind is productively utilizing reason, combined with will, to gain greater knowledge through greater learning. The one who is familiar with the process of Self learning will discover the ability to become a knower (Jesus) is very near, and is possible during this lifetime. The door symbolizes the doorways into the inner levels of consciousness.

The *"present generation"* of that time did pass away before Jesus physically came again. So the Bible is inaccurate as a report of physical history. The Bible is incorrect and Jesus is incorrect when one tries to interpret the Bible, physically, literally, and historically. However, interpreted in the Universal Language of Mind, the present generation represents *you* — existing *this* lifetime with the opportunity for Enlightenment. The heavens and earth pass away for one who has gained full Self understanding. For such a one there is no more entrapment, no further lessons to gain from the physical experience thus no further need to reincarn. Still the Truth, awareness, and understanding the knower has gained will always exist and reside forever in the Enlightened One. Truth lasts forever. Truth is eternal. Limitations, the conscious mind, and physicalness, are limited and restrictive therefore untrue or only holding the lesser awareness of Truths.

³⁶ *As for the exact day and hour no man knows it, no, not the angels of heaven nor the son, but my Father only.*

Because each person has free will, only he or she decides — through the choice made by the soul — the time of departure from the physical life. One consciously chooses and decides how swiftly to mature as a spiritual being and how quickly to evolve through desire and free will.

Notes:

> [37] *But as the days of Noah were, so will also the coming of the Son of man be.* [38] *For as in the days that were before the flood they were eating and drinking, marrying and giving in marriage, until the day that Noah entered into the ark,* [39] *and knew not until the flood came, and took them all away; so shall also the coming of the Son of man be.* [40] *Then shall two be in the field; the one shall be taken, and the other left.* [41] *Two women will be grinding at the mill; the one will be taken, and the other left.* [42] *So keep awake; for you know not what hour your Lord does come.*

Both the recorded account of Noah and of the coming of the Son of Man indicate a mutation has taken place. The older aspects attempt to retain control so they must be removed or eliminated to facilitate the change. A gardener will pull the weeds out of the garden so the new crop of fruitful plants can grow. The new plants are more tender and not as strong as the weeds, which are the unwanted older and more established plants. The individual is like a gardener. The gardener must root out all the unproductive and stifling parts of Self so that the young, immature and more evolved aspects of Self that are productive can grow and mature.

> [43] *Know this, if the goodman of the house had known in what watch the thief would come, he would have watched and would not have allowed his house to be broken into.* [44] *Therefore be ready: for the Son of man is coming at a time when you least expect it.* [45] *Who then is a faithful and wise servant, whom his lord has made ruler over his household, to give them meat in due season?* [46] *Blessed is that servant, whom his master discovers at work when he returns.* [47]

Verily I say unto you, That he will put him in charge of all his property.

No one knows exactly when they will become Enlightened or exactly when in the life they will have the urge toward caused Enlightenment. Proper perspective indicates one needs to respond to the inner urge immediately. One lifetime is short, yet much can be accomplished. The Self needs to remain in motion to prepare the stilled conscious mind to receive the inner level awareness.

> [48] *But if that evil servant will say in his heart, My master delays his coming;* [49] *And will begin to beat his fellowservants, and to eat and drink with the drunkards;* [50] *The master of that servant will come on a day when he looks not for him, and in an hour that he is not aware of,* [51] *And will punish him severely and will settle with him as is done with the hypocrites: there will be wailing and grinding of teeth.*

To eat and drink with drunkards is to forget who you are, refusing to exercise will power and reasoning thus becoming engrossed in the physical existence and its sensory entrapment. Wailing and grinding of teeth occurs when one experiences the pain of having refused knowledge and learning. The teeth ingest and assimilate the knowledge (food) from experience. This refusal to change and grow causes pain in one's physical existence. Use every moment of every day for learning and growth. Never allow time to be your enemy. Young children learn from everything and have no blockage to their learning. In essence, be prepared to expand your consciousness completely and totally. Use every opportunity to change, grow, mature, discipline, and devote the whole lifetime and attention to knowing the whole Self.

Notes:

Symbols and Their Interpretation

Chapter Twenty-Five

1. Bridesmaid - desire in conscious mind aspects to make full commitment to inner Self
2. Torches - ability to create awareness
3. Sheep - righteous, productive
4. Goats - habits, that protect alignment of the minds such as making a habit of meditation
5. Left - unproductive, repeated mistake
6. Home - superconscious mind and awareness

Chapter Twenty-Five

This chapter is exceptional in that it contains some of Jesus' final parables. Anytime a parable is presented it shows there is an understanding of both the activity of the physical, day-to-day life and of a deeper insight from the mental or spiritual level. Parables are presented outwardly as a story or allegory about a physical event. They always have a hidden and elevated meaning. The use of parables shows there is an understanding of the Universal Language of Mind upon the part of the knower. The knower can explain a concept and Truth in the language of mind because the knower is fluent in the language of inner consciousness. Everything in this chapter revolves around the day and the hour of the coming of the master — meaning Jesus, the knower, the Enlightened One.

> [1] *The reign of God may be likened to ten bridesmaids, which took their torches, and went forth to meet the bridegroom.* [2] *Five of them were wise, and five were stupid.* [3] *They that were stupid took their torches, and took no oil with them:* [4] *But the wise took oil in their vessels with their torches.* [5] *While the bridegroom tarried, they all slumbered and slept.* [6] *At midnight there was a cry made, Behold, the bridegroom comes; go you out to meet him.* [7] *Then all those bridesmaids arose, and trimmed their torches.* [8] *The stupid said to the wise, Give us of your oil; for our torches are gone out.* [9] *But the sensible ones replied, Not so; there may not be enough for us and you: but rather go to them that sell oil, and buy for yourselves.* [10] *While they went to buy, the bridegroom came; and they that were ready went in with him to the wedding: and the door was shut out.* [11] *Afterward came also the other bridesmaids, saying, Lord, Lord, open to us.* [12] *But he answered and said, Verily I say unto you, I do not know you.* [13] *So stay awake, keep your eyes open; for you know neither the day nor the hour wherein the Son of man comes.*

The essence of the story or the parable of the ten bridesmaids is always keep your awareness moving and expanding. Always apply your awareness and perception to seek and create the opportunities for learning and growth. Align the inner and outer minds making the commitment to know the whole Self. The wedding indicates the commitment made between the inner or subconscious mind and the outer or conscious mind. Torches are a tool for causing awareness (light). The bridesmaids who had extra oil for their torches represent aspects of the conscious mind who are without experience concerning harmony with subconscious mind yet prepared for the greater awareness available. The wise and sensible bridesmaids represent those aspects of the conscious mind who make every effort to gain greater awareness through learning about, and imaging greater commitment to, their soul or subconscious mind.

The reign of God is called by the Lamsa <u>Bible</u>, *"the kingdom of heaven"*. The kingdom of heaven is superconscious awareness, also called Christ consciousness or cosmic consciousness. A step to gaining Christ consciousness is causing consistent awareness of the learning in each experience. Another step is the full commitment to know Self, inner and outer. The door symbolizes the doorway to the inner mind. This is the method of movement from outer to inner levels of mind. Eyes symbolize perception. To keep one's eyes open is to constantly give the full attention to the experience at hand in order that mental perception can be applied to the problem or situation. Use one's perception fully to gain the learning necessary to move into Enlightenment.

[14] *For the kingdom of heaven is as a man travelling into a far country, who called his own servants and gave them his goods.* [15] *Unto one he gave five thousand silver pieces, to another two, and to another one he gave one thousand silver pieces. Then he departed on a journey.* [16] *He who had received the five talents went and traded with the same, and*

made them another five thousand silver pieces. [17] *And like-*
wise he that had received two, he also gained another two.
[18] *But he that had received one went and dug in the earth,*
and hid his lord's money. [19] *After a long time the lord of*
those servants came and reckoned with them. [20] *He who*
had received five thousand silver pieces came and brought
another five thousand silver pieces, saying, Lord, you de-
livered unto me five thousand silver pieces: behold, I have
gained beside them five thousand silver pieces more. [21] *His*
lord said unto him, Well done, you good and faithful ser-
vant: you have been faithful over a few things, I will make
you ruler over many things: enter into the joy of your lord.
[22] *He also who had received two thousand silver pieces came*
and said, Lord, you delivered unto me two thousand silver
pieces: behold, I have gained two thousand silver pieces
beside them. [23] *His lord said unto him, Well done, good and*
faithful servant; you have been faithful over a few things, I
will make you ruler over many things: enter into the joy of
your lord.

The parable of the silver and the man going on a journey is the story of the value of using everything in the physical existence without attachment so one can gain the abundance of understanding the expansion of consciousness as a creator. The man on a journey symbolizes Self in the journey of life. This journey can include many lifetimes. The purpose for incarning is to build permanent understandings of Self and creation. Servants are aspects of Self that do one's bidding. An aspect's abilities are dependent on one's use of that particular part of Self this lifetime.

To one servant he disbursed five thousand silver pieces, which the Lamsa and King James translations interpret as *"five talents"*. In ancient Hebrew times a talent was a unit of weight used for measurement equal to 93 3/4 pounds. So five talents of silver was a lot of money in Biblical times. Five is the number that symbolizes reasoning. The servant who received five talents and created five more talents of silver from the first five, symbolizes the aspect and area of life in which one uses reasoning to wield the Law of Cause and Effect thereby producing not only greater abundance in the life but greater and more elevated reasoning. The highest reasoning moves the Self closer to the sixth day of creation which is application of the intuitive faculty. The aspect who produced two more talents of silver or two thousand pieces of silver from the two he was given symbolizes one's ability to gain in understanding of the Universal Law of Duality. The aggressive and receptive principles make it possible for all of the structure of creation to exist. This one knows how to initiate new and different activity towards desire creation and ideal realization. Such a one also carries the ability to receive without limitation or constriction. In this highly developed aspect, learning through experience occurs unimpeded and full processing of learning occurs. This makes for rapid understanding of the whole Self and relationship to all of creation. The aspect of Self who received one talent of silver (each according to his ability) represents that area of Self that does not understand receptivity. Therefore activity occurs without openness to receive. Then a part of Self thinks, I have to hoard what I have because I will never receive more. This hoarding, which is a refusal to produce energy, is motion which retards the movement of Self and keeps Self bound to the object of attachment.

The servant (aspect) addresses the master as Lord which symbolizes I AM. I AM is lord of all aspects of Self. I Am is the one true identity of Self, I AM is to rule and direct all aspects of Self, thus unifying them in the progressive march of creation and forward evolution. The one who uses and applies reasoning will create greater spheres of influence to practice and learn. The one who uses both the initiatory quality and the receivership quality will find their opportunities for further investment in Self increased.

> [24] *Then he who had received the one thousand silver pieces came and said, Lord, I knew that you are a hard man, reaping where you have not sown, and gathering where you have not scattered:* [25] *And I was afraid, and went and hid your money in the earth: lo, here is your money back.* [26] *His lord answered, saying, You wicked and slothful servant, you knew that I reap where I did not sow, and gather where I have not scattered:* [27] *You ought therefore to have invested my money with the bankers, and then at my coming I should have received mine own with interest.* [28] *Take therefore the silver from him, and give it unto him who has ten pieces of silver.* [29] *For unto every one that has more will be given, and*

*he will have abundance: but from him that has little it will
be taken away what little he has. ³⁰ Throw this worthless
servant into outer darkness: where there will be wailing and
grinding of teeth.*

Those who have created will create more until they grow rich, while
those who refuse to expand consciousness through creation and Self understanding will lose what they have. Those who have symbolize the ones who
are wielding the Universal Laws and understand the value of the commitment
to the whole Self. As creation is practiced, creation is understood. Self can
then create wealth anytime, anywhere and more and more of it. Once on the
spiritual path, the whole time frame of evolution from the present to full Enlightenment shortens because the keys to causing awareness and the keys to
using Universal Law are understood. Those who have not symbolize the ones
who do not understand the Universal Laws and are not operating in harmony
with the laws. They do not place their learning and growth above wealth,
position, and physical temporary sense gratification. They will lose what
little they have because they are not operating in harmony with Universal
Law. The end result will be they will die and lose all that they thought was so
important such as the temporary, physical objects. Because one does not use
Universal Law, possessions will tend to slip through his or her fingers because life will pass him or her by. The one who refuses to change and grow
finds that life changes and grows faster than they do and therefore life passes
them by.

*³¹ When the Son of man will come in his glory, and all the
holy angels with him, then will he sit upon the throne of his
glory: ³² Before him will be gathered all nations: and he
will separate them into two groups, as a shepherd divides
his sheep from the goats: ³³ He will set the sheep on his
right hand, but the goats on the left. ³⁴ Then will the King
say unto them on his right hand, Come, you blessed of my
Father, inherit the kingdom prepared for you from the foundation of the world: ³⁵ For I was hungry, and you gave me
food: I was thirsty, and you gave me drink: I was a stranger,
and you took me in: ³⁶ Naked, and you clothed me: I was
sick, and you comforted me: I was in prison, and you came
to visit me. ³⁷ Then will the righteous answer him, saying,
Lord, did we see you hungry, and feed you? or thirsty, and
gave you drink? ³⁸ When did we welcome you away from
home and took you in? or naked, and clothed you? ³⁹ Or
when did we see you sick, or in prison, and came to you? ⁴⁰
And the King will answer then and say to them, Verily I say
unto you, As often as you have done it for one of the least of*

Notes:

my brothers, you have done it unto me. [41] *Then will he say also unto them on the left hand, Depart from me, you are cursed into everlasting fire prepared for the devil and his angels:* [42] *For I was hungry, and you gave me no food: I was thirsty, and you gave me no drink:* [43] *I was a stranger, and you did not take me in: naked, and you did not cloth me: sick and in prison, and you did not visit me.* [44] *Then will they also answer him, saying, Lord, when did we see you hungry, or thirsty, or away from home, or naked, or sick, or in prison, and did not minister unto you?* [45] *Then will he answer them, saying, Verily I say unto you, Inasmuch as you refused to do for the least of these, you would not do for me either.* [46] *And these will go away into everlasting punishment: but the righteous into life eternal.*

Angels represent thought forms from I AM moving through the superconscious mind. They are in alignment with the plan of creation. Create strong thought forms of being God-like; then cause actions to match the thoughts. When this thought form occurs within the Self followed with motion then this ideal image is fulfilled.

The Knower draws the analogy of sheep and goats. Sheep are docile creatures. In olden times, shepherds placed a goat with the sheep to protect the sheep. The goats and sheep lived well together. The shepherds kept the goats in the same flock with the sheep because the goats were strong and had an affinity for fighting, so they would protect the sheep as well as themselves from any wild animal that came around such as a wolf or a lion. The goats didn't produce much wool so they were mainly used to protect the sheep. At the time of shearing, the animals were separated — the goats were put on the left, and the animals that produced wool, the sheep that were productive for the shepherd, were put on the right. The right hand, or the right path, or the right side, always indicates what is productive or righteous symbolizing value, abundance, and prosperity for the inner Self. On the left hand side indicates that which is temporary.

The goats symbolize one whose attention is placed on making a habit of productive actions such as meditation. Most people perpetuate mannerisms and habits as a way to attempt to protect themselves from the painful experiences they have received in the past and therefore expect to receive in the future. As the person physically matures, these walls and actions of protection become a barrier to learning and growth. The fort which once protected becomes a prison and you become the prisoner. People go to extreme lengths and behave in strange ways just to maintain their walls of separative, protective behavior. The first step to causing renewed learning is to let one's walls down by giving to others. Then one can begin to receive the new learning. Goats, the non-producing habits, were used to protect the productive, wool-producing sheep. But when one has outgrown protecting Self and is ready to open Self to vast new vistas of consciousness-raising learning, then the walls of protection are seen as restrictions.

As often as you have aided others in your environment you have also aided the Son of Man, here called Lord. The Lord represents I AM. One who is practicing abundance, giving to others, and aiding others is actually learning about the Universal Law of Abundance and how to use it. The Self needs to learn where the real prosperity exists. What you have physically is only temporary. By giving to others one learns what causes personal prosperity and builds security within. Then the understanding of Universal Law is with Self wherever one goes and it is also built as permanent understanding. By filling subconscious mind with understanding, the individual moves closer to the day when there is no longer any need to reincarn or be entrapped in a physical body. The person seriously desiring Enlightenment, and who would make rapid strides in soul awareness, will not ignore any opportunity to learn nor will they ignore any area of Self. Rather they will have and continuously experience -- life eternal.

Notes:

Symbols and Their Interpretation

Chapter Twenty-Six

1. Passover - moving out of entrapment
2. Caiaphas - physical security based on spiritual information
3. Jar of costly perfume - using receptivity to develop and store value
4. Judas Iscariot - the motivating ego
5. 30 pieces of silver - the value of unifying aggressive and receptive qualities
6. Feast of unleavened bread - recognition of the duty and capability of moving out of entrapment by acquiring permanent knowing
7. Covenant - commitment to love all aspects; love your neighbor as your Self
8. Sword - tool for change
9. Sanhedrin - being governed by one's memory and rules

Chapter Twenty-Six

¹ It came to pass, when Jesus finished all these sayings, he said to his disciples, ² You know that after two days time will be the feast of the passover, and the Son of man is to be handed over to be crucified. ³ Then the chief priests, the scribes, and the elders of the people assembled at the palace of the high priest, Caiaphas, ⁴ They all plotted that they might take Jesus by some sly way, and kill him. ⁵ But they said, Not during the festival for fear there might be a riot among the people.

Those who have not been immersed in overinflating their conscious ego, conscious satisfactions, and physical gratifications are willing to change. Those who have put all their value on fake authority, false pride, and physical accumulation, resist the expansion of consciousness that knowing and understanding provide. One who changes produces new more expansive thought images and awareness that overrides the old memory attachments of Self protection and false comfort. Some people hate changing because they dislike themselves. The high priest connotes the highest value that you place upon your physical possessions, spiritual ideas, and physical attachments while still being without commitment to change and caused forward motion soul growth. The physical existence is made of temporary associations rather than permanent interconnectedness.

⁶ When Jesus was in Bethany, at the house of Simon the leper, ⁷ There came unto him a woman having an alabaster jar of costly perfume. She poured it on his head while he sat at the table. ⁸ When his disciples saw it, they were indignant, saying, To what purpose is this waste? ⁹ For this perfume might have been sold for a good price, and the money given to the poor. ¹⁰ When Jesus understood it, he said to them, Why do you criticize the woman? It is a good deed you have done for me. ¹¹ For the poor you will always have with you; but you will not always have me. ¹² For she has poured this perfume on my body and in that contributed to my burial preparation. [13] Verily I say to you, Wherever this good news will be proclaimed in the whole world, what this woman has done will be told as a memorial to her.

This woman represents an aspect of the conscious mind who recognizes the value of the knower; the value of directing one's thoughts toward knowing the whole Self. The head of Jesus symbolizes the identity of the knower. In other words, the woman recognizes who the knower-Jesus is and his tremendous understanding, awareness and enlightenment. The greatest value one can give is their full attention to the knowing quality. If one gives their valuable time and attention solely to the part of Self that refuses to learn, a lifetime will pass. There will be no return on Enlightenment for the attention was not on Enlightenment. The knower instructs the disciplined aspects to appreciate the conscious mind and its aspects. The conscious mind is the division of mind that produces the knower. The highest priority is to be given to the knower and receiving the value of the knower. Burial preparation represents the steps one goes through in preparation for the next step forward in growth and awareness. Then one can free the attention to move toward the imaged future. The world symbolizes the whole mind. The good news is that we have the *textbook to Enlightenment* here at our fingertips and within our grasp. These collective works, written in the language of mind, are called the <u>Bible</u>. The whole Self will remember any conscious aspect that gives value to the knower.

[14] Then one of the twelve, called Judas Iscariot, went unto the chief priests, [15] And said unto them, What will you give me, if I hand him over to you? And they paid him thirty pieces of silver. [16] And from that time he sought an opportunity to hand him over.

Judas is the Greek form of the name Judah. Jesus was a descendant of Judah of the *Old Testament* and was therefore a member of the tribe of Judah. Hence, the term Jew or Ju-dah. Thirty pieces of silver may be contrasted and compared with the talents of silver the master gave to his servants to invest in the parable given by Jesus in *Matthew 25:14-30*. Silver in both instances represents value. Three is the number of unification of aggressive and receptive qualities to create a third quality. Judas, an aspect of the motivating ego, is attempting to gain value in the Self by combining aggressive and receptive principles in the knower. Judah, often referred to as Judas Iscariot, is actually Judah of Iscariot, or Judah of Kerioth in the Hebrew language. Iscariot (Kerioth) is the area where Judah-Judas originated. He went to the chief priests and got thirty pieces of silver in payment for turning the knower (Jesus) over to them. With this action, Judah-Judas became known as the betrayer. Judah is the actual name; Judas is the Greek translation.

Judah was the name of one of the twelve tribes of Israel. Jesus was of that tribe of Judah. The name Judas shows the one who desires authority and is motivated to achieve it. Kerioth, or its Greek name Iscariot, was a city of Moab against which Jeremiah prophesied *(Jer. 48:24-41)*. Judah or Judas represents a major aspect in alignment. That aspect represents the *intention* to motivate; similar to the ego whose duty is to motivate one to move forward. Judas is always trying to motivate Jesus in order to fulfill his assignment of being a King. However, Judas-Judah gets caught up in thinking Jesus is going to be an earthly king instead of king of the spirit, king of the mind, and authority of all the inner levels of mind. Judah exemplifies thinking physically. He wants a physical kingdom commanded by the knower without realizing there must be a mental and spiritual kingdom of the knower in order for the kingdom to be permanent.

> *17 Now on the first day of the feast of unleavened bread the disciples came to Jesus, saying unto him, Where do you wish us to prepare the passover supper for you? 18 And he said, Go into the city to this man, and say to him, The Teacher said, My time is at hand; I will celebrate the passover at your house with my disciples. 19 The disciples did as Jesus had appointed them; and they made ready the passover.*

The meaning of passover is derived from a story in the *Old Testament*. The Hebrews were in Egypt, preparing to leave and be led by Moses out of their entrapment in Egypt. Several plagues were visited upon the Pharaoh and his people. Of these, the plague causing the death of the first born of each household convinced the Pharaoh to let the Israelites go. The Israelites were told to sacrifice a lamb and place the blood of the lamb above the door in every house where they lived so the angel of the Lord would pass them by and not kill their first-born. In this way, they were "passed over". Thus, by death, their first-born were spared. This theme is repeated following the birth of Jesus when Herod orders the killing of all the boys two years old and younger.

Jesus represents the knowing quality. Jesus' father, Joseph, represents perception and knowing builds upon the foundation of perception. Jesus' ability to perceive is evident as he is aware of what Judah is creating and the contacts he has made.

> [20] *Now when the even was come, he sat down with the twelve.* [21] *As they did eat, he said, I assure you, one of you is about to betray me.* [22] *They felt very sad, and began to say to him one by one, Is it I, my Lord?* [23] *He answered and said, He that dips his hand with me in the dish, the same will betray me.* [24] *The Son of man goes as it is written of him: but woe unto that man by whom the Son of man is betrayed it had been good for that man if he had not been born.* [25] *Then Judas, which betrayed him, answered saying Surely it is not I, Rabbi? Jesus said to him, You said it.*

During the course of the meal, Jesus said, *"I assure you, one of you is about to betray me."* Jesus knows this because he is doing everything to fulfill the scriptures. The scriptures predicted all these steps that he is accomplishing. The scriptures he refers to are recorded in what is now known as the *Old Testament.* The fulfillment of the goal of becoming Enlightened and becoming a whole functioning Self is accomplished by the knower. The fallacy of putting your value, trust, and security in physical possessions is that they are temporary and you will be separated from them sooner or later. Lamsa translates the disciples questioning as; verse 22, *"they felt very sad, and began to say to him one by one, Is it I, my Lord."* In verse 25, Judah asks in a similar fashion: *"Then Judah, the traitor answered, saying, Master, perhaps it is I? Jesus said to him, you say that."* Thus the Lamsa translation (which agrees with the King James version) clearly shows all the disciples as having doubts as to whether or not they would be the one to betray the knower. All disciplined aspects will seek to imagine themselves like one who is gaining the Christ consciousness. The conscious ego aspect will attempt to push or pull, draw or drive Self forward.

> *26 As they were eating, Jesus took bread, and blessed it, and broke it, and gave it to the disciples, and said, Take this and eat it; this is my body. 27 He took the cup, and gave thanks, and gave it to them, saying, All of you drink from it; 28 For this is my blood of the covenant, which is shed for many for the forgiveness of sins. 29 But I say unto you, I will not drink henceforth of this fruit of the vine, until that day when I drink it new with you in my Fathers kingdom. 30 And when they had sung a hymn, they walked out to the mount of Olives.*

Blood represents Truth and wine represents wisdom. The new covenant, that is the *New Testament*, is an injunction to live your life according to the Truth and according to wisdom which comes from practicing and applying knowledge rather than living your life in a state of wanting to learn the quality of believing through practicing rules and regulations. Rather, use rules and regulations in order to build and move to the higher step; use them to create the new structure for the higher step. Self builds the structure. The individual has the inner authority. The symbolism of bread (knowledge) and wine (wisdom) representing Jesus' body (structure) and blood (Truth) is clear. Self understanding through the use and practice of Universal Truths is the way to build the structure needed for using all of mind and all of creation.

> *31 Then said Jesus unto them, your faith in me will be shaken this night: for it is written, I will strike the shepherd, and the sheep of the flock will be scattered abroad. 32 But after I am risen again, I will go to Galilee ahead of you. 33 Peter answered and said to him, though all men may forsake their faith in you, mine will never be shaken. 34 Jesus said to him, Verily I say to you, This night, before the cock crows, you will deny me three times. 35 Peter said to him, Even if I should die with you, I will never disown you. Likewise also said all the disciples.*

Peter represents the will. Peter is a disciple. The will is being developed and is being disciplined. The will is not fully empowered for it is not yet completely developed. The knower always has greater perception and has built more than the aspect of will. The cock or rooster is an animal and as such represents the compulsive or habitualness of the conscious mind. Animals represent habits and compulsion. This aspect called Peter still somewhat identifies with the limitations of the physical environment. These limitations of Peter will not be overcome until after the death of the knower, Jesus, because then Peter becomes a teacher and leader of the new Christian church. The disciples go out and preach the good news throughout the world.

> *36 Then came Jesus with them to a place called Gethsemane, and said unto the disciples, Sit here, while I go and pray over there. 37 He took with him Peter and the two sons of Zebedee, and began to experience sorrow and distress. 38 Then he said to them, My heart is nearly broken with sorrow, even unto death: remain here, and stay awake with me.*

Zebedee's two sons are the disciples James and John. The disciple John, the beloved, symbolizes the incorporation of the believing factor into the whole Self. John the Baptist represents believing; however, since believing is now incorporated as one of the aspects of the Self, as represented by the disciple John, the quality of believing is seen to have been surpassed by the knower. Jesus is the teacher of his disciple John. Believing is now integrated into knowing for the development of the whole Self. Respect and value is given to the powerful and valuable quality of believing. Will and imaged desire of Enlightenment are those important qualities anyone utilizes and builds in their quest for Enlightenment.

> *39 He went a little further and fell on his face, and prayed, saying, O my Father, if it be possible, let this cup pass from me: nevertheless, not as I will, but as you will. 40 He came to the disciples, and found them asleep, and said to Peter, Could you not stay awake with me for one hour? 41*

Watch and pray that you not enter into temptation: the spirit indeed is willing, but the body is weak. ⁴² He went away again the second time, and prayed, saying, O my Father, if this cup may not pass away from me except I drink it, your will be done. ⁴³ He came and found them asleep again: for their eyes were heavy. ⁴⁴ He left them and went away again, and prayed the third time, saying the same words. ⁴⁵ Finally he returned to his disciples, and said to them, Sleep on now, and enjoy your rest: behold, the hour is at hand, and the Son of man is to be handed over into the hands of the godless. ⁴⁶ Wake and rise, let us be going: behold, he is at hand who does betray me.

The fulfillment of the plan in the superconscious mind is the creation of a whole functioning Self which is to be Enlightened. This ideal must always come first. We enjoy our physical pleasures, our physical comforts, but if it means sacrificing pleasure and experiencing a little temporary pain or discomfort in order to have the permanent joy and bliss of Enlightenment then in the long run we will gladly do so. An intelligent thinker will gladly exchange the temporary for that which is permanent and joy-filled.

⁴⁷ While he spoke, Judas, one of the twelve, came, and with him a large crowd with swords and clubs, including the chief priests and elders of the people. ⁴⁸ Now he who betrayed Jesus gave them a sign, saying, Whomever I will kiss, that is he; capture him. ⁴⁹ Immediately he came to Jesus, and said, Peace Rabbi; and kissed him. ⁵⁰ Jesus said unto him, Friend, do what you are here to do. At that moment, they stepped forward and laid hands on Jesus and took him. ⁵¹ Behold, one of them who were with Jesus stretched out his hand, drawing his sword struck a servant of the high priest's, severing his ear. ⁵² Then said Jesus unto him, Put your sword where it belongs: for all they that use the sword sooner or later will die by it. ⁵³ Do you think that I cannot now pray to my Father, and he will give me more than twelve legions of angels? ⁵⁴ How would the scriptures be fulfilled, that say this must be? ⁵⁵ In that same hour said Jesus to the crowd, Am I a thief that you have come out armed with swords and clubs to take me? I sat daily with you teaching in the temple, and you laid no hold on me.

Jesus, of course, knew exactly that this embrace was the signal for the Romans to recognize and to take hold of him. One of his followers cut off the high priest's servant's ear. This shows that the quality symbolized by the high priest is only physical. The servant symbolizes an aspect who refuses to hear the Truth. This aspect of Self identifies with the physical instead of the inner Truth. Jesus tells them to stop for those who use the sword are sooner or later destroyed by it. The sword symbolizes a tool for change. There is a connection with karma here. The intention behind the energy of an action moving from Self into the environment toward others, is the way energy will return to the Self as an opportunity for learning and until there is understanding of that intention. Understanding fulfills karma and intention sets karma into motion. Destroying one's learning opportunity (death-killing) returns to Self as the destruction of one's own learning opportunity.

> [56] *But all this was done, that the scriptures of the prophets might be fulfilled. Then all the disciples abandoned him, fleeing.*

Enlightenment is the completion of the goal that was started with the first chapter of *Genesis*. The ideal is to produce a creation and in that creation to build thinkers who will be compatible with their maker; like and similar, or image and likeness to their creator. This is the fulfillment of the goal of which the prophets spoke. The Christ is one who is Enlightened or full of the light of Divine Radiance and therefore is compatible with the Creator.

> [57] *They that had laid hold of Jesus took him to Caiaphas the high priest, where the scribes and the elders were assembled.* [58] *Peter followed him from afar to the high priests palace, and going in and sat with the servants, to see the end.* [59] *The chief priests, the elders, and the whole Sanhedrin, wanted false testimony against Jesus, to put him to death;* [60] *But they found none: even though many false witnesses came, yet found they none. At the last came two false witnesses,* [61] *And said, This fellow*

said, I am able to destroy the sanctuary of God and to build it in three days. [62] *The high priest arose, and said unto him, Have you no answer to the testimony given against you?* [63] *Jesus remained silent. And the high priest said unto him, I order you by the living God, that you tell us whether you are the Messiah, the Son of God.* [64] *Jesus said unto him, It is you who have said it: nevertheless I say unto you, Hereafter will you see the Son of man sitting on the right hand of power and coming in the clouds of heaven.* [65] *Then the high priest tore his clothes, saying, He has spoken blasphemy; what further need have we of witnesses? behold, now you have heard his blasphemy.* [66] *What is your verdict? They answered and said, This is punishable by death.* [67] *Then did they spit in his face and hit him; and others slapped him with the palms of their hands,* [68] *Saying, Prophesy for us, you Messiah, Who just struck you?*

The knower admits and affirms the restriction of physical life in order to identify and commit more powerfully to the real and permanent life which transcends the physical. The knower identifies the restriction and limitation of memory and brain pathways which produce no new learning keeping one in the compulsive state. The aspect of will power symbolized by Peter is available and somewhat usable but not yet fully effective. This indicates there has not yet been the full commitment to move ever consistently and constantly forward, without hesitation, with will power. Guards represent the way one tries to protect Self from life and thereby limit the learning. The chief priests could discover no false testimony because one who is true to the Self and practices universal Truth has no dichotomy. Such a one insures the thoughts of Self are fully manifested in the actions of Self. The Realized One causes the words to correctly and accurately describe the mental images and thoughts of Self. God's sanctuary is the superconscious mind. The one who gains freedom from entrapment transcends the physical limitations. As the awareness of superconscious mind develops, the old way of relating to the structure of mind as something far away is overturned. In its place is instituted the constant awareness of, and existence in, superconscious mind called Christ consciousness. Life is motion. The living God *is* creation in motion. The son of God is one who constantly causes motion toward the Enlightenment that Self desires to construct within Self. The forward motion producing thinker will understand how to create experiences to gain further Self knowledge. He knows the righteous or correct and productive manner of causing permanent learning.

Self understanding is power. It is the power of the universe. The torn robes of the high priest symbolize the recognition on the part of the conscious mind that the outer expression has changed. The former method of behavior and relating to others is outmoded and no longer appropriate. The conscious mind, being habitual and limited, recognizes the new identity of Self as knower and re-acts. The experiences of the old Self in the conscious mind still tend to intrude on the knower's identity until one is firmly established in Christ consciousness and Enlightenment. The knower does not need to be or pretend to be the prophet, for the knower has fulfilled the prophecies and has thus transcended *goal* creation. He has evolved to *ideal* creation. For the knower, gaining cosmic consciousness is the *goal* and cosmic consciousness exists as the *ideal*.

Jesus uses the words *"the right hand of power."* He doesn't say the right hand of God. The power is given in *Genesis, chapter one. "God made man in his image and likeness."* Likeness means with like attributes; the power to create was given through the imager called the imagination. The right hand of the power connotes the use of that imager to develop that visualized image of what is desired to occur, successfully and with will power. The power is in holding the whole picture in mind until it has been matched with activity and it has been created, enabling Self to move into that picture and create a new, more expanded Self. This, of course, is at odds with any aspect that thinks physically because this will be threatening to such a one's false sensation of security which derives from an effort at non-changed fixity.

[69] Peter sat in the courtyard when one of the serving girls came to him, saying, You also were with Jesus of Galilee. [70] He denied this before them all, saying, I know not what you say. [71] When he had gone out to the gate, another maid saw him, and said unto them that were there, This fellow was also with Jesus of Nazareth. [72] And again he denied with an oath, I do not know the man. [73] And after a while others who stood by came to him, saying, Surely you also are one of them; for even your accent gives you away. [74] Then he began to curse

The Book of Matthew Interpreted

and to swear, saying, I do not know the man. And immedi-
ately the cock crowed. 75 Peter remembered the word of
Jesus, which said to him, Before the cock crows, you will
deny me three times. And Peter went out, and wept bitterly.

Everyone needs will, as symbolized by Peter, to be in unison with
the reasoning abilities to develop Self awareness. In the instance of Peter, the
will is still in its development stage. There are hesitations at times. Doubt
will always arise in the conscious mind in various aspects and forms until the
full commitment to know Self is firmly formed in Self. Then one's overriding
passion for food, sex, and money will be transcended. At that point the physical is something to appreciate and enjoy without the attention ever leaving the
creative infinite.

Symbols and Their Interpretation

Chapter Twenty-Seven

1.   Daybreak - dawning of new awareness with new opportunity for learning
2.   Potter's field - subconscious mind substance used to build receptivity
3.   Cemetery - emotional attachment, stagnation
4.   Foreigners - unknown aspects of Self
5.   Blood field - subconscious Truth
6.   King - authority
7.   Barabbas - Bar-Abba, Son of the Father; a knower who has limited Self.
8.   Dream - communication from subconscious mind to conscious mind
9.   Crown of thorns - control over doubts
10. King of the Jews - authority over faith
11. Golgotha (Skull Place) - facing one's identity
12. Bandits (insurgents) - stealing value from Self
13. Curtain of the sanctuary - wall between conscious and subconscious minds
14. Mary Magdalene - the nurturing quality of love in the conscious mind focused on adulthood
15. Other Mary - the nurturing quality of love in the conscious mind focused on adolescence
16. Joseph of Arimathea - disciplined perception
17. Sealing the stone - stubbornness to block will power

Chapter Twenty-Seven

¹ At daybreak, all the high priests and elders of the people took formal action against Jesus to put him to death: ² When they had bound him, they led him away and delivered him to Pontius Pilate the governor.

Chapter Twenty-seven portrays the final days of Jesus in his physical body leading up to and including the time of his death. Death represents change, for death is not an ending. Death is not the end to consciousness or the cessation of being. Death is a process of change from one point of reference, the outer conscious mind, to another, the inner subconscious mind. What change could the knower make? — The change from knowing to full Enlightenment; from Jesus to Christ. Change from being a knower entrapped in a physical body to a knower who is free to transcend the physical by understanding the spiritual lessons available through experience. The knower is tied up or bound which symbolically represents the process of one feeling very restricted when it is time to change. This restrictive, constricted feeling continues until such a time as the expansion of consciousness occurs.

The word Christ is a title indicating Enlightened. The word Christ is not a proper name. Christ was not Jesus' last name. Christ is an earned title, as is Doctor. Our English word Christ comes from the Greek word *Cristos*, meaning *Enlightened*. The word Cristos or Christ had been used by the Greeks for centuries before the birth of Jesus of Nazareth to indicate the state of Christ or cosmic consciousness achieved by several highly evolved beings living before the time of Jesus the Christ. The Greek *Christ* or *Cristos* was the word chosen to translate the Hebrew *Messiah*, meaning *anointed one*. So the actual name and title of Jesus in his own original language was Jeshua or Yeshua or Yoshua, the Messiah, the anointed.

³ Then Judas, who had betrayed him, when he saw that Jesus was condemned, regretted his action and brought the thirty pieces of silver to the high priests and elders, ⁴ Saying, I have sinned in that I have betrayed the innocent blood. And

Notes:

*they said, What is that to us? It is
your affair. [5] And he threw down the
pieces of silver in the temple and left.
He departed; and hanged himself. [6]
And the chief priests took the silver
pieces, and said, It is not right to put
this in the temple treasury, because
it is blood money. [7] They took coun-
sel, and used it to buy the potter's
field as a cemetery for foreigners. [8]
That is why that field was called, The
blood field to this day. [9] Then was
fulfilled that which was spoken by
Jeremiah the prophet, saying, And
they took the thirty pieces of silver,
the price of him that was valued,
whom they of the children of Israel
did value; [10] And paid it for the
potter's field, as the Lord has commanded me.*

The end of Judah shows a change in the ego.
The knower is going to change. This quality of motivation inherent to the ego is going to change, for death
indicates change. Self hanging is accomplished by
putting a rope around the throat and allowing the weight
of the body to break the neck or suffocate the lungs.
The throat is that area of the body which symbolically
is associated with will and will power. The will chakra
is physically located in the area of the throat. This
shows that there is a need and a desire on the part of
the ego — identity of Self — to develop a stronger
will! The different disciples keep trying to develop
greater willpower. Peter rejecting Jesus and saying *"I
don't know him"* three times before the cock crowed
shows the undeveloped will practicing fear instead of
desire and courage. Fear is created by an undisciplined
imagination and lack of awareness. An undisciplined
mind, leads to fear which leads to terror. Each time
this occurs, the disciples show that they are not fully
strengthened. They have yet to become fully matured
aspects of the Self so they must follow the one teacher,
the one committed to the whole Self and that is Jesus,
the knower. It is also significant that a mention of what

Jeremiah the prophet said was fulfilled. This quote comes from *Jeremiah 32:6-9.* They took thirty pieces of silver — the value of a man, the price on his head, the price set by the Israelites — and they paid just as the Lord had commanded. Jeremiah was a prophet so therefore he symbolizes a goal creator. The zero in the number 30 indicates power which comes from understanding the process of using the aggressive and receptive principles in conjunction to create anew. Three indicates in itself a new creation produced through the use of unity of what has come before. The number one represents the aggressive quality. Two represents the receptive quality. Three represents the aggressive and receptive coming together to produce a child, a new idea, or a new creation. In the case of lines or geometric drawings, one can be represented by a line. Two represented by two lines. Three represented by three lines that come together and touch to form a triangle. Now instead of an open figure the lines have come together to form a new geometric figure which is a triangle having two dimensions instead of one. The two dimensions being width and breadth.

> [11] *Jesus stood before the governor: and the governor asked him, saying, are you the King of the Jews? And Jesus said to him. You are the one who has said it.* [12] *When he was accused by the chief priests and elders, he answered nothing.* [13] *Then said Pilate unto him, Hear you not how many things they witness against you?* [14] *He answered him not a word; inasmuch that the governor marvelled greatly.* [15] *Now at that feast the governor was accustomed to release to the people a prisoner, whomever the crowd would choose.* [16] *They had then a notable prisoner named Barabbas.* [17] *Therefore when they were gathered, Pilate said to them, Whom will you ask that I release unto you? Barabbas, or Jesus who is called Christ?* [18] *For he knew it was out of jealousy that they had delivered Jesus.* [19] *When he sat down on the judgment seat, his wife sent to him a message, saying, Do not interfere with this Holy man, for I have had a dream about him today that has upset me greatly.*

The main question that Jesus is asked over and over is, *"Are you the King of the Jews?"* The chief priests and elders ask various questions but Jesus, for his part, remains mostly silent. This seems to amaze the people and amaze the Romans; that someone wouldn't even defend himself. All he would say to these questions is, *"You are the one who has said it."* This was a way of saying that even the Romans and the Sanhedrin admitted that Jesus was King of the Jews. Barabbas is accurately translated as Bar-Abba which means son of the Father. This name, meaning son of the Father, shows a fascinating similarity to Jesus' title which was son of God (or son of his father in heaven).

Notes:

Abba means *father* as given in *Mark 14:36.*

> *Mark 14:* [36] *And Jesus said, Abba, Father, all things are possible unto you; take away this cup from me: nevertheless, not what I will, but what you will.*
>
> [20] *But the chief priests and elders persuaded the crowd that they should ask for Barabbas, and destroy Jesus.* [21] *The governor answered and said unto them, Which of the two do you wish me to release to you? They said, Barabbas.* [22] *Pilate said to them, What will I do then with Jesus the so called Messiah? They all said, Let him be crucified.* [23] *And the governor said, Why, what evil has he done? But they cried out the more, saying, Let him be crucified.* [24] *When Pilate saw that he could prevail nothing, but that a riot was breaking out, he took water, and washed his hands before the multitude, saying, I am innocent of the blood of this just person: see you to it.* [25] *Then answered all the people, and said, His blood be on us, and on our children.* [26] *Then he released Barabbas to them: and when he had scourged Jesus, he delivered him to be crucified.*

Now the story is, because it was the time of the festival the procurator was accustomed to releasing one prisoner whom the crowd would designate. Besides Jesus there was another such man, a notorious prisoner named Bar-abba who has been mistakenly called Barabbas. The man who is a notorious prisoner is Bar Abba. *Bar* means *son* and *Abba* means *father.* Son of the father. This is a very similar name to the title Jesus gave himself. Jesus called himself *"son of my father in heaven".* Son of the Father! Both have a similar meaning name. The indication is that there is the potential in every aspect of us to be a whole functioning Self. When anyone identifies with just the physical part of Self, refusing to change and move forward in the life by releasing the old worn out mental pictures, they become jealous. They are jealous toward someone who has changed, grown, and built permanent learning because they have not. The mob of undisciplined and out of control aspects chose something they were familiar with, Bar-Abba. Bar-Abba is physically-oriented even though he has the potential to align with the whole Self. When one is not participating in change and soul growth, but instead sitting in silent judgment, one is either alone or in the prison of Self created limitations. Being negatively judgmental towards those who are advancing in soul progression arises because one is jealous; lacking the will power and personal drive necessary to change Self. One never makes Self bigger or better by trying to tear down those who are successful.

In Jesus' final days, a dream proved to be important just as when Jesus was born. Joseph, his father, had a dream that contained important information about Jesus' destiny. Now, the wife of Pilate has a dream which says do not interfere with the goings on and just let it be played out. This step of Enlightenment is part of the plan. This action is in fulfillment of the prophecies of the prophets. The Jews, that is the priests and the people themselves, not the Romans, choose to crucify Jesus. It is the people themselves, the people living in that area, the Jewish people, who give the directive to crucify Jesus. To be hung on the cross and crucified is to be at the exact point of the coming together of vertical time symbolized by the vertical bar and horizontal time symbolized by the horizontal bar. Vertical time is mental time and is gauged by the understandings of permanent learning Self has built. Horizontal time is measured by the clock, the rising of the sun, and other regular and consistent physical motion and physical events, and is thus a gauge for the experiences of the Self. Being crucified on a cross shows that the knower would not be limited by physical time nor by mental time, but that he would use all to produce everything that is desired and needed to transcend physical existence and limitation. Pilate, the Roman governor for that particular area of the Roman Empire, symbolizes a leader or an authority aspect concerning physical discipline and structure.

> [27] Then the soldiers of the governor took Jesus into the common hall, and gathered unto him the whole band of soldiers. [28] They stripped him and put a scarlet robe on him. [29] When they had platted a crown of thorns, they placed it on his head and put a reed in his right hand: they bowed the knee before him and mocked him, by saying, Hail, King of the Jews [30] They spit on him, and took the reed, repeatedly striking on the head. [31] After that they mocked him, they took the robe off from him and put him in his own clothes, and led him away to crucify him.

Stripping off his clothes and wrapping him in a scarlet robe shows that the old expression of Self is no longer needed. The old outer presentation is no longer needed because Self is being prepared to be filled with light and have the complete Enlightenment which eliminates entrapment. The aspects who refuse to change will see what they habitually want to see but it will not be true or accurate and their perception will not show the knower accurately. The crown of thorns shows control of doubts and indecisions. The way to control doubts and indecisions and have power over them is to be in full control of one's creation, attention, and thoughts. The crown on top of the head symbolizes the authority of the crown chakra. When understood, this chakra is creation and Enlightenment. Jews represent those aspects who have not recognized that they have the opportunity to bring the second coming of the Christ into themselves in the present. Their limitation is living for the future as an excuse to be unproductive in the present. One who has attained Christhood is the leader, the royalty, the director of all those aspects that are still physical.

> [32] *As they came out, they found a man of Cyrene, Simon by name: him they compelled to bear his cross.* [33] *And when they were come unto a place called Golgotha, that is to say, Skull Place,* [34] *They gave him a drink of wine flavored with gall: and when he tasted it, he refused to drink.*

Simon was the earlier name of Peter and indicates that even in the last stages of the transformation of the knower there is a reliance on and use of the will but without the full development and use of will power. Head symbolizes identity in the Universal Language of Mind. Skull place (Golgotha) symbolizes the stage of the change of identity for the knower from being earthly bound to transcending physical entrapment in the light of full Enlightenment.

> [35] *They crucified him, and parted his garments, drawing lots: that it might*

be fulfilled which was spoken by the prophet, They parted my garments among them, and upon my vesture did they cast lots. ³⁶ Sitting down they watched him there; ³⁷ And set up over his head the charge against him saying, THIS IS JESUS THE KING OF THE JEWS. ³⁸ Then were there two bandits crucified with him; one on the right hand, and another on the left. ³⁹ And they that passed by insulting him, tossing their heads, ⁴⁰ saying, You are the one that was going to destroy the temple, and rebuilt it in three days, save yourself. If you be the Son of God, come down from the cross. ⁴¹ Likewise also the chief priests mocking him, with the scribes and elders, said, ⁴² He saved others; but he cannot save himself. If he is the King of Israel, let him now come down from the cross, and we will believe him. ⁴³ He trusted in God; let God deliver him now, if he will have him: for he said, I am the Son of God. ⁴⁴ The bandits also, which were crucified with him, kept taunting him in the same way.

Verse thirty-five is a fulfillment of a prophecy or statement in *Psalms* in the *Old Testament*, Chapter 22:18 *"They part my garments among them, and cast lots upon my vesture."*

Psalms 22 ¹ My God, my God, why have you forsaken me? why are you so far from helping me, and from the words of my roaring? ² O my God, I cry in the daytime, but you hear not; and in the night season, and am not silent. ³ But you are holy, O you that inhabit the praises of Israel. ⁴ Our fathers trusted in you: they trusted, and you did deliver them. ⁵ They cried unto you, and were delivered: they trusted in you, and were not confounded. ⁶ But I am a worm, and no man; a reproach of men, and despised of the people. ⁷ All they that see me laugh me to scorn: they shoot out the lip, they shake the head, saying, ⁸ He trusted on the Lord that he would deliver him: let him deliver him, seeing he delighted in him. ⁹ But you are he that took me out of the womb: you did make me hope when I was upon my mother's breasts. ¹⁰ I was cast upon you from the womb: you are my God from my mother's belly. ¹¹Be not far from me; for trouble is near; for there is none to help. ¹² Many bulls have compassed me: strong bulls of Bashan have beset me round. ¹³ They gaped upon me with their mouths, as a ravening and a roaring lion. ¹⁴ I am poured out like water, and all my bones are out of joint: my heart is like wax; it is melted in the

Notes:

midst of my bowels. [15] My strength is dried up like a potsherd; and my tongue cleaves to my jaws; and you have brought me into the dust of death. [16] For dogs have compassed me: the assembly of the wicked have enclosed me: they pierced my hands and my feet. [17] I may tell all my bones: they look and stare upon me. [18] They part my garments among them, and cast lots upon my vesture. [19] But be not you far from me, O Lord: O my strength, haste you to help me. [20] Deliver my soul from the sword; my darling from the power of the dog. [21] Save me from the lions mouth: for you have heard me from the horns of the unicorns. [22] I will declare your name unto my brothers: in the midst of the congregation will I praise you. [23] You that fear the Lord, praise him; all you the seed of Jacob, glorify him; and fear him, all you the seed of Israel. [24] For he has not despised nor abhorred the affliction of the afflicted; neither has he hid his face from him; but when he cried unto him, he heard. [25] My praise will be of you in the great congregation: I will pay my vows before them that fear him. [26] The meek will eat and be satisfied: they will praise the Lord that seek him: your heart will live for ever. [27] All the ends of the world will remember and turn unto the Lord: and all the kindreds of the nations will worship before you. [28] For the kingdom is the Lords: and he is the governor among the nations. [29] All they that be fat upon earth will eat and worship: all they that go down to the dust will bow before him: and none can keep alive his own soul. [30] A seed *will serve him; it will be accounted to the Lord for a generation. ³¹ They will come, and shall declare his righteousness unto a people that will be born, that he has done this.*

The outer expression of Self will be cast to the four winds when death occurs. Whatever effect one has had on people, it will be dispersed to them. They will contact other people and from them others will be contacted until one affects the whole world with the goodness of Self. The physical body, the outer presentation of Self, will no longer exist in the physical. No man needs to prove their abilities and skills of Enlightenment to another person, except their teacher. The only person who can prove the Truth and facts about Enlightenment to anyone is one's Self. It is proved by the willingness to meditate everyday, the willingness to discipline, to focus, and to still the mind. Then one proves with results the Truth of the Real Self and the benefits thereof. By writing down one's dreams every day, learning to interpret them, and learning the language of mind, one comes to know the messages of the inner Self. A little temporary discomfort does not deter the knower from the ideal of Enlightenment. To a person or aspect who is not learning to know Self, the actions of the knower may be threatening or at least strange. One who is engrossed in physical life is incapable of understanding one immersed in spiritual life.

⁴⁵ Now from noon onward there was darkness over all the land unto mid afternoon. ⁴⁶ And about mid afternoon Jesus cried with a loud voice, saying, Eli, Eli, lema sabachthani? (Lamsa, Eli, Eli, lemana shabakthani, which means "My God, My God, for this I was spared.") *that is to say, My God, my God, why have you forsaken me? ⁴⁷ Some of them that stood there, when they heard that, said, This man calls for Elijah. ⁴⁸ And immediately one of them ran, and took a sponge and filled it with vinegar, and put it on a reed, and gave him to drink. ⁴⁹ The rest said, Let him be, let us see whether Elijah will come to save him. ⁵⁰ Jesus, when he had cried again with a loud voice, yielded up the ghost. ⁵¹ Behold, the curtain of the sanctuary was torn in two from the top to the bottom; and the earth did quake, and the rocks rent; ⁵² And the graves were opened; and many bodies of the saints which slept arose, ⁵³ And came out of the graves after his resurrection, and went into the holy city, and appeared unto many. ⁵⁴ Now when the centurion, and they that were with him, watching Jesus, saw the earthquake, and those things that were done, they feared greatly, saying, Truly this was the Son of God. ⁵⁵ And many women were there beholding from afar, some of whom had followed*

Jesus from Galilee, ministering unto him: [56] *Among which was Mary Magdalene, and Mary the mother of James and Joseph, and the mother of Zebedee's children.*

"Eli, Eli lema sabachthani that is, my God, my God why have you forsaken me?" is a direct reference to *Psalms* 22. However the correct interpretation of the verse is "*about the ninth hour, Jesus cried out in a loud voice and said, "Eli, Eli, lemana shabakthani"* instead of lema it is lemana and instead of sabachthani it is shabakthani which means, *"My God, my God for this I was spared."* And so now the full statement makes complete sense. It presents a whole clear picture of the reason Jesus was not killed before by the scribes and the Pharisees, the Sadducees, the chief priests, the Romans and all the people who could have had his life before. It was necessary for the knower to be put on the cross so that all these prophecies would be fulfilled. It showed the Messiah, the Christ, had come to mankind so all would believe and so everyone could see that it was possible to gain their Christhood and thus raise the consciousness of the whole planet. It is necessary for the Christ consciousness to awaken inside as the fulfillment of the plan so that all the other aspects can see this and can move into alignment. Then the whole Self is completely filled with light, and awareness.

The cheap wine stuck on a reed to make him drink indicates there is still some value seen in wisdom even though Enlightenment goes beyond and supersedes wisdom. Others say *"see if Elijah comes down"* because Jesus says *"Eli"* which is the first half of the name Elijah. El is God. The centurion referred to earlier in *Matthew* as commanding a hundred, is again referenced. He always sees the Truth of Jesus' Enlightenment for he says, *"Surely this was the son of God."* Mary Magdalene and Mary, the mother of James and Joseph and the mother of Zebedee's sons were all there. These two Marys are shown because they represent the quality of love and the nurturing quality in the conscious mind. The compassion displayed by the knower results from an awareness of each individual being divine and having divine capabilities. The knower recognizes the stage of development of each individual in their own point of growth. The knower has completely surrendered the conscious ego up to a greater power; to the Creator and to all of humanity. The element of surrender always occurs immediately preceding a major initiation. The acceptance of the fact that the old life and its limitations no longer suffice and that the new life is more expansive, leads then to the full movement of the Self into the next stage of evolution.

> *57 When the evening came, a rich man, Joseph of Arimathea, who was himself a disciple of Jesus: 58 went to Pilate and requested the body of Jesus. Then Pilate commanded the body to be delivered. 59 When Joseph took the body, he wrapped it in a clean linen cloth, 60 And laid it in his own new tomb, which he had hewn out in the rock. Then he rolled a great rock across the entrance to the tomb, and departed. 61 And Mary Magdalene, and the other Mary remained sitting there facing the tomb.*

The true translation is when it was evening there came a rich man from Ramtha whose name was Joseph who had also studied under Jesus. This is called Arimathea in the Western versions but the actual name of the place was Ramtha. This Joseph is the one who wraps the body in linen and lays it in his own new tomb. Jesus' physical father was Joseph who was with Jesus at the beginning of his physical life. A man called Joseph is the one who completes Jesus' sojourn in the physical by putting his body in the tomb. The body will then be closed off and the physical part of Self sloughed off. Joseph, symbolizing perception, is again part of this process. The quality of perception, which is use of subconscious mind, is again being displayed. Perception always works hand-in-hand with knowing and Enlightenment, and is a part of the sixth day of creation called intuitive man. Man meaning thinker, whether male or female.

The name Mary is used in this chapter several times to refer to more than one woman. Woman or wo-man indicates extension of man, the thinker. The extension of the subconscious soul thinker is the reasoning conscious mind. There must be love for spiritual progression to occur. Mary was present at the birth of Jesus the knower as his earthly mother. Mary was also present at his death in the form of several Marys. The knower's death is the expansion of consciousness beyond its earthly confines. Each Mary, representing love, shows that love must be present for spirituality to expand and soul growth to occur. Love is the nature of spirit. Love is beyond affection and love is beyond the physical.

Notes:

> ^{62} *Now the next day, that followed the day of the preparation, the chief priests and Pharisees came together to Pilate,* ^{63} *Saying, Sir, we remember what that imposter said, while he was yet alive, After three days I will rise again.* ^{64} *Command therefore that the tomb be kept under surveillance until the third day, otherwise his disciples may come by night, and steal him away, and say to the people, He is risen from the dead: so the final imposture will be worse than the first.*

The rock indicates the will being placed over the tomb of stagnation and attachment to the past. The tomb in the earth indicates there is some use of subconscious mind but not yet full awareness of what has been caused in the full Self. The physical body is the past. The Knower will not remain attached to it. Stationing a guard to keep Jesus under surveillance does not work because this is not a physical transfiguration; it is an actual transfiguration to freedom from attachment from the physical body into the Spiritual Self of Divine Radiance.

The Pharisees had excellent memories but were very poor in listening, which is a deadly combination that forms a barrier to soul growth. This is because such a person is willing to receive into the memory, brain information that is comfortable to previously accepted limitations in thought. One does not listen to anything that will cause the consciousness to expand. Therefore such a person thinks memory gives them power, when actually it makes them more like an animal because they operate from compulsion. Animals have memory but no imagination. This is how the Pharisees are portrayed in the Bible.

> ^{65} *Pilate said unto them, You have a guard: go and secure the tomb as best as you can.* ^{66} *So they went, and made the tomb secure, sealing the stone, and setting a guard to watch.*

The hypocrites and those unwilling to change are still, to the very end, attempting to stop the process of Enlightenment from occurring. Through attachment to money, food, or other physical-entrapping objects these aspects attempt to go against the motion of the universe by trying to remain as they are without changing. Yet, there is no physical power on earth capable of holding the one who has gained and earned Enlightenment. The knower can always exercise the will (stone) and break any seals of limitation. The knower, in gaining Enlightenment, gains freedom over death (change) by transcending the slow rate of movement and change in the physical existence.

Symbols and Their Interpretation

Chapter Twenty-Eight

1.   Angel of the Lord - thought form from I AM
2.   Garments white as snow - full use of understanding, creation, and consciousness
3.   Mountain of Galilee - superconscious awareness while in the physical
4.   Peace - aspects causing cooperative motion
5.   Soldiers - aspects that have physical discipline
6.   Culmination of time - end of entrapment, full consciousness, superconscious awareness, and Divine Radiance; light radiating from inner Self outward

Chapter Twenty-Eight

¹ In the end of the Sabbath, as it began to dawn toward the first day of the week, Mary Magdalene came with the other Mary to inspect the tomb.

The first day of the week was dawning — which is Sunday because the Sabbath was celebrated on Saturday. The Sabbath is the seventh day of the week in commemoration of God having rested on the seventh day of creation as recorded in *Genesis 2:2*. Sunday has been traditionally the first day of the week and that is why it is still the first day of the week appearing on the calendars of today. This is why the first day of the week is named the Sun's day or Sunday. Just as each day of the week is named after one of the Gods of the ancient religions. The moon's day on Monday. Twigg's day on Tuesday. Woden or Oden's day called Wednesday. Thor's day or Thursday. Frigg's day or Friday. Saturn's day or Saturday. The early Christian church celebrated the Sabbath mass on Saturday. It wasn't until a few hundred years ago that this got switched to Sunday.

Mary Magdalene, that is Mary of Magdala, came with the other Mary to inspect the tomb. As indicated earlier, Mary symbolizes the nurturing quality of love in the conscious mind. The presence of the Marys at the tomb and their inspection thereof indicates Jesus, the Knower, is about to achieve the sixth day of creation called Intuitive Man. The stage of Reasoning Man (whether male or female) has been completed and love is understood as the essence of creation. The Knower has overcome the entrapment of the physical body and is about to achieve the freedom of absolute motion and Universal consciousness which Jesus refers to in this chapter with the statement, *"Know that I AM with you always"*. A new day dawning symbolizes the new light of awareness coming into the Self. Mary again shows there is the receptive factor nourishing the conscious mind and the new awareness.

² Behold, there was a great earthquake: for the angel of the Lord descended from heaven, and came and rolled back the stone from the door, and sat upon it. ³ His appearance was like lightning, and his garments white as snow: ⁴ And for

Notes:

fear of him the guards did shake, and became as dead men. [5] The angel answered and said to the women, Fear not: for I know that you seek Jesus, which was crucified. [6] He is not here: for he has risen, exactly as he promised. Come, see the place where he has laid. [7] And go quickly, and tell his disciples that he is risen from the dead; and, remember, he goes before you into Galilee; Remember, I said that to you.

Jesus is not there to tell them himself he has arisen, but he gets by the guards and is raised up showing there are no physical limitations. Physical limitations cannot control or entrap one who is Enlightened. This shows the complete freedom from entrapment in the physical existence. The cycle of reincarnation and of karma has been overcome. There is no need to incarn again. The Self Christ, or Cristos, Messiah, or Godman, never needs to incarn again, never needs to reincarn.

Lightening represents the flash of new awareness of the Self that accompanies the movement forward in evolutionary development and soul growth from Reasoning Man (thinker) to Intuitive Man (thinker). Garments white as snow symbolize that the outer expression has been changed to that of light or awareness. The outer conscious mind is in alignment with the angel which is the superconscious mind thought representative of I AM. The disciples, the disciplined aspects, are always following the directives of the knower. He is raising them up so the whole Self benefits and evolves into the divine being.

[8] The women departed quickly from the tomb with fear and great joy; and did run to bring his disciples the good news. [9] And as they went to tell his disciples, behold, Jesus stood before them, saying, Peace. And they came and held him by the feet, and worshipped him. [10] Then said Jesus unto them, Be not afraid: Go and tell the

*good news to my brothers that they are to go to Galilee,
where they will see me.*

This shows that even though one is Enlightened and moving among
people who are engrossed in the physical entrapment they can choose to ignore the Enlightened One. They can ignore and avoid the opportunity even
though deep down they know that they are lying and avoiding oneness with
others, that is, non-separation. Nevertheless the Enlightenment will still exist
and they will try to maintain and live in their limitations. History is full of the
names of spiritually evolved beings who have been ignored by the vast majority of the populace while some who were willing to change latched onto the
good fortune of being near the spiritually aware teacher. For those *with eyes
to see* the enlightened, spiritually awakened teacher is available and present
on earth awaiting the students who are prepared and ready to learn.

> *11 Now when they were leaving, behold, some of the guards
> came into the city, and reported to the chief priests all the
> things that had occurred. 12 When they were assembled
> with the elders, and had worked out their strategy, they gave
> large amounts of money to the soldiers, 13 Saying, Say you,
> His disciples came by night, and stole him away while we
> slept. 14 And if this comes to the governors ears, we will
> persuade him, and make sure you are not punished. 15 So
> they took the bribery money, and did as they were told. This
> saying is the story that is commonly reported among the
> Jews even to this day.*

Any dishonest aspects will lie to themselves and others and refuse to
acknowledge change even when it is in their midst. Those aspects who do not
believe it is possible in the present life to transcend the physical existence
refuse proof that is right in front of them.

> *16 Then the eleven disciples went to a mountain of Galilee
> where Jesus had summoned them. 17 When they saw him,
> those who had entertained doubts fell down in homage. 18
> And Jesus came and spoke to them, saying, Full authority
> has been given to me in heaven and in earth. 19 Go there-
> fore, and make disciples of all nations, baptizing them in
> the name of the Father, and of the Son, and of the Holy
> Ghost: 20 Teaching them to keep everything I have com-
> manded you: and, know I Am with you all ways, even unto
> the culmination of time. Amen.*

A challenge and obstacle has been overcome as symbolized by the mountain. Self is operating from a high and expanded consciousness in mind; the superconscious mind the highest vantage point having clear perception. Authority goes to the one who has the experience to know what he is doing, knows where he wants to go (that being Universal consciousness), and has a clear mental image of how to do it. This is the Truth for one that operates from superconscious mind with full awareness.

The Enlightened know the plan of creation. They are operating from that plan so they have full awareness — in superconscious mind, subconscious mind, and in conscious mind. *"Go therefore and make disciples"* symbolizes the need for the disciplined aspects of the whole Self, indicated by the *nations*, to gain Universal Truth. The root word for discipline and disciple is the same. The nations represent all the aspects of the Self. Discipline all aspects so there is full awareness in all parts of the mind and Self. *"Baptize them"* indicates the commitment made to the one living God; to creation and to knowing Self. Be a creator in the name of the Father (superconscious mind), the Son (the aggressive one who is striving to understand the whole mind and the superconscious plan) and the Holy spirit (the whole mind). The Greek word for spirit can be translated as mind or spirit. *"Teach them to carry out everything I have commanded you"* indicates the full use of the Universal Laws.

Know that I Am is with you always. I AM is with oneself always because the I AM is Self. You *are*, I AM. The culmination of time means you, the thinker, have moved fully into the sixth day of Creation which is called Intuitive Man. Therefore, you have ended your fifth day of creation world by leaving it behind. Then I AM will not be with the conscious mind anymore because there is no conscious mind. This is superconscious awareness, and Christ consciousness, and Divine Radiance of the one who is everywhere; being beyond time and space yet connected to all, aware of all and giving to all.

AMEN

Epilogue

Imagine! You find yourself in a foreign country, unable to speak the language of this new land. Everything the people of this foreign country say sounds like gibberish to you. It is incomprehensible to you. However, the people of that country seem to understand what they are saying to each other. At least, to a degree.

So you set yourself to the task of mastering this foreign language for you have little, if any, idea of when you may be returning to the place you call home.

You notice, as you begin to learn this new, strange language, that you begin to forget your native language. The new language doesn't seem to be quite as efficient or accurate as your old language but you persevere, and over time learn to comprehend and speak the new language.

By the time you, the stranger, have resided in this strange land for seven years, you have completely forgotten the language of your origination. Your native language has been forgotten and you are communicating daily in the new, once foreign language. In fact, you are so caught up in your existence in this foreign country that you no longer recall living anywhere else. You have forgotten your origination point. You have forgotten where you came from and you have forgotten therefore who you really are.

You exist in a world of limitations, using a language that limits you in your ability to communicate clearly and effectively the exact mental image you hold in your mind. Some people have mastered this ability to communicate in clear, complete, and accurate statements of words that clearly describe the image they hold in their mind's eye. But these people are few and far between. They seem to be enlightened or wise in ways that you do not quite understand.

You live out your life in this way, caught up in your life, having forgotten where you came from. Once in a while faint recollections and brief urgings motivate you to do something more with your life and rise above the morass of your countrymen. But your efforts in this direction are usually brief as you haven't developed a lot of discipline.

This story of a person's movement to a foreign land is the story of the soul's entrapment in a physical body for a lifetime.

The soul — that is you, the individual — exists without a body in subconscious mind when not incarned in a physical body. The question is: where did you exist before you were born? Some people and some religions say you existed with God. This is true in many ways for your existence in subconscious mind prior to this lifetime is "closer" to God, being higher in mind as presented on the mind chart earlier in this book.

I AM is the famous *I Am* that Moses saw in the burning bush described in *Exodus 3:1-14* . The *"I Am that I AM"* is who you are. *I Am* is the *Living God.* You exist as an identity and individual; an I Am. I Am, the identity that is you, exists in the eternal now. That is why I Am is not I was or I will be. I Am, the Real Self, does not exist in the past or the future. You, which is I Am, exist in the eternal now. I Am is the Prodigal Son referred to in the Bible in the *Book of Luke 15:11-31.* The Prodigal Son leaves home, makes mistakes, learns the lessons of life and creation, and returns home much wiser than when he departed.

You, the I Am that God created, exist as spirit in superconscious mind and as soul in subconscious mind. The soul that is your vehicle in subconscious mind, moved your attention out into physical existence — choosing a time, place, mother and father, and physical body, baby-vehicle that was being birthed — for physical incarnation. You chose that body vehicle and now are entrapped in it for a lifetime. You have probably forgotten this fact, just as most people do, on or before the age of seven. Someday, however, you will remember and re-cognize all of your existence. Then you will remember and know where you came from and who you are.

You will awake into Real Life.

You will know the purpose of life and the truth will set you free.

You will experience the joy and fullness of eternal, continual existence while still inhabiting a physical body.

You will know the reason for the limitations of communication in our physical existence is due to the limitations of the five physical senses plus the need for people to learn to develop the ability to communicate using the Universal Language of Mind.

As you, and others, learn to form clear mental images in your mind's eye and describe those images with words that explain and define those images clearly, you discover the satisfaction of clear and open communication. As you learn to receive the messages communicated by others, completely, you translate their words into mental images that convey their thought image accurately.

As you develop this process aligning yourself with and remembering your real language, you will again know the language of your native land — the Universal Language of Mind.

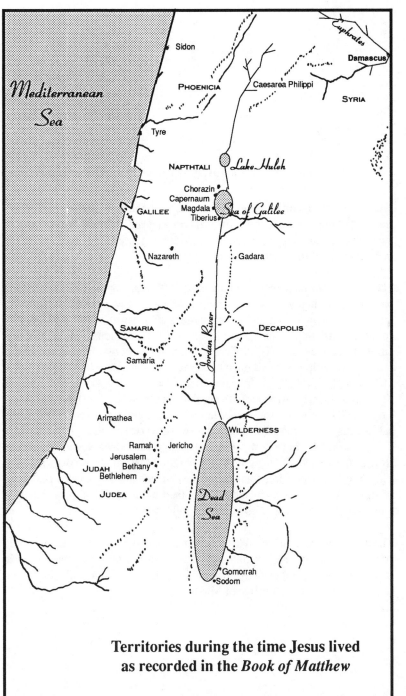

**Territories during the time Jesus lived
as recorded in the *Book of Matthew***

Acknowledgment

This work is the result of decades of research into the mind, the use and understanding of the mind, and the Universal Language of Mind. This discovery of the Universal Language of Mind was then applied, used, and employed in the interpretation of the *Book of Matthew*.

The *Book of Matthew* was written almost 2000 years ago and since that time has undergone many translations, new translations, new translations from old translations, new translations of translations after new manuscripts were discovered, translations of manuscripts from Greek, translations from Latin, translations from Aramaic. The Biblical text used in this book is the author's interpretation of scripture based upon his research in many available translations, including <u>The Lamsa Bible</u> from the Ancient Eastern Text, George M. Lamsa's Translation from the Aramaic of the Peshitta published in 1993 by A.J. Holman Co., which is quoted several times in the interpretation of texts in the Universal Language of Mind. The author suggests two other outstanding resources in English for further study: <u>The Holy Bible</u> authorized version edited by Rev. C. I. Scofield, D.D., published in 1909 by Oxford University Press and <u>The New American Bible</u> translated from original languages with critical use of all the ancient sources by members of the Catholic Biblical Association of America published in 1971 by Catholic Publishing Inc.

The author wises to thank all those who have come before who have worked so diligently to provide accurate translations so they may now be utilized in this volume to present them to the world in the inner, interior, and mind meaning in the Universal Language of Mind.

About the Author

Daniel R. Condron has as his assignment, his commission, for this lifetime giving to the world the Universal Language of Mind. In order for there to be world peace, there must not only be peace in each individual, there must also be a universal language to communicate the peace and understanding of one individual to another. The interpretations given in this Holy Work is the sourcebook and textbook for beginning to understand the Universal Language of Mind which the subconscious mind or soul uses to communicate to the conscious mind. This language is universal and applies to anyone, anywhere, anytime. One Universal Truth is stated thusly: *"As Above, So Below,"* meaning everything in our physical existence is a reflection of, or was first created in, the inner mind. Therefore, as mankind (whether male or female) progresses, our physical human languages will begin to and finally completely take on the attributes of the inner language of the subconscious mind which is universal. Thus, the Universal Language of Mind herein presented is a great discovery which will hasten that time of universal and complete communication of mankind. May peace and communication be with you.

This assignment Dr. Condron chose gladly and with great joy as it is the willful culmination of eons of preparation on his part in building permanent understandings in the full utilization of the Universal Language of Mind. His sagacity and insight into "The Universal Language of Mind," he gives freely to the world to enhance and quicken humanity's movement forward into the full flowering of the reasoning attributes in order that the time of the Age of Intuitive or Spiritual Man (thinker, whether male or female) may rapidly dawn upon the whole world.

Daniel R. Condron, D.M., D.D., M.S., Ps.D., was born in Chillicothe, Missouri. Raised on a farm ten miles from that town, he excelled in sports and academics during his high school years. Condron furthered his education at the University of Missouri-Columbia where he earned Bachelors and Masters degrees. He traveled through Europe and South America, and was named to *Who'sWho in American Colleges and Universities.*

He has devoted the last thirty years of his life to Self awareness and to understanding the Universal Language of Mind. Serving as a teacher of mind and spirit to people throughout the country, Dr. Condron has shared his knowledge and research with thousands through formal study, seminars and conferences, and all forms of media. His major address on *Permanent Healing - Breakthrough to Awareness* was warmly received at the 1993 Parliament of the World's Religions in Chicago.

Dr. Condron is Chancellor of the College of Metaphysics and serves as President of the Board of Directors of the School of Metaphysics, an educational and service institute with centers throughout the United States and headquartered in Missouri. His influence continues to reach around the globe as a conductor of readings, including the Health Analyses, offered through the institute.

Dr. Condron looks forward to aiding millions more people to lead a richer and more rewarding life.

Additional titles
available from SOM Publishing include:

Permanent Healing
Dr. Daniel R. Condron ISBN 0944386-12-1 $9.95

Dreams of the Soul
The Yogi Sutras of Patanjali
Dr. Daniel R. Condron ISBN 0944386-11-3 $9.95

Kundalini Rising
Mastering Your Creative Energies
Dr. Barbara Condron ISBN 0944386-13-X $9.95

Shaping Your Life
The Power of Creative Imagery
Laurel Jan Fuller ISBN 0944386-14-8 $9.95

Total Recall
An Introduction to Past Life & Health Readings
Dr. Barbara Condron, ed. ISBN 0944386-10-5 $9.95

Going in Circles
Search for a Satisfying Relationship
Dr. Barbara Condron ISBN 0944386-00-8 $9.95

Will I Do Tomorrow? Probing Depression
Dr. Barbara Condron ISBN 0944386-02-4 $4.95

Who Were Those Strangers in My Dream?
Dr. Barbara Condron ISBN 0944386-08-3 $4.95

Meditation: Answer to Your Prayers
Dr. Jerry L. Rothermel ISBN 0944386-01-6 $4.95

Symbols of Dreams
Dr. Jerry L. Rothermel   ISBN 0944386-03-2 $4.95

HuMan, a novel
Dr. Jerry L. Rothermel   ISBN 0944386-05-9 $5.95

Discovering the Kingdom of Heaven
Dr. Gayle B. Matthes   ISBN 0944386-07-5 $5.95

Autobiography of a Skeptic
Frank Farmer   ISBN 0944386-06-7 $7.95

To order write:

> **School of Metaphysics**
> **National Headquarters**
> **Windyville, Missouri 65783**

Enclose a check or money order payable to SOM with any order. Please include $2.00 for postage and handling of books.

A complete catalogue of all book titles, audio lectures and courses, and videos is available upon request.

About the School of Metaphysics

We invite you to become a special part
of our efforts to aid in enhancing and quickening
the process of spiritual growth and mental evolution
of the people of the world. The School of
Metaphysics, a not-for-profit educational and
service organization, has been in existence for more
than two decades. During that time, we have taught
tens of thousands directly through our course
of study in applied metaphysics. We have elevated
the awareness of millions through the many services
we offer. If you would like to pursue the study
of mind and the transformation of Self to a higher
level of being and consciousness, you are invited
to write to us at the School of Metaphysics National
Headquarters in Windyville, Missouri 65783.

The heart of the School of Metaphysics
is a three-tiered program of study. Lessons
introduce you to the Universal Laws and Truths
which guide spiritual and physical evolution.
Consciousness is explored and developed through
mental and spiritual disciplines which enhance
your physical life and enrich your soul progression.
We teach concentration, visualization (focused
imagery), meditation, and control of life force
and creative energies. As a student, you will develop
an understanding of the purpose of life and your
purpose for this lifetime.

Experts in the language of mind,
we teach how to remember and understand the
inner communication received through dreams.
We are the sponsors of the National Dream Hotline
an annual educational service offered the last

*weekend in April. Study centers are located
throughout the Midwestern United States.
If there is not a center near you, you can receive
the first series of lessons through correspondence
with a teacher at our headquarters.*

There is the opportunity to aid
*in the growth and fulfillment of our work.
Donations are accepted and are a valuable way
for you to aid humanity by supporting the expansion
of the School of Metaphysics' efforts.
Currently, donations are being received
for Project Octagon, the first educational building
on the College of Metaphysics campus.
The land for the proposed campus is located
in the beautiful Ozark Mountains of Missouri,
less than four hours from St. Louis and Kansas City,
and one hour north of Springfield.
The four-story octagon design will enable us
to increase headquarters staff and enrollment
in our College workstudy program. This proposed
multipurpose structure will include an auditorium,
classrooms, library and study areas, a cafeteria,
and potential living quarters for up to 100 people.
We expect to finance this structure through
corporate grants and personal endowments. Gifts
may be named for the donor or be designated
as an ongoing memorial fund to a family member
or special friend. Donations to the School of
Metaphysics are tax-exempt under 501 (c) (3)
of the Internal Revenue Code. We appreciate
any contribution you are free to make.
With the help of people like you, our dream
of a place where anyone desiring Self awareness
can receive wholistic education
will become a reality.*

We send you our Circle of Love.